*Kings, Lords
and Wicked Libellers*

Kings, Lords and Wicked Libellers

SATIRE AND PROTEST
1760–1837

John Wardroper

JOHN MURRAY

Printed in Great Britain by
W & J Mackay Limited, Chatham

0 7195 2912 3

Contents

Illustrations

Illustrations

Illustrations

viii

Illustrations

Acknowledgments

I HAVE HAD the privilege of being graciously permitted to consult manuscripts in the Royal Archives at Windsor. I am grateful to Earl Waldegrave for kindly permitting me to quote some unpublished passages in the Walpole manuscripts; and to Earl Spencer and Sir Sacheverell Sitwell for kindly allowing me to inspect manuscripts in their possession. I extend my thanks to the staffs of the Public Record Office, the Historic Manuscripts Commission and National Register of Archives, the Guildhall Library, the Victoria and Albert Museum's department of prints and drawings, and above all, the British Museum, the chief begetter of this book. In particular I thank the British Museum's department of prints and drawings for permitting me to reproduce all the caricatures used here—a few among the thousands that the department's staff tirelessly laid before me.

1

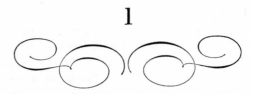

If you Funk, Goodbye
to you

NEVER HAVE MEN in power been so honoured by the impudent attentions of satirists as during the reigns of George III and the two elderly sons who succeeded him. These three kings and their courtiers and ministers were often so pained by the assaults of the insufficiently gaggable press that they declared society to be in danger. From below, the danger looked different, as it usually does. The ruling men seemed foolishly deaf to every reminder that their power could be questioned and that things-as-they-were might be changed. It was a conflict that nourished the arts of the caricaturist, balladeer, lampoonist, pamphleteer and newspaper polemicist. They made their age something braver than an age of illusion.

Satire is a stripper-off of alluring and lulling disguises. Unaided, humble men can easily forget that the great personages of their day may well be as fallible and passionate as themselves. We need such help still more when we try to seize the truth of an earlier time; and especially perhaps the truth of the dazzling and unquiet Georgian age. We do not have our eyes, and our doubts, sharpened by the direct experience of the errors, insolence and expense of ministers now long dead. We cannot see those princes misbehaving or learn of their follies from men in the know; or catch those fine gentlemen in moments of indignity, reeling perhaps out of White's Club at dawn, broken at faro. We see them instead in portraits displaying them as they wished to be remembered, in moments of grace amid the artifacts we now long to possess. The rapid work of the London printshop artists helps us to come nearer to the truth. And the words flung back and forth then, the weapons fashioned in the heat of the skirmish, can give better clues to the hopes and agitations of the day than what was written later to justify a disaster or patch up a reputation.

Some historians have little taste for what was said by the dissidents and the losers, who perhaps seem like fractious impractical students. We are warned against misjudging such a man as George III: some ideas of his time, we are reminded, quite rightly, were different from ours. But if we attend to all the voices in the Georgian dialogue, and look for them in caricatures and broadsides and the corners of newspapers, we are struck by something else at least as important. We find ideas that were indeed strange to George III, but were clear enough to many of his subjects. 'Privileges of the people' and 'rights of mankind' are not late-invented phrases. They came to life in the seventeenth century. By the time of George III, unprivileged men were talking of rights with a new insistence. That is one reason why there was trouble in the reign of this not so much misunderstood as misunderstanding king.

Visitors from the absolutist Continent were struck by the way Britons asserted their right to speak their minds. Nobody in Louis XV's or XVI's France or Frederick the Great's Prussia —or George III's own German domain of Hanover—could openly sell political broadsides and caricatures, or publish anything like London's contending newspapers. As early as 1726 a Swiss traveller, César de Saussure, noted that the newspapers provided in the London coffee-houses were a great attraction, and not only for gentlemen: 'All Englishmen are great newsmongers. Workmen habitually begin the day by going to coffee-rooms to read the latest news. I have often seen shoeblacks and other persons of that class club together to buy a paper. Nothing is more entertaining than hearing men of this class discussing politics and news about royalty.' Another witness among many is Johann von Archenholtz, a widely-travelled German who was in England in the 1770s. 'Among the privileges of this nation,' he writes in his *Tableau de*

2

l'Angleterre, 'must be counted the free manufacture of satirical prints that expose the events of the day to ridicule. The Frenchman makes songs; . . . the Englishman has chosen engraving as the best way to bring satire to the public.' Some political prints were made in France under the old régime, but it was an under-the-counter trade. When caught, engravers and printsellers went to jail and their stocks were destroyed. Even the Frenchman's songs were furtive: 'They are not sung in public as in London,' says Archenholtz. He describes the London balladmongers, usually women, gathering crowds by singing their broadside songs about politics or some passing event—'They sell them by thousands.'

Archenholtz too was surprised to find that the most ordinary people talked politics. 'One is sometimes dumbfounded to hear people of the meanest sort very seriously discussing laws, property rights, privileges, etc., etc.,' he says. And again: 'Often nothing is more difficult than to make an Englishman converse; he replies to everything with Yes or No; but if one has the address to start him off on politics, suddenly his face is alive, he opens his mouth, he becomes eloquent.'

The common man did not have to be literate before he could talk politics, but the ability to read was certainly widespread. Some historical guesses seem to put the figure too low. At the artisan-shopkeeper-clerk level there were many schools— often run by nonconformists—at which children got basic teaching for a small fee. For the poorest families there had been charity schools since the 1690s, and by 1746 England and Wales had nearly 1,500 of them. Even children lodged in workhouses were often taught to read and cipher. Daily stagecoaches from London ensured that the minds of the country people were kept alert with the news of every controversy. In 1721, when daily journalism was young, a government informant in Birmingham wrote agitatedly to London about attacks on Robert Walpole in *The London Journal:* 'The general cry among the common people is of late, "Oh, this is a fine paper! This paper contains nothing but the truth!" . . . Last Saturday's paper is now become the general talk of not only this place but Coventry, Warwick, etc. In every alehouse people have the London Journal in their hands, showing

3

to each other with a kind of joy the most audacious reflections therein contained. . . . The fellows who have this paper to sell are the only market-men.' At about the same date another informant wrote about the oppositionist *Mist's Journal:* 'It is scarcely credible what numbers of those papers are distributed both in town and country, where they do more mischief than any other libel, being written *ad captum* of the common people.' And the reading public was to grow much larger before the end of the century. Here is the evidence of a London bookseller, James Lackington, writing his memoirs in 1792: 'According to the best estimation I have been able to make . . . more than four times the number of books are sold now than were sold twenty years since. The poorer sort of farmers, and even the poor people in general . . . now shorten the winter nights by hearing their sons and daughters read tales, romances, etc. . . . You may see Tom Jones, Roderick Random and other entertaining books stuck up on their bacon racks. . . . In short, all ranks and degrees now READ.'

Although power was in a very few hands, political argument and political laughter were the privilege of all. Politics could throw tenuous bridges across the gulf between gentlemen and poor labourers. They had more than newspapers in common. In times of conflict, gentlemen as well as plebeians joined noisy street parades, and pasted libels or scribbled slogans in chalk on the Georgian walls that now speak to us of elegant order. They assisted at the execution of hated ministers in effigy, and were not above helping to inspire that popular form of eighteenth-century protest, the smashing of great men's windows. But nowhere was there such lively cross-fertilizing in the language of politics as in the vast activity of lampooning and caricaturing.

Ballads had been political weapons long before Cavaliers and Roundheads used them in Cromwell's day. A little later 'Lilliburlero', the work of a lord, was credited with singing James II out of his kingdom. George I and his ugly German mistresses were mocked by Jacobite gentlemen:

> To quench their lewd fire
> They were forced to retire,

4

If you Funk, Goodbye to you

Though dinner was scarce down their throats.
>But alas! in this hurry,
>While with too much fury
The rampant old lecher embraced her,
>Her ladyship's weight,
>Which we all know is great,
Brought down on 'em both the bed's tester. . . .

The courtier Lord Hervey, the 'thing of silk' abhorred by Pope, tells of lampoons and ballads being 'handed about, both publicly and privately, some in print and some in manuscript', attacking George II for keeping Sir Robert Walpole in power. Hervey wrote pro-Walpole ballads, and the queen sang them. On the other side a high-born balladeer was William Pulteney, later Lord Bath. In 1733, when Walpole tried to enforce a new excise law, Pulteney was one of the men who 'ballad-sung the mob out of their senses', as a Walpole newspaper put it, with mass-produced broadsides distributed round the country.

At the height of an even greater storm nearly thirty years later, against Lord Bute and his friend, George III's mother, even John Wilkes wrote a ballad, with some help from his patron Lord Temple.

>To be knight of great Edward's blue riband and star,
>Oft beyond the fair's garter this bold Scot pushed far;
>A lance so upright went well couched to the root
>And won England's famed trophies for John Earl of Bute. . . .

By this time ballads were being surpassed by the political weapon that became an English speciality, caricatures run off from engraved copper plates. It was in the 1750s that they were given a new sharpness, stimulated by the political infighting early in the Seven Years War. One man who put new life into the trade was an ambitious intriguer at the heart of affairs, George Townshend, heir to one of the Whig magnates. He seems to have been in a constant frenzy of caricaturing. Walpole's son Horace, the famous memoirist and letter-writer, reports in 1756 that Townshend 'adorns the shutters, walls and napkins of every tavern in Pall Mall' with impromptu caricatures of the Duke of Newcastle, William Duke of Cumberland, and other contenders in the political game. Townshend extended the power of his wicked pencil far beyond Pall Mall. He began supplying caricatures to Matthew Darly, an artist and engraver who for many years had one of the leading printshops at 39 The Strand. And Townshend devised something new: compact caricatures printed on cards measuring $2\frac{1}{2}$ inches by 4 for sending messages by hand or in the post. The first, 'which had amazing vent', says Horace Walpole, showed Newcastle and Henry Fox looking at each other at the time of the loss of Minorca—a disaster for which they were shifting the blame to Admiral Byng—and saying, like the two rogues in *The Beggar's Opera*, 'Brother, brother, we are both in the wrong.' One thing that struck Walpole about Townshend's prints was 'his genius for likenesses'. He knew these men and pictured them realistically, never turning them into symbols as earlier artists had often prudently done.

Soon Matthew Darly was advertising that his caricatures were on sale at 'all the book and printsellers in Great Britain and Ireland'. He encouraged other gentlemen to supply material: 'Sketches, or hints, sent post-paid, will have due honour shown them.' He and his wife Mary also inspired talent in the best houses by giving drawing lessons, and in 1763 Mary Darly published a guide to the art of caricaturing, illustrated with work by Townshend and others. 'Some of our nobility and gentry,' she wrote, 'at this time do equal if not excel anything that ever has been done in any other country.' The Darlys of course dealt in, and taught, non-political caricaturing as well: the two were never segregated. Either helped to repel hypochondria: ' 'Tis a diverting species of designing, and will certainly keep those that practise it out of the hipps or vapours.'

The 'amazing vent' of political prints is confirmed in many ways. For ten years from 1756 the Darlys reissued the year's work of Townshend and others in pocket-size bound volumes entitled *A Political and Satirical History*, with comments on each item to twist the knife further. At the time of the furor over Lord Bute these books were pirated—always a proof of high demand—under such titles as *The Scots Scourge* and *The Butiad*. Forthcoming prints were advertised in the newspapers. A popular one could easily sell in thousands. In 1766, one on the American Stamp Act, 'The Repeal, or the Funeral of Miss Americ-Stamp', sold two thousand copies in its first four days at a shilling each (now over £1); on the fifth day a sixpenny piracy came out, soon followed by at least three others; these piracies alone were said to have sold sixteen thousand copies; and others were issued in America.

The audience that caricatures reached was far larger, too, than the sales figures suggest. All the scores of printshops from St Paul's to St James's displayed their best things in every pane of their windows, and no doubt the other shops of Great Britain and Ireland did the same. These displays drew knots of people, in which the politically literate could be heard explaining every subtlety. Caricatures, besides, are less ephemeral than newspapers. Like broadside ballads, they were pasted up on the walls of alehouses and select coffee-houses, in barber-shops and gentlemen's clubs. Gentlemen collected folios of caricatures and brought them out for their guests. George IV, when Prince of Wales, bought hundreds of them. Ladies covered folding screens with them. (An age later, when Lady Conyngham, George IV's last mistress, was an ancient dame and feeling the cold, her hostess brought out a screen— and saw too late that it displayed her in her days of notoriety.)

The better printshops became social centres, places to lounge and gossip, and no doubt to offer scandalous hints to the proprietor. In the 1780s several shops set up exhibitions and charged a shilling admission. The first to do this was William Holland, a radical-minded man who published books, wrote political songs and supplied ideas and words for his caricaturists. In September 1789 he advertised that his shop at 50 Oxford Street had 'all the French caricatures'—for the revolution had brought every kind of satire out into the open in Paris. A few months later he boasted of 'the largest collection in Europe of political and other humorous prints, with those published in Paris'. Then as now, radicalism was sometimes associated with eroticism. Holland denied allegations by 'defamatory characters, envious printsellers and others . . . that a number of the prints exhibited were of that complexion that would suffuse the cheek of modesty with the blushes of aversion'. Perhaps this was simply advertising; at any rate, Holland's booklist included *Female Flagellants* and the lascivious poems of the Earl of Haddington.

One of Holland's chief rivals was the Tory-inclined S. W. Fores of No. 3 Piccadilly. He opened an exhibition in 1789 that was 'the largest in the kingdom'. By 1793 it was 'the completest in Europe' and included a six-foot model of the guillotine. Fores hired out folios of caricatures for the evening, at half-a-crown plus a £1 deposit; and the wide influence of the art is well illustrated by the further services he was soon offering: 'Prints and drawings lent to copy. . . . Prints and caricatures wholesale and for exportation. Also prepared for screens, assorted for folios, arranged for scrapbooks, etc., etc. Private subjects designed, executed and published. Gentlemen taught to etch.'

During the 1790s Holland and Fores were surpassed in importance by a woman printseller, Hannah Humphrey. She did not offer such a variety of services; but she acquired a monopoly in the work of the great James Gillray. This son of a Scottish ex-soldier was born in London in the year that George Townshend was beginning his innovations. Gillray's ambition was to be a portrait artist, engraver and illustrator, but by the mid-1780s his restless, ambiguous talent—his cool, luminous, playful savagery—had fixed him in the less respected craft which he quickly raised to a subtle art. He set standards that made this the golden age of English caricature. He was soon famous even on the Continent, and Swiss, French and German caricaturists paid him the compliment of using his name on their prints.

His finest prints are complex structures in which dozens of details convey messages that often question each other. Words stream, characters swarm. He could count on being savoured at leisure, for he was selling a self-contained product, not a newspaper cartoon to be glanced at over breakfast. He poses a further problem for later ages. Inspired perhaps by a newspaper paragraph, or a clash between Pitt and Fox which he had gone to witness from the Commons gallery, he would produce an instant realistic-fantastic image of the state of affairs, crowded with characters familiar to his customers, characters who might well be passing his shop in St James's

Street as he worked. But now only a Pitt, a Fox and a few others are remembered, so his finest works cannot quite give us their first full delight.

What is known of Gillray tells us a good deal about the caricature trade. In his earlier years, when he worked for various printsellers—the Darlys, Holland, Fores—he charged up to two guineas (an artisan's monthly wage) for one engraving, which might measure 10 by 14 inches. When he was Hannah Humphrey's star and mainstay, and lodger and probably lover, he earned much more. He worked on a profit-sharing basis, and his prints sold, when coloured, for at least two shillings, and sometimes, when outsize, for five shillings. In 1805, when he sold Hannah Humphrey his remaining rights in all the plates he had engraved for her till then, he got £500, which would be well over £10,000 now—a demonstration of the lasting selling-power of good prints.

The Humphrey–Gillray shop was in Bond Street until 1797. Then they moved to 27 St James's Street (the site is now No. 24). This move was good for custom and convenient for Gillray, for St James's Street was a political and social microcosm. Across the street was Brooks's Club, where Charles James Fox and the rump of the Whigs dined, drank, gamed, gossiped and powerlessly conferred. Not far up the street was White's Club, where most of the ruling Tories dined, drank, gamed, gossiped and decided the future. Gillray moved here as a subversive, detached observer. He descended from his attic room above the shop and went for morning walks, slouching and untidy, eyeing the world, and always carrying with him a pencil and a few sketch cards. A few dozen of these cards survive, all bearing portraits of heads. Some of the cards are as small as 1½ inches by 3, easy to conceal in the palm. When Gillray said on a print that his people were drawn *ad vivam*, it was the truth. He generally used little exaggeration of feature—far less than most modern cartoonists. In his prints, his public could find, and we can find, a realistic gallery of public faces.

Gillray took great care with words as well as images. Draughts of some of his prints survive, with the margins filled with trial dialogue and variant titles. He went to the

9

Commons to find ideas as well as to sketch faces. He took notes from the morning papers. Men on both sides sent suggestions. 'As an old friend and customer I subjoin a hint or two which the papers of this morning have suggested,' says a typical letter among Gillray's papers. Another, giving a detailed outline for a caricature of George III in his privy ('the fundamental privy-ledge in use'), says humbly, 'These nasty ideas (if worthy of notice) will no doubt be properly corrected by your most ingenious and ever-diverting pencil.'

For years Gillray lashed everyone with almost equal ferocity. Fox was a shifty bankrupt, Pitt was 'a toadstool on a dunghill'. George III was a graceless miser, his heir was a bloated voluptuary. Reformers were terrifying sans-culottes, the rich lived in heartless luxury. In 1788, briefly, Gillray sold his services to Pitt's side during a hotly contested election in the Westminster constituency. Among the Treasury's papers there survives a bill itemizing newspaper support, bill-stickers, handbill distributors, cockades—and £20 for Gillray. But the few caricatures he did were weak; and then within a fortnight he produced a signed print, 'Election Troops Bringing in their Accounts,' exposing the use of hired opinion-makers. Journalists, ballad-singers and others queue at the Treasury door for Pitt, and he says, 'I know nothing of you, my friends. . . . Go to the back door in Great George Street under the Rose'— meaning the office of George Rose, the Treasury secretary then in charge of news-management. Gillray was back to normal.

But then in 1795 the twenty-five-year-old George Canning, a rising friend of Pitt and an ardent anti-Jacobin, began to make indirect approaches to Gillray. Canning hoped, in that revolutionary time, to stifle criticism of the government; he also hoped to get himself into a caricature, for that was a sign, as it is still, that a man had arrived. Canning's go-between was a rich clergyman whose amateur caricatures were published by Hannah Humphrey. The two men fed Gillray with ideas, but he was a wary fish. In January 1796, when a print Canning had helped to inspire appeared in the St James's Street window, he 'looked with trembling anxiety for something that I might acknowledge as a resemblance of myself'— in vain. Nine months later Canning did appear, but perhaps he was not delighted, for Gillray showed him, in 'Promis'd Horrors of the French Invasion', hanged from a lamp-bracket outside White's Club. Later he became a tiny figure kissing the toe of a gigantic Pitt. But Gillray was yielding. He stopped savaging Pitt and the royal family. And in November 1797 a friend of Canning wrote to the go-between, 'Gillray is to be here tomorrow, and Canning is to have his will of him'— which meant that Gillray was accepting a secret pension. The following year a Tory peer wrote to Gillray, 'The opposition are as low as we can wish them. You have been of infinite service in lowering them and making them ridiculous.'

The best proof of the importance of the satirists is that men in high places deplored, threatened, prosecuted, wooed and employed them. There are many witnesses to the power of satirical prints. A memoir-writing Tory MP, Nathaniel Wraxall, remarks that in 1770 they were 'dispersed throughout the kingdom' and 'inflamed the public mind' against George III and his mother. One man who had reason to deplore caricatures was Charles James Fox, whose questionable private life was a boon to his enemies. In the first month of his surprising coalition with Lord North in 1783, Horace Walpole wrote, 'If satirical prints could dispatch them, they would be dead in their cradle; there are enough to hang a room.' Caricatures undoubtedly had a hand in the death of the coalition before the end of the year; in particular, several created by a Pittite lawyer, James Sayers. When Fox introduced his bill to bring the East India Company under government control, Sayers drew Fox as a thief running away with East India House, and as a great potentate, Carlo Khan, riding in triumph into Leadenhall Street on an elephant. 'Fox said that Sayers's caricatures had done him more mischief than the debates in parliament or the works of the press,' recalled the Tory Lord Eldon; they had 'certainly a vast effect upon the public mind'. Fox even complained of them in parliament. He was used to abuse, but he knew the danger of charges that he hoped to profit by a usurpation of power, and that he wished to put himself above the king. Soon afterwards a print showed Fox looking in a mirror and seeing the reflection of Cromwell. The French ambassador is recorded as saying, 'I know from a good source [Fox himself?] that Mr Fox was sensitive about this caricature.' Another caricature that is said to have pained him is Gillray's 'A Democrat', in which Fox, just after Louis XVI's execution, is a bestial sans-culotte holding a bloody dagger and singing 'Ça ira'.

In 1795 the playwright and radical Thomas Holcroft protested in a pamphlet about the methods used 'to enflame the populace of London' against the opponents of war with France: 'Charles Fox, holding the gore-dripping head of the late king of France by the hair; Mr Sheridan feasting with him at a banquet of decapitated kings; monstrous figures of pretended Frenchmen devouring the bodies of their murdered fellow citizens, and other infernal devices . . . in every printshop.' Holcroft is addressing William Windham, one of the Whigs who had deserted Fox for Pitt; and he protests about another piece of visual propaganda used by Windham at an election at Norwich: 'You went to a carpenter, in person, and directed him to make a guillotine, and to place a female figure on the platform of the horrid instrument, with its head in the act of being struck off, and bleeding: over which was an inscription in large letters, *This is French liberty!*' Windham paraded this round the city to convert its traditionally Whiggish voters.

Sometimes caricaturists were said to be defeating themselves. In 1813 one writer took the lofty line that to be attacked in caricatures was 'now considered as the necessary consequence of holding a place under the government, or wishing to obtain one, and in both instances little more is occasioned than a laugh by, and at the expense of, the parties'. Yet he conceded that 'it has its use in checking many aberrations'. A good example had occurred a few years earlier.

A man called Frome was an agent for army commissions serving the Duke of York, the less than immaculate commander-in-chief. A caricature, 'The New Military Road to York by Way of Frome', pictured Frome barring scarred veterans at a tollgate and letting young dandies pass in return for bribes. The effect of this is recorded by Elizabeth Ham, a journal-writing governess who met Frome later in Guernsey.

If you Funk, Goodbye to you

A young officer there gave her a copy of the caricature (it clearly circulated widely in the army), and Frome found her looking at it. 'He told me that caricature had lost him his office. It had been shown to the king, and he sent for the duke immediately and ordered him to close the office.' Frome seems not to have borne a grudge: his first remark to Miss Ham was, 'Do you think it like?'

The power of caricatures is shown more comically in a story about Addington, the failed prime minister, who in 1804 was heading for the Lords and was talking of calling himself Lord Raleigh. 'I was determined he should not if I could help it,' Pitt's uninhibited niece Hester recalled years later. She said to Pitt, 'What a pretty caricature they have made about Addington,' and invented one with Addington in a ridiculous encounter with Queen Elizabeth and George III. Pitt told Addington. 'Immediately half a dozen people were dispatched to all the caricature shops to buy up the whole impression at any price.' In the event, 'the fright they had been thrown into was so great that another title was chosen'—which is why Addington, the scourge of regency radicals, is remembered as Lord Sidmouth.

To buy up the whole impression: that was the best defence ministers and other victims had. In earlier days, Robert Walpole had prosecuted prints and even ballads as well as newspapers as treasonable libels. In 1731 printers and book-sellers were charged over, among other things, a series of caricatures entitled 'Robin's Reign', and a pamphlet giving a commentary on them, 'Robin's Game'. A theme of both was Walpole's effort to curb the press. One caricature was labelled 'Hail Typographic Art', and the pamphleteer commented that he was 'persuaded this will never give offence to great R[obin], because 'tis a point he himself strained his throat about formerly'. It cannot have done Walpole much good to bring this into court.

After Walpole's day, political caricatures seem to have been safe from the law (save for alleged blasphemy) until two were prosecuted in the first year of George IV's reign—a measure of his desperate unpopularity. Those prosecutions, which are dealt with in a later chapter, only confirmed that legal action was self-defeating, for it publicized the caricature and loaded the victim with ridicule. The privilege of the caricaturist is with us still: a politician can be pictured as a beast, a tyrant, a fool, but one must be wary of saying the same in simple prose.

Free-speaking newspapers were time and again denounced as licentious. Ministers tried to contain the threat in several ways. To price newspapers out of the hands of the lower orders, they imposed taxes and stamp duties which were eventually put so high that a four-page paper cost sevenpence, or nearly half a poor man's wage. This was what sent so many readers to the coffee-houses and taverns; and in the 1790s artisans' reform societies began establishing newsrooms, which incidentally saved workmen the expense of unholy taxed coffee and beer. The newspaper taxes put a limit on sales (3,000 a day was a good figure), but each overpriced copy was read perhaps by dozens; read or *heard* by hundreds in anxious times.

The hunger for news and comment could not be suppressed. The founding of the first London daily in 1702 (seventy-five years before Paris could achieve one) was soon followed by many more. Political conflict was a great stimulus. In 1769, nine years after George III's accession, *The Middlesex Journal* said, 'The numberless and almost daily violations of our rights for *nine* years past have produced a spirit of inquiry amongst the people. . . . To gratify this inquisitive temper— or to take advantage of it—publications have been multiplied beyond all former example.' By then there were in London alone six daily papers, eight evening papers appearing tri-weekly, and numerous weeklies and monthlies. The American conflict helped to increase the number by 1783 to nine dailies and ten evenings. Most of these papers had country circulations carried by the stagecoach service. And the provinces had a growing force of papers; about fifty as early as 1760.

A little of the newspaper tax revenue was returned in-directly to chosen papers in the form of secret subsidies—a practice much followed by Robert Walpole, and long con-tinued. As for the writers and printers of unbribable trouble-making papers, they always had hanging over them the threat of fines, prison and (until the early nineteenth century) the pillory. It was often prudent to say things between the lines. Such words as 'minister', 'parliament' and 'king' were commonly written m------, p--------- and ----, which could force the prosecution into having to demonstrate that the cap fitted. Walpole set an example for later governments by jailing a number of newspaper proprietors—one of them for attacking his play-licensing law of 1737, which was itself a measure to suppress political satire. But juries would not always give governments the libel verdicts they wanted; least of all in the City of London, the old redoubt against royal or ministerial encroachment. Dissident newspapers could be silenced or financially crippled, however, by arbitrary arrests on attorney-generals' warrants which in the end were often not tested in court. To give heart to the printer-proprietors of newspapers, writers of dangerous political articles would undertake to indemnify a printer for any costs that might arise. This is well illustrated by a note among the papers of Henry Sampson Woodfall, proprietor of *The Public Advertiser* in Paternoster Row. Bonnell Thornton, an ally of John Wilkes, is persuading Woodfall to publish an outspoken anti-government article at the height of the first Wilkite storm in May 1763:

Harry—Your answer to Stanhope [a Treasury lawyer] is simply no more than that you took it in as a common advertisement, of which you have a proof. (Keep it, keep everything in a snug place.)

Don't Be Afraid. (If you funk, goodbye to you.) Don't show my indemnification to anybody, not even to *father*.

Harry Woodfall had some reason to fear. Dozens of printers had just been rounded up. At the same time, the government of the young George III was laying out on the purchasable part of the journalistic world amounts far exceeding the great sum of £5,000 a year that Walpole had expended in his heyday. Such was the delicate state of things in the first years of this king's reign. For the next fifty years, until his mind withdrew from the world, he was to learn that the press in all its forms could never quite be lessoned out of absurd, disorderly, licentious ways.

2

The Wickedest Age

WHEN GEORGE III came to the throne of a growing empire at the age of twenty-two, he was sadly unsure of himself. But of this he was sure: he must deliver the crown from a lordly gang of self-interested men, and then reign as a king should, 'adored by a happy, free and generous people'.

He did begin amid some goodwill. He was the first British-born king for seventy-five years. His country was glorying in a victorious war. He was young, tall, apparently obliging—a visible improvement on Old Squaretoes, as courtiers called his grandfather, the short, strutting, fussy, short-tempered George II who had just died at seventy-seven. 'This young man,' Horace Walpole reported after watching him at his first levee, 'don't stand in one spot, with his eyes fixed royally on the ground, and dropping bits of German news. He walks about, and speaks to everybody.' And yet very soon he was distrusted and abused. His reaction was as simplistically royal as his dream had been: he lamented that it was his fate to be king of an ungrateful people in 'the wickedest age that ever was seen'.

It is true that his inheritance could not have been wholly pleasing to any royal mind. He was expected to glory in being that anomalous thing, a limited monarch, a parliament-created heir to the Glorious Revolution of 1688: surrounded from childhood with the scarcely abated pageantry of absolutism, yet forbidden to toy with the notions that had doomed the Stuarts. He was asked to remember that his family possessed the throne because the English had a right to rebel against

16

an overweening king. Such talk never had to be tolerated by other sovereigns, George III's continental cousins.

Englishmen had modified the ancient custom of giving a man high power by an accident of birth. George III was meant to believe that his glory was truly served only by the employment of ministers who had the confidence of his people, as expressed in parliament. It was a vulnerable compromise. Kings naturally did not love it. As early as 1689, William III complained that he was 'like a king in a play' and the Commons 'used him like a dog'. The immediate example before George III's eyes, George II, had felt much the same. He had thought of the English as king-killers and republicans (in the previous century they had after all got rid of two kings within forty years). If pressed to accept men or policies he disliked, he would kick his hat across the royal closet, and sometimes kick his ministers. When put right on the subtle nature of his limited powers, he replied plaintively, 'Ministers are the kings in this country.' George III despised him and believed he had been 'a cypher', had been 'in fetters'.

A man who protests about fetters is determined to throw them off. During his slow-maturing and secluded youth, George III was tutored in this determination by his widowed German mother and by her one close friend, John Stuart, Earl of Bute. Alarm over this couple's influence was what so soon shattered the young king's dream. When flippant Londoners saw him being carried in his sedan-chair from St James's Palace along Pall Mall to visit his mother at Carlton House, they shouted, 'Are you going to suck?' Handbills were posted up, even in Westminster Hall where the high courts sat, saying 'No petticoat government—no Scotch favourite.' Soon the king's mother gave up going to the theatre because she was greeted with insulting shouts from those turbulent satirists, the gallery crowd. There is no need to wonder what sort of things were shouted. We need only look at the halfpenny ballads and sixpenny caricatures that were being spread through the kingdom.

> With pleasure he sees her both early and late,
> To kiss her and clap her no scruple does make,

17

> And at her desire he can her well shake,
> So stout and so able is Sawney.

This ballad is entitled 'The Wanton Widow', and for the guidance of political innocents it is headed with a picture of Bute (Sawney the Scot) and the king's mother standing lovingly together. She was then a little over forty:

> The widow is neither so young nor so old,
> But still loves a Scotchman that's active and bold,
> For all other men are but lifeless and cold
>   Compared to the vigorous Sawney.

> He busses and smacks her by night and by day:
> So well he does please her, she never says nay. . . .

Were Bute and the widow lovers? It is not a frivolous question. The rise and fall of royal favourites of both sexes was vital news in many capitals. The forces that shaped the young mind of George III were to affect the course of British politics for seventy years, and with results still to be seen.

Even before Princess Augusta of Saxe-Gotha arrived in England at the age of seventeen to be the bride of George II's heir-apparent, Prince Frederick, she was advised by Frederick's worldly mother 'to be easy with regard to amours'. She found Frederick in the grip of an ambitious mistress ten years his senior. She found too that he was a small, ill-formed, childish, devious spendthrift, whose character had not been improved by his parents' unremitting attacks on him as 'a monster and the greatest villain that ever was born'. Augusta's skill in courtly tactics was soon remarked: she ousted the mature mistress, but winked at lesser amours. No doubt Augusta learned about earlier mistresses, notably Anne Vane, a plump and promiscuous Maid of Honour (a title that was often doubly a joke). A few years earlier, Anne Vane had convinced Frederick that he was the father of her baby son, though Lord Hervey and other courtiers might have claimed the honour; and Frederick had established her sumptuously in Soho Square and settled £3,000 a year on her. She is celebrated in a set of verses, 'Vanella in the Straw':

In vain your rivals laugh and make their jest:
The *settlement* sets you above the rest . . .
None suffer scandal but the mean and poor . . .
Madam who sins at Drury or the Fleet,
When placed in coach-and-six and dressed most neat
Laughs at the drudging fools who sin for hire.

The poem hopes the baby boy may look like Frederick, with
his prominent oscillating Hanoverian eyes:

May the same *stare* dart from his rolling eyes;
May he be just as *good* and just as *wise*.

Other lampoonists remark on the witlessness of the man who
expected to be Britain's first King Frederick. The diplomat-
wit Sir Charles Hanbury-Williams calls him 'the prattling
monkey' and says:

From Freddy's lips the royal nonsense flows,
And fools and ladies catch it as it goes.

A song attributed to the great Lord Chesterfield says:

God send the prince, your babe of grace,
A little whore and horse,
A little meaning in his face,
And money in his purse.

Frederick and Augusta are remembered now only because of
their son George, born in 1738 on the day that was to become
known as the Glorious Fourth of June. He was a shy, dull,
sulky child; and Frederick, true to a Hanoverian compulsion,
made him worse by scorning and abashing him, and praising
his quicktongued younger brother. If George 'faltered out an
opinion', says one of Bute's daughters in her memoirs, it was
either ignored or knocked down with, 'Do hold your tongue,
George, don't talk like a fool.' Augusta, too, treated him with
great contempt. But then George suddenly acquired great
importance: when he was not yet thirteen, Frederick died.
Now the despised child was heir to the throne. Augusta
'changed her manner', says another memoirist, Lord Shelburne, 'caressing her eldest son, and keeping his brothers and
sisters at the greatest distance possible'. Yet the prospect of

power could not change Augusta's unmotherly nature; she still showed George 'great want of feeling'. It is not surprising that the boy did not respond to her efforts to make him into a promising prince. However, a man who could help her was already a member of her household.

In 1746, just after the Battle of Culloden had made clear to Scottish peers where future power lay, the Earl of Bute had emerged from a five-year retirement in the Isle of Bute. He took a house at Twickenham and began to move in society. He was no rough outlander; but born in Edinburgh, schooled at Eton, and, more important, nephew to the Duke of Argyll, a political magnate in Scotland. Argyll seems to have had a hand in bringing Bute to the notice of Prince Frederick. Before long Bute was one of the prince's inner circle—a £600-a-year Lord of the Bedchamber. When the prince died, outsiders thought Bute's hopes were dashed. But he was secure in the friendship of the princess.

Champions of the princess's virtue sometimes picture her as a dim elderly lady. She was thirty-two when she was widowed, and Bute was six years older. In contrast to the 'prattling monkey' whose amours she had observed for fifteen years, Bute was impressive. He was tall, handsome, redhaired, had 'a good person, fine legs, and a theatrical air of the greatest importance'—and indeed had taken leading parts in plays presented for the amusement of Frederick and Augusta. He excelled Frederick in other ways too: 'There is an extraordinary appearance of wisdom both in his look and manner of speaking,' says the journal of Earl Waldegrave, who spent some years as a tutor to the young Prince George. 'He would be thought a polite scholar and a man of great erudition.' Frederick called him 'a fine showy man who would make an excellent ambassador in a court where there was no business', says Waldegrave. Then comes this: 'But the sagacity of the Princess Dowager has discovered other accomplishments, of which the prince her husband may not perhaps have been the most competent judge.' This is not the only such oblique but telling remark about Bute in Waldegrave's journal, written in 1755, years before Bute was lashed by satirists.

The Wickedest Age

A more direct statement comes in the memoirs of Horace Walpole, who had close friends at court, and whose niece was married to Waldegrave and later to Princess Augusta's third son. He says of the widowed princess: 'The eagerness of the pages of the back-stairs to let her know whenever Lord Bute arrived, a mellowness in her German accent as often as she spoke to him, and that was often and long, and a more than usual swimmingness in her eyes, contributed to dispel the ideas that had been conceived of the rigour of her widowhood. . . . The favoured personage . . . seemed by no means desirous of concealing his conquest. His bows grew more theatric . . . and the beauty of his leg was constantly displayed in the eyes of the poor captivated princess.' Walpole is sure they were lovers. The princess 'passed the critical barrier', he says, as a consequence of Frederick's flaunted infidelity.

Bute's 'attachment' to the princess, as he himself called it, might not have mattered much if he had not also become the prince's tutor, father-figure and adored 'dearest friend'. The mother's friend took several years to win the son's confidence. When the boy was seventeen, Bute wrote him a long letter (one of many) devoted to quieting his doubts.

The prospect of serving you and forming your young mind is exquisitely pleasing to a heart like mine, but how many rocks and quicksands do I see! . . . It will sooner or later be whispered in your ear, 'Don't you know Lord Bute was your father's friend, and is strongly attached to the princess? He only means to bring you under your mother's goverment. Sure you are too much a man to bear that!' Hear, sir, what Lord Bute will say: 'I glory in my attachment to the princess, in being called your father's friend, but I glory in being yours too. . . . She alone can wish you great and happy for your own sake; all others must have interested views—riches, ambitions, honours.'

The letter goes on to tell the prince that when he comes to the throne he must accept the united guidance of the princess and Bute himself until he has had 'years of application and experience in business'. Any man 'who attempts to breed suspicions in your breast against her' is the prince's 'most

21

determined enemy'. Having said he is indispensable, Bute
then pretends he is not. 'Should secret malice paint me to you
in a villain's dress', the princess will be able to find someone
else with 'I dare say as honest a heart and I am sure a much
abler head than I can boast of'.

A royal heir grows up in an environment likely to do him
harm. This is true especially if he is destined for real power.
He is unique by chance, whatever his talents. His household
is organized to adorn and flatter him. He is tutored for a role
that is part fantasy, but it will not seem so within his palace.
While he waits for an ageing king to die, ambitious men woo
him. All this would put a strain on the wisest of princes.
George had neither a subtle head nor a generous heart; and
his faults were reinforced by Bute.

The two had traits in common. (Bute, like George, had lost
his father as a boy.) Both indulged in fits of pique and melancholy. They felt betrayed when opposed. Men who served
them were self-interested, men who opposed them were
villains. Lord Shelburne, who for a time was a protégé of Bute,
describes his contradictory nature. 'He was insolent and
cowardly . . . rash and timid . . . had a perpetual appre-
hension of being governed . . . was always upon stilts, never
natural, except now and then upon the subject of women'.
And there was 'a gloomy sort of madness' in his character.

At eighteen, George was calling this man 'my Friend'; at
nineteen, 'my Dearest Friend'. In a hostile world he was the
one man to be trusted and emulated. When Bute had been
'forming his young mind' for three years, George's character
was summed up by Earl Waldegrave in his journal: 'He has a
kind of unhappiness in his temper, which, if it be not conquered . . . will be a source of frequent anxiety. Whenever he
is displeased . . . he becomes sullen and silent, and retires to
his closet . . . to indulge the melancholy enjoyment of his
own ill humour.' George's own letters confirm this. Even nine
years later he writes: 'Nothing pleases me but musing on
my cruel situation.' Waldegrave also points to other faults that
were to stay with George throughout his reign: 'Too much
obstinacy. . . . It will be difficult to undeceive him. . . . Has
strong prejudices. . . .'

22

1 Matthew Darly's printshop at 39 The Strand (see page 6). The passing figures (like the prints in the windows) satirize oddities of wig and costume. In 1772, when this print was issued, Darly had temporarily turned away from political caricature.

2 *Good Humour:* Wellington enjoys a look at caricatures of himself in the window of Thomas McLean's printshop in the Haymarket, 1829.

AN ENGLISHMANS DELIGHT OR NEWS OF ALL SORTS.

All Englishmen delight in News
In London there's enough to chuse
Of morning papers near a Ream
Fill'd with every kind of theme
At Noon there's such a duced Clatter
Strangers must wonder what's the matter
And E'en that day the Lord hath blest
Is now no more a day of rest

Forth from the Press the Papers fly
Each greedy reader to supply
Of battles fought, and numbers slain,
Of Towns besieg'd, and prisoners ta'en.
Engagements both by Sea and Land
Eccho from Aldgate to the Strand
Hail! happy land, sure none's so blest
With News to comfort every breast.

Published as the Act directs 30 Dec.r 1780 by W. Richardson No 68 high Holborn.

Every day newsboys ran through the streets blowing horns. As the verses here show, the hottest news in 1780 was of the American war. Even a Sunday paper had appeared —an innovation that did not establish itself, however, until the 1790s.

4. *A Meeting of City Politicians*: A dozen men of the humbler sort (the apron of the beer-drinker indicates an artisan) gather round a tavern table to read and discuss the news. They are distraught because it is 1779 and the war is going badly. Newspapers depicted: *London Chronicle, Daily Advertiser, London Gazette, Evening Post, Morning Post*

5 *The Scotch Broomstick & the Female Besom*: Bute and George III's mother have a suggestive aerial encounter. Watching Scots are much impressed. A George Townshend caricature of 1762. (See page 27).

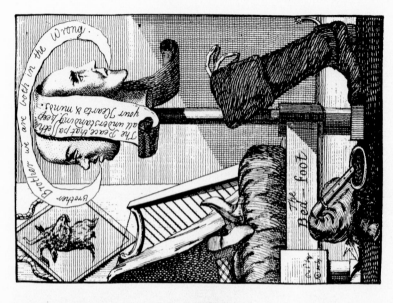

6 *The Couchant Lion, or Saxeney in the Secret:* Bute finds the way to preferment with one hand and twists the lion's tail with the other. A Darly print, evidently by Townshend. (See page 33)

7 *The Bed-foot:* Bagpipe and boot, and widow's armorial lozenge with goat's head, announce the bed's occupants. The wig-block heads are Bute (right) and the Duke of Bedford, Britain's peace negotiator in 1762. A Darly print.

8 *Resignation:* Bute, heading for the flames of hell, pleads with the devil viciously attacking him—'O spare my manhood.' The Scot-smiting Duke of Cumberland speeds his going, supported by George III's brother Edward. The bare-breasted Princess Dowager weeps. (See page 34) Caricature published by John Williams, who was soon to be jailed and pilloried for selling Wilkes's *North Briton* (see next plate).

9 *The Pillory Triumphant*: John Williams, pilloried in 1765 for reprinting the North Briton, is made the hero of a demonstration for press liberty and against Bute, whose jackboot symbol is being hanged while another flies in the air. This print would be very near to a realistic picture of the scene in Palace Yard. Note pugilist punching a Scot; gentlemen drinking to 'Wilkes, Williams and the Glorious 45'; King's Messengers, right. (See page 48)

10 This portrayal of the shooting by Scots guardsmen of an innocent youth during the 1768 St George's Fields riots was dedicated to George III. It is decorated with grim hints for him. (See page 54)

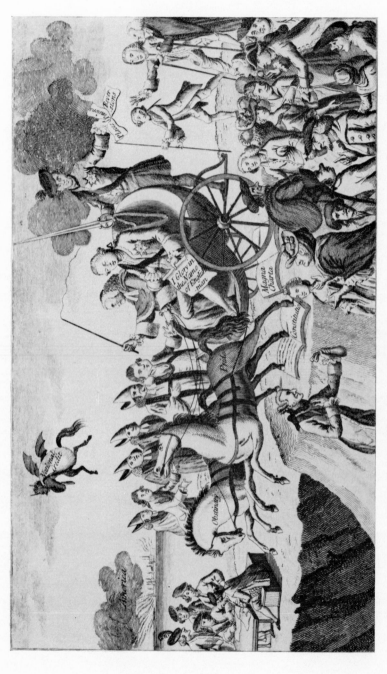

11 *The Political Cartoon for the Year 1775:* Obstinacy and Pride prophetically lead George III toward the abyss, with Bute riding

12 *The Last Stake*: It is 1779; Spain and France attack the British bull, on which fat Lord North rides, dozing. Holland insults a British diplomatic protest. An insult descends too on George III, and the crown is falling.

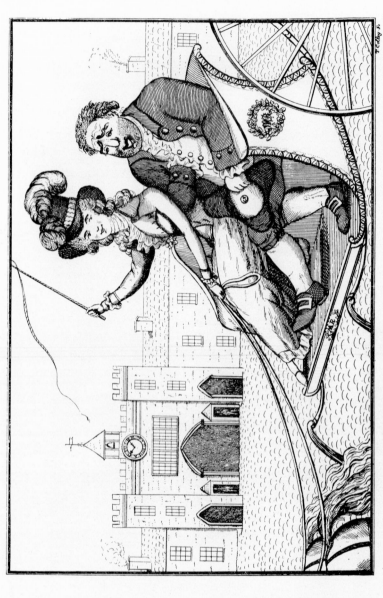

T. Colley, sc.

13 *Perdito & Perdita or the Man & Woman of the People*: St James's street scene, 1782—realistic except for the facial caricaturing of Charles James Fox. Mary 'Perdita' Robinson did drive him about in her monogrammed gig. (See

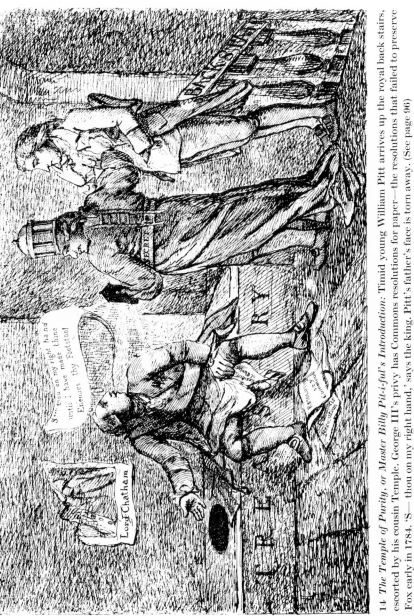

14 *The Temple of Purity, or Master Billy Pit-i-ful's Introduction:* Timid young William Pitt arrives up the royal back stairs, escorted by his cousin Temple. George III's privy has Commons resolutions for paper—the resolutions that failed to preserve Fox early in 1784. 'S— thou on my right hand,' says the king. Pitt's father's face is torn away. (See page 96)

15 *Political Affection*: A fox ousts the Duchess of Devonshire's baby—an odd conceit by Thomas Rowlandson at the height of the 1784 Westminster election. (See page 102)

16 *The Devonshire Minuet, danced to Ancient British Music:* Butchers beat time with marrow-bones and cleavers while another (with double-meaning slogan on his apron) dances with the duchess. Her Fox favours and foxtail are realistic; 'Love & Liberty' is an addition. Other prints went much further. (See page 102–3)

Wishes of the People

Air Balloons

Air Balloon

Wishes of the People

NEIGHBOURS I HAVE LOST the SEAL

Proclamation for Afflatation from a Bread Bottom

H.Y.L

Inflamable

AIR

PITT

17 *Solomon in the Clouds!!*: The king personally contributes to his aerial propulsion, 17?
Lord Chancellor Thurlow, Temple and Pitt are supported (a few months after the fi
balloon ascent in England) by balloons representing the swing of opinion against Fox.

The Wickedest Age

Bute stood high enough to upbraid his prince—not for these faults, however, but for faults that might put him in fetters: his indolence, forgetfulness, lack of spirit, bashfulness, irresolution, and, soon, his distracting interest in 'the fair sex . . . those divine creatures'. Bute disciplined the prince by threatening to abandon him—'to set me adrift', as George put it. George swore to do better; for otherwise 'I shall lose the greatest of stakes, my crown, and what I esteem far beyond that, my Friend'. It is an astonishing scale of values. A year later, aged twenty, George writes that if Bute gives him up he will resign the crown: 'I have too much spirit to accept the crown and be a cypher.' He must be a strong king for his Dearest Friend's sake. It is an ominous infatuation.

If the Hanoverians sometimes surpassed the conceptions of satirists, they also outran the fears of statesmen. In May 1760, Bute approached William Pitt, who was prime minister in all but name, and who as the architect of victory was a national hero. Bute wanted Pitt to help him to become prime minister after George II died. Pitt spurned him, and said he could best stay where he was, as Groom of the Stole (chief Lord of the Bedchamber). Prince George reassured the downcast Bute:

> You will for all that be [prime] minister, for all men will find the only method of succeeding in their desires will be by first acquainting you with what they mean to request. . . . Whilst my Dearest is near me I care not who are the tools he may think necessary to be in ministry, provided the blackest of hearts is not one of them.

The blackest of hearts is Pitt. George also called him 'the most ungrateful, most dishonourable of men' and 'a snake in the grass'. His crime was that a few years earlier, when barred from power by George II, he had been associated with Bute in opposition. Now he was too high. His victories displeased the prince who dreamed of being a Patriot King: 'I can't help feeling that every such thing raises those I have no reason to love,' he wrote to Bute.

George II fell dead in his water-closet at Kensington Palace at sunrise on 25 October 1760. The sudden death was 'a most

23

favourable circumstance', his successor wrote a few years later; 'parties had not previous warning, as they might otherwise have formed cabals that might have been unpleasant'. A messenger galloped out to Kew to let the prince know that he had become George III, and the first letter of his reign went at once to Bute. '. . . An extraordinary thing is just happened to me. . . . I thought I had no time to lose in acquainting my Dearest Friend of this.' The next arrival at Kew was William Pitt in his coach-and-six. He expected to be entrusted with summoning a privy council, but George said he would 'give his own orders'. The hour had come to tame Pitt, the Great Commoner (or, to his enemies, the Great Dictator). George hurried to town, passing Kensington Palace without turning aside to pay his last respects; and sent a second message to Bute: 'I am coming the back way to your house.'

The back way: how the politicians and the news-writers would have delighted to see that unmajestic message, or to espy the coach of the as yet unproclaimed king entering the stable yard of Bute's town house in South Audley Street! George never doubted his right to be devious to outwit the unpleasant cabals which would otherwise make him a cypher. He and Bute instantly began a Whig-splitting operation. They summoned Pitt's chief partner in the imperfectly united government, the ageing, jealous, dithering Duke of Newcastle, and assured him that Bute was his 'good friend'. Newcastle found these words 'remarkable', for he was the ministerial embodiment of the alliance of old Whig families—the Cavendishes, the Russells, the Grenvilles, and so forth—which Bute and the new king were determined to master. But their first concern was the blackest of hearts.

When Pitt, no patient man, was brought into the presence after hours of waiting, he was outraged to find that a speech had already been devised in which George was to say he was mounting the throne 'in the midst of a bloody and expensive war'—a phrase aimed at the aggressive Pitt. If politicians fight over a phrase, it is because much more is at stake. Pitt was daunting when roused; his grey eyes had an almost manic power. He challenged Bute, who was still a mere courtier, and got the phrase changed to 'an expensive but just and necessary war'.

This pained the king. He wrote to Bute, 'I plainly see, if every ill humour of a certain man is to be soothed, that in less than a couple of months I shall be irretrievably in his fetters; a state of bondage that an old man of seventy-odd [George II] groaned, and that twenty-two ought to risk everything rather than submit.' The broken syntax is characteristic of George III under pressure. Still more characteristic is the talk of fetters and of risking everything.

When the king had reigned five months, Bute exchanged the gold key of Groom of the Stole for the seals of a Secretary of State. This first step toward the premiership made him pour out an extraordinary trembling letter to his master. 'I have just took off the gold key . . . . an awful change . . . I have passed the Rubicon . . . my heart cries out . . . violent emotion and unpleasant forebodings. . . . How fares it with my Prince?' It goes on for thirteen hundred words. He insists and insists on the purity of his motives. He has never 'entertained a selfish view or one interested thought since the princess first entreated me to apply my life to your education'. His favour with the king has been won 'by honest, noble means, and not the wretched arts through which minions have too often fascinated their Prince'. But he adds something less reassuring. 'I may want talents for business, faction may overwhelm me, and court intrigues destroy me'—and so he asks for 'your royal promise to ensure me a safe retreat again near your person'. At times the satirists seem the only stable men in an age of unreason.

Any favourite would have caused alarm. That he was a Scot only made him easier to attack. Fifteen years had scarcely passed since the Young Pretender's defeat at Culloden, and the heads of two executed Jacobites still mouldered on spikes at Temple Bar. Besides, the self-admiring English could easily be roused to condemn all Scots as poor immigrants, pushing interlopers. 'Every man has at some time or other found a Scotchman in his way,' wrote Henry Fox in his journal when he was Bute's chief collaborator, 'and everybody has therefore damned the Scotch; and this hatred their excessive nationality [nationalism] has continually inflamed.'

They were also credited (like other strangers from simpler

lands) with great carnal vigour. And now no Scot was more
vigorous than Bute. His attachment for the German widow
was celebrated to many tunes:

> Quoth he, 'Bonny lassie, your Flute gangs weel
> And keeps gude time wi' my Bagpipe clear.
> Sic music as this is can surely ne'er fail
> In time to accord wi' an English ear . . .'

> 'Play away, bonny lad, I have good store of gold.
> Your Bag shall be full while your Pipe it can play.
> You ne'er shall return to a climate so cold,
> For your kisses are warmer and sweeter than May.'

A much-relished lampoon was *Gisbal, an Hyperborean Tale*,
a sequel to the Ossian fabrication which one pushing Scot,
James Macpherson, had just published with a dedication to
Bute. In Macpherson's archaic style, it tells of the progress of
Gisbal, whose 'staff, which he always bare *upright*, was equal
in bigness unto a weaver's beam'. This staff commends him
to Bathsheba. 'My palace and lofty roof be thine,' she says;
'thine be also the care of my Household: for well I ween that
in man the best quality is an *upright staff*, and his stature that
of a hero of gigantic size.' They celebrate the death of George
II 'as a day of triumph', with Gisbal contributing 'the pleasing
voice of the soul-lulling bagpipe'. Soon Gisbal's people, the
Hebronites, prevail everywhere; 'their croaking was heard
even in the king's chamber . . . and this begat great mur-
murings'. The same lampoonist was probably the author of a
ballad, 'The Staff of Gisbal', published as a broadside with a
handsome portrait of Bute:

> When this notable chief of the Hebronites' land
> Before Bathsheba stood with his staff in his hand,
> The damsels around her cried out one and all,
> 'What a wonderful staff is the Staff of Gisbal!'

> From the days of old Adam there has not been found
> Through the world's ample circuit a staff so renowned:
> Not the Cherokee King* or Nabob of Bengal
> Can boast such a staff as the Staff of Gisbal. . . .

*The virility of the Cherokee King, an ally of Britain then visiting London,
was honoured in several songs.

26

No staff ever made of gold, silver or wood
Could compare with this compound of pure flesh and blood.
A staff so upright I may venture to call
A staff for a Princess—this Staff of Gisbal. . . .

Caricaturists seized on the Gisbal theme. In 'Gisbal's Pre-ferment', Bute stands proudly with a suggestive staff; the princess speaks the 'My palace and lofty roof' passage; and a cluster of court ladies rhapsodize—'Never was such a staff seen in Israel!—What a ravishing length!' Pitt, grieving, says, 'O liberty, O my country!' And a horde of Scots approach from the north in covered wagons.

Again and again the Scots are pictured swarming in, hungry, tattered, ready for anything. One tells new arrivals, 'You'll be as welcome as if you had fought for the family [the Hanoverians]. Treason's a joke.' Another says to Bute, 'Oh, I desire a trifle! Only to be an admiral or so.' More than once Bute is a mountebank; his miracle medicine is gold.

Awa' wi' ye to the de'il, ye southern loons, but aw ye bonny lads frae the north o' Tweed, make haste and I'll relieve ye of the Scotch itch wi' my never-failing Golden Nostrum. . . . If I had not travelled early and late to find out a passage through Wales [the princess] I should never have had it in my power.

Bute certainly was being pursued for jobs. One eager Scot among many, James Boswell, applied to him for a Guards commission. It is our good fortune that Bute was intent on a peace.

The Scots queue for the princess as well, and with double-meaning remarks. She says of one of them, 'He shall have any place I can put him in.' With wilder obscenity, a caricature entitled 'The Scotch Broomstick and the Female Besom' shows the princess and Bute flying toward each other through the air. She has the bushy head of a besom ready to receive the end of his broomstick. People gaze up at them.

LADY: I wish my Sawney had such a broomstick.
MAN (peering through telescope): I see the road to prefer-ment.

LADY: I wonder if Mary Queen of Scots was so well served.

BUTE: Come, lassie, let's make the most of the game, for I am strong in hand, and we are above the vulgar.

PRINCESS: The Russian bear is not more carnivorous. I love power as well as she.

The princess's words show how quick London was to react to international as well as domestic scandal. This caricature, probably by George Townshend, appeared in 1762 soon after the lustful (carnivorous) Empress Catherine—a German cousin of the princess—had seized power in Russia. It is striking to find the two women associated, too, just at this time, in the journal of Henry Fox. He says they have been 'in constant correspondence', and he goes on, 'And a correspondence of another sort, I mean of constitution, made her think it would be very agreeable to send to that court one Mr [Thomas] Wroughton, a handsome young man . . . and maybe he is by this time at Petersburg, in an employment which probably Her Imperial Majesty will not suffer to be occupied only by native Russians.' Furthermore, when Fox laments in his journal that Bute is attacked as a Scot, he adds that Bute is also 'told of his intrigue with the Princess Dowager'. In the context, 'told' is a powerful word.

'The Scotch Broomstick' is one of about twenty anti-Bute caricatures that have been ascribed to Townshend, the high-born caricaturist discussed earlier. His younger brother Charles, it is worth noting, was married to one of Bute's cousins. Bute suspected nothing, regarded George Townshend as his friend, and made him a privy councillor.

Besides his card-size caricatures, Townshend is credited with having invented caricatures incorporating a transparency which when held up to the light reveals a hidden scene. In one, Bute and the princess are discovered freely caressing each other. In another, George III stands with a scroll saying *amor vincit omnia*, and with a petticoat above his head to symbolize his mother's domination; and the princess says to Bute, 'Your love's too large for a vulgar body'—at once a lewd joke and a hit at Bute's notorious hauteur.

The finger was pointed at Townshend a few years later in a

letter to *The Public Advertiser*. It complains, or pretends to complain, of the vast output of caricatures—'Every window of every printshop is in a manner glazed, and the shop itself papered, with libels'—and goes on: 'One arch-libeller in particular has rendered himself more than a hundred times liable to prosecution. . . . He has dealt his grotesque cards from house to house and circulated his defamatory pictures from *Town's end* to *Town's end*.' The letter is signed 'George Bout-de-ville'. By this time Bute had withdrawn behind the scenes. Using blanks for his name, the same paper addressed some 'Hints for a Political Print' to Townshend:

> Your friendship for the ---- of ---- will naturally secure a corner in the retirement for him and his curtain. Provided you discover him on a bed, with a magic wand in his hand, any one of Aretine's postures will suit him; for if fame be not too partial, there is certainly a bed upon which he has exhibited with uncommon grace and activity in them all.

No print went so far; but more than one takes us into the princess's bedchamber, offers a glimpse of activity through the bed-curtains, and scatters such Butian symbols as a boot and bagpipe. In one of these, a dog is sniffing Bute's breeches, and some commenting verses say:

> Oh, oh, is it so? Bonny Sawney, thou'rt blest.
> This petticoat tumbling brings on all the rest.
> We guess who you've got, and the dog at your breeches
> Proclaims by the smell, you can scratch where it itches.

That abuse like this could be found in the shops is a measure of the detestation in which Bute was held. A still more impressive clue to the public's mood is the fact that among all the caricatures that survive, four hundred attack Bute and only four support him.

Before the reign was two years old, Bute was pleading for his 'safe retreat'. 'He made the king so uneasy,' says George Grenville, then in Bute's cabinet, 'that he frequently sat for hours together, leaning his head upon his arm without speaking.' Here is an early example of George III's indulgence in wounded melancholy. Why was his Dearest Friend not triumphant? He had the most potent single asset a prime minister could have—the unquestioning favour of the king. Together they had eased out first Pitt and then the Duke of Newcastle. The way was open for Bute and the king to break up the Whig oligarchy which for so long had managed affairs by an artful distribution of jobs, pensions, titles, favours and bankbills. All honours and rewards would then flow from one royal fountain. There would be 'an end of faction'—a constant phrase of Bute's. They would, in the king's words, 'put an end to those unhappy distinctions of party called Whigs & Torys'. Bluntly, that would mean there was no organized opposition to challenge the king's chosen ministers. George, guided by Bute, would be king indeed.

Having plunged the king into despair, Bute the rash/timid, the arrogant/inept, was persuaded by the princess to fight on. But then he gave the attackers an additional target.

He was offering France peace terms which were thought by much of the country, in its John Bullish mood, to be far too soft. He wanted a resounding Commons majority for the peace—a majority to demonstrate the impotence of the 'wicked faction' that opposed him. He must employ an expert in the influencing of MPs. Bute and the king had been telling the country, and even each other, that they were innocent of the old gang's 'dirty arts'. Now a gap was revealed between professions and practice. They brought in Henry Fox: a man notorious as a self-seeker and a master of corruption. 'We must call in bad men,' said the king, 'to govern bad men.' That is, dirty arts were permissible if he used them. The Duke of Devonshire, Lord Chamberlain, wrote bluntly to Fox that he was doing no good to Bute or the king: 'The nation is mad and ready to break out into a flame.' He added this advice: 'If a king of England employs those people for his ministers that the nation have a good opinion of, he will make a great figure; but if he chooses them merely thro' personal favour, it will never do.'

The nation was learning indeed to see the king as a figure of contempt. Caricatures show him as a lion in child's clothing, led by Bute. Or he and the young Queen Charlotte are two tiny lions in a coach driven by his mother. Or he serves as a footman (with rattle and fool's cap) to Bute and the princess. Bute's name, then pronounced 'boot', inspires endless puns. In 'The Loaded Boot' the king and queen are degraded into a horse and zebra pulling a boot-shaped carriage in which Bute and princess snugly sit.

PRINCESS: This is a pleasing Boot to me.
BUTE: Our power is almighty. As you have often *raised* me, so will I now support you.
FOX: I'll lead 'em till I get 'em in the mire, and then I'll leave 'em.

'The Loaded Boot' is attributed to Townshend; and just at this time, comically enough, Bute is writing to him ('My Dear George') to defend his employment of Fox. 'I have hardly met with anything but cruel abuse and base ingratitude.' (Did Townshend laugh?) 'Fox . . . has very nobly abandoned retreat and security to stand the storms of faction, without any motive on earth but that of obedience to the king's commands. This is the naked truth. The king has flung the last die for his liberty.'

The naked truth about Fox was that he expected to be rewarded with an earldom (he became only a baron, Lord Holland); and that he had a financial incentive. Fox was paymaster general of the army. The official income, magnificent then, was £3,000 or £4,000, but the post yielded much more, for Fox took full advantage of the fact that he was not forbidden to speculate with the money entrusted to him. In 1761 he put £773,000 in government stocks before Bute opened a first round of peace talks, sold out just before the talks collapsed, and made £103,000—which more than two hundred years later would be well over £2 million. When he 'nobly' stepped forward in 1762, he had again bought stock; ratification of the peace was to give him a further £56,000.

'The king has flung his last die': the nation had reason to be enflamed. The Whig system, though oligarchic and corrupt, had at least maintained a partial freedom (the envy of sufferers under absolutism) by setting parliamentary power in an uneasy interplay with royal prerogative. MPs had been bought and sold; this royal gamble went further.

When parliament assembled, Bute was hissed, jeered, and pelted with rubbish, and had to be rescued from the mob. The king was 'insulted at the door of his parliament, in getting out of his coach, in the midst of his guards'—so Bute bitterly described the scene—and the 'rascal' who insulted him was 'rescued in his sight' by the mob. Bute seems to have wished that the guards had opened fire, for he adds (writing to Fox), 'There are minutes when great prudence and caution animate rebellion and encourage faction and riot'—a line of thought that George III later followed.

A self-pitying man can be dangerous. 'Little do they know what passes in my breast,' Bute writes the next day to a friend. He has been 'forced' into high office. He is the target for 'all that malice, faction and disappointed ambition can invent to destroy me'. It is true he has to use bribery, but it pains him: 'How little nature has formed me to practise those arts by which ministers support themselves! I hate to offer what I despise a man for accepting.'

In the first crucial division on the peace, those arts helped to win a majority of 316 to 65. Nobody can now say how many MPs Bute had to despise; but in 1762 the outlay on 'secret service' and 'special service' was £125,000, or £52,000 more than the year before (itself a costly year). Banknotes were moreover only one of the forms of influence enjoyed by MPs and by the peers who controlled many of them. Grants of pensions, for example, went up sharply. And in calculating how much temptation a single MP might face, one must remember that the rewards did not need to be shared among anything like a majority of the 558 members, for there was no point in wasting them on men already inclined the right way. The king himself wrote to Bute afterwards, 'Has this whole winter been anything else but a scene of corruption?'

There was besides the enormous carrot-and-stick power of the thousands of posts now commanded by a united court and Treasury. A purge of Whigs had begun before the vote. The king, roused from his melancholy, had made his will clear by dismissing several magnates with great rudeness. Bute quoted the king as saying, 'Will more great men follow? Let them. I prefer six open enemies to two secret ones.' Bute himself raised the odds in another letter: 'Ten open enemies are preferable to one secret one.' After the vote, Fox the turncoat Whig told Bute that the king must 'pursue his victory' and purge even the lowliest Whig job-holder: 'His Majesty has it in his power to make his reign easy'. Bute agreed: the party must now either be destroyed or else 'lead him in chains'. The king agreed: 'Vigour and violence are the only means of ending this audacious faction.' Fox worked ruthlessly. Out went every placeman who would not turn his coat—excisemen, tidewaiters, all the men whose jobs nourished party loyalty.

Fox managed to feel offended by the alarm he was helping to cause. 'Nobody can prevent such clamour as was never before heard,' he complained to his journal. 'And prints come out without number, all stupid, and some so indecent they would not be suffered to hang up in a bawdy-house. I have one now before me—' But he crossed out this phrase, recoiling from describing, perhaps, 'The Couchant Lion or Sawney in the Secret', in which a huge boot crushes the British lion, the princess sits astride on the boot, and Bute reaches up her skirts.

> BUTE: I have found out the way to preferment, and will go a great way in my politics.
> PRINCESS: You're right for my favour.

Or perhaps Fox was looking at a caricature of himself, for he went on, 'I am not forgot in some of these prints (not the indecent ones), which I mention more because of the singularity than any importance it is of. . . . A people whom I never offended cannot let me alone.' Another misunderstood man! Common people are getting above themselves: 'To this pass are we brought by newspapers and libels, and the encouragement given to the mob to think themselves the government.'

Bute was pictured as a barber holding Britannia by the nose and shaving her, with words inspired by a popular song, 'My eye, that's the barber!'

> Well, wonders sure will never cease—
> Thank God we've got a glorious peace!

That commerce, arts and wealth increase
    We owe to Scot the Barber.

The greatest lady in the land
Can see with pleasure Sawney stand
And *lather* muckly at command,
    And then she thanks the barber.

So clean he moves his instrument
The nation stares at the event,
And every man would be content
    Were he like Scot the Barber.

In fact Bute was no longer the picture of a virile Scot. His nerves were shattered, he could not sleep, constipation plagued him. 'The vessel's safe in harbour,' he wrote to Fox. 'Firmness and resolution are no more necessary; but a thousand little arts, sinister arts and unworthy trafficking, become the proper talents for the fresh-water pilot.' With true Butian tactlessness, he followed these words by asking Fox to be the fresh-water pilot. (Fox the realist was not unwilling, but his wife dissuaded him.)

On the day Bute retired, 8 April 1763, he unburdened himself once more to his friend George Townshend the unsuspected caricaturist. 'What treatment have I not met with! I allude not to the mere vulgar clamour against me. No, I speak of the interior of government. . . . I have seen myself single in a cabinet formed by my own hand . . . though opposed to the most violent attacks of the enemy.' He has a further reason for quitting: the king is suffering from 'popular clamour in a manner none of his predecessors ever did. This, I am afraid, has been in some measure owing to me. The national prejudice against me; the use that faction has made of the odious name of Favourite to poison the minds even of well-intentioned people; has not failed to blacken this most amiable character.' Satire had proved its power to influence public events.

Bute's retirement inspired delighted comments. The devil, leading him away, claws for his genitals and says, 'I'll soon spoil your piping.' Or the princess kneels by a fallen Bute and says—

The Wickedest Age

> My feeble hand, alas! in vain
> Attempts to make thee stand again.

But sober second thoughts told Bute's enemies that he was still a power behind the scenes. Just after the resignation, George III is caricatured as a mule-headed lion led by Bute, who is mounted on a she-goat.

BUTE: Damn your sauls, ye loons, I dinna mind ye, I can make the animal do as I please—and I am well mounted.

GOAT: I love Jockey should ride me. He gives me the greatest pleasure.

Accompanying verses say of the king:

> Some say he's a lion, and some say a mule,
> But most people say he's an obstinate fool. . . .
> But if this poor Brute had but reason and sense
> He would give him [Bute] a kick and drive him from thence.
> The people would hollo and give a great shout. . . .

A mere retreat by Bute is not enough to free the king from 'popular clamour'. In two years he has sunk very low. He is not only a fool; he is obstinate, a deeper accusation. ''Tis an obstinate creature,' says another caricature; 'he'll be guided by none but that d----d Scotchman and his villainous gang.'

The bitterness of the attack only made the king more certain he was right, and confirmed him in his bad opinion of mankind. Nothing made him so furious in his certainties as the impudent demagogue John Wilkes.

3

An incomparable Subject
for a Print

AUDACIOUS polemical journalism raised John Wilkes to fame. It was a late-developed talent. When he entered his thirty-eighth year he had served William Pitt in parliament, eagerly but without reward, since 1757; was deep in debt but unquenchably devoted to women and high living; and Pitt's fall had cheated him of his hopes of a lucrative post. His best resource was to join in the paper war to topple Bute.

Since the first months of George III's reign, Bute had been laying out public money to influence newspapers and buy writers. On becoming prime minister in mid-1762 he launched a new weekly paper, *The Briton*, edited and largely written by an irascible Scot, Tobias Smollett—a good novelist, but unhappy as a propagandist. Wilkes was to call him 'a wretch hired to ring the alarum bell of discord'. After only a week, Wilkes hit back with *The North Briton*, so named in mockery of Bute and all Scots. Wilkes was backed financially by Pitt's ungainly, rich and plot-loving brother-in-law, Lord Temple, known as Lord Gawkee. *The Briton* struggled for circulation and perhaps never passed a few hundred. Its antagonist is said to have reached two thousand, and its readers were uncountable, especially when the unministerial papers soon began reprinting each issue (containing about two thousand words). Wilkes had the art to speak equally to gentlemen and to what he called 'the middling and inferior set of people'. He dignified his arguments with Latin and even Greek quotations;

he shamelessly appealed to the mob's prejudice against Scots. He appealed too—and his heart, it must be said, was in this— to English ideas of freedom.

The first words of Wilkes's first issue are: 'The liberty of the press is the birthright of a Briton.' This liberty, he says, is 'the terror of all bad ministers'; they will use every art 'to check the spirit of knowledge and inquiry'. This was not mere rhetoric. Wilkes knew that threats of prosecution were being held over the head of another weekly, *The Monitor*—and because of articles he himself had written. He had tried out in *The Monitor* a technique he was soon to use again: attacking Bute, without naming him, by finding in history alarming instances of royal favourites.

One favourite only glanced at by Wilkes was the Emperor Tiberius's Sejanus, who ended by being thrown headless into the Tiber. Smollett, in his first issue, blundered into Wilkes's rapier (no doubt pushed by Bute) and fumed at the scandalous insinuation that there was 'some resemblance between Tiberius and the r------g prince, between Sejanus and the present M------r', for 'Sejanus was the most wicked minister of one of the most execrable tyrants'. Wilkes urbanely retorted: 'He and only he has mentioned a resemblance between the reigning prince and Tiberius, which I believe has never occurred to anyone else'. But Wilkes did not offer to say there was no resemblance between Sejanus and Bute.

A royal favourite nearer home, doubly so, was Roger Mortimer, the lover of young Edward III's mother. In *North Briton* No. 5, Wilkes pointed up the story for his purposes, and concluded: 'Oh, may Britain never see such a day again, when power acquired by profligacy may lord it over this realm; when the feeble pretensions of a *court minion* may require the prostitution of royalty for their support!' Messengers from the Treasury were going out every Saturday to buy copies of *The North Briton*, *The Monitor* and other unpleasant papers so that Bute's law officers could study them. But how could they prosecute a historical essay, or argue that Wilkes's fine peroration was a libel on Bute and his king's mother? Bute chose not to have the delicate point debated before the Court of King's Bench.

Smollett could only rage at 'these tides of scurrility and treason, these deluges of filth and sedition', which flowed from 'the rabble, hedge coffee-house politicians, bankrupt mechanics soured by their losses, and splenetic sots who change their no-opinions oftener than their linen'. These warring papers were written anonymously, but Smollett knew that Wilkes, a former friend of his, was behind *The North Briton*. Smollett printed a diatribe against the ugly, cross-eyed Wilkes under the name of Jahia Ben Israel Ginn—for Wilkes's father Israel was a gin distiller:

> His external form was such as happily expressed the deformity of his mind. His face was meagre, sallow and forbidding, as if he looked pale and haggard from the consciousness of guilt. His eyes were distorted with such a hideous obliquity of vision that the sight of him alone had frightened some matrons into miscarriage. . . . His jaw was furnished with large, irregular tushes. . . . By dint of perpetual talking, sneering, laughing, shrugging and slabbering, he acquired some reputation as a satirist and buffoon. . . .

This was hardly the John Wilkes whose wit and good humour charmed even his enemies; even, years later, that Tory bear, Sam Johnson. Wilkes was not wounded. On reading this portrait of himself, he wrote cheerfully to his partner on *The North Briton*, his fellow-lecher Charles Churchill, poet and lapsed clergyman, 'I am excellently portrayed in Saturday's Briton. Why do not the printshops take me? I am an incomparable subject for a print.'

His day of fame was approaching. In November 1762 Bute rounded up the editor and printers of *The Monitor* on charges citing 'gross and scandalous reflections and invectives' written in part by Wilkes many months before. Wilkes's own printer was frightened out of touching any more of his copy by being shown a warrant drawn up ready to arrest him for the first twenty-five *North Britons*. Wilkes found another printer, but soon this man had 'fallen ill to avoid printing the paper'. He found yet another. He had a lawyer vetting everything, and sometimes at the last minute Charles Churchill had to find a way to fill an entire issue. As an MP Wilkes had wide privileges against arrest, but was he safe? He wrote in *North Briton* No. 27:

> Almost every man I meet looks strangely on me. Some industriously avoid me—others pass me silent—stare—and shake their heads. Those few, those very few, who are not afraid to take a lover of his country by the hand, congratulate me on being alive and at liberty. They advise circumspection—for they do not know—they cannot tell—but—the times—liberty is precious—fines—imprisonment—pillory—

The *Monitor* charges, he wrote, were 'of excellent use to stop the mouths of those who . . . exclaim against the Minister'. And in fact they were never brought into court.

Circumspection was not for Wilkes. He went on finding ways to pursue Bute, the 'hot-brained and overbearing Minister'. When he could, he named him—which made Lord Temple write nervously, 'Ld B's name at full length may be attended with unhappy consequences,' for Wilkes was flouting a pamphleteering convention that the names of peers and MPs must be disguised with blanks. In March 1763 Wilkes caused a sensation by reprinting a seventeenth-century play, *The Fall of Mortimer* (which thirty years earlier had been used against Robert Walpole), with an artful dedication to Bute:

> . . . I have felt an honest indignation at all the invidious and odious applications of the story of Roger Mortimer. I absolutely disclaim the most distant allusion, and I purposely dedicate *this play* to Your Lordship because history does not furnish a more striking contrast than there is between the two Ministers in the reigns of Edward the Third and of George the Third. The former prince was held in the most absolute slavery by his mother and her Minister, the first nobles of England were excluded from the king's councils, and the minion disposed of all places of profit and trust. . . . This excellent prince is held in no kind of captivity. . . . No discord now rages in the kingdom, but every tongue blesses the Minister. . . .

Wilkes recalls Bute's love of play-acting, and says one part in which he was perfect was 'the famous scene of Hamlet, where you *pour fatal poison into the ear* of a good, unsuspecting king'. The knife-twisting goes on to the end of the dedication:

> The play is quite imperfect. . . . It is the warmest wish of my heart that the Earl of Bute may speedily complete the story of Roger Mortimer [who was executed]. . . . And wherever the name of Roger Mortimer shall be mentioned, that of Bute will follow to the latest times.

In the week this came out, young James Boswell overheard a bit of dialogue in Child's Coffee House on Ludgate Hill, next-door to Wilkes's publisher, George Kearsley:

> CITIZEN: Bless me! how this play, *The Fall of Mortimer*, has sold, and all for the dedication.
> PHYSICIAN: Yes, 'tis an old play and not worth sixpence.

'Inclination there is, no doubt, to silence *The North Briton*,' Wilkes wrote in No. 44. 'That impudent libeller, as they are pleased to call, but cannot or dare not prove him, shall still pursue the path in which he hath hitherto trod.' He forecast that Bute was going, and six days later he went. For two Saturdays Wilkes produced no *North Briton*. Then came the issue that was to make 'No. 45' a rallying cry for years. Its chief crime was to say that the King's Speech that George III had just read to parliament, commending Bute's peace treaty, was 'the most abandoned instance of ministerial effrontery ever attempted to be imposed on mankind', and that the honour of the crown was 'sunk even to prostitution'.

Here at last, it seemed to the king, was the opening he needed to punish the man who had been wounding him for so long with innuendoes against his mother and Bute. Here too was the chance to teach all wicked libellers a lesson.

But the first round in the well-known story of Wilkes as martyr-hero ended a fortnight later with his being brought from the Tower to the Court of Common Pleas and freed, by a judge friendly to Pitt, on the ground that an MP was privileged against arrest for a libel. A great shout of joy filled Westminster Hall, and as Wilkes bowed to the crowd he heard the

cry that was to delight him and torment George III for years
to come: 'Wilkes and Liberty!' A mob escorted him home to
Great George Street. With Pitt in eclipse and the Whig
machine crumbling, the 'middling and lower' people were
seizing on Wilkes as the champion of their liberties. Even
opponents of Bute found it alarming.

Now Wilkes was indeed 'an incomparable subject for a
print'. One that soon appeared was far from pleasing him. Up
in the gallery in Westminster Hall, the ageing William
Hogarth had been sketching Wilkes; as Charles Churchill put
it,

> Lurking, most ruffian-like, behind a screen . . .
> The murd'rous pencil in his palsied hand.

Hogarth was paying off a score. An old friendship between the
two men had been broken eight months before—and all over a
caricature. Wilkes had learned that Hogarth, who had a small
court sinecure, was working on a print depicting Pitt and
Temple fanning the flames of war while Bute strived to put
them out. Hogarth ignored an appeal from Wilkes to suppress
the print. In retaliation Wilkes devoted an entire *North Briton*
to an abusive attack on him. Hogarth does seem to have
regretted caricaturing Pitt: he said later that he did it, after
an illness, 'to stop a gap in my income'. But he made no
apology for his portrait print of Wilkes, which did more than
justice to his squint and his irregular tushes, and made him
into a sly, devilish figure who hardly looked like a believer in
the cap of liberty that he held aloft. 'The ridiculous was
apparent to every eye,' Hogarth wrote. 'A saviour of his
country with such an aspect!' It galled Wilkes and his friends,
Hogarth said—and the venom Churchill then poured on
Hogarth confirms this. But Wilkes's excited followers, who
were able to make even his squint a virtue, were no doubt
among the buyers of the print. According to a printer, 'nearly
four thousand copies . . . were worked off in a few weeks.'
Other prints were rushed out which even made Wilkes
handsome. Songs extolled him:

> His pen was like a two-edged sword,
> His wit was sharp and pat;

And keen North Britons he could write,
　　But not a word of that. . . .

The Tower then received the guest
　　But he cared not a f--ta;
They soon were glad to let him go
　　By dint of Magna Carta. . . .

Beware, *guid laird*—for tho' this work
　　By others' hands is done,
So bunglingly 'tis brought about
　　We ken 'tis all thine own.

Unprivileged printers and publishers, however, were as
vulnerable as ever. Wilkes therefore set up a press on the
second floor of his privileged house to produce a reprint of his
North Britons in book form. But he also put his printers to work
on a job he was later to regret: *An Essay on Woman*. The chief
author of this obscene parody of Alexander Pope had been
one of Wilkes's guides in dissipation: Thomas Potter, son of an
Archbishop of Canterbury, one-time secretary to George III's
father, Wilkes's precursor as MP for Aylesbury, and a junior
minister under Pitt. Though no rake, Pitt did not discounte-
nance bawdry, and called Potter 'one of the best friends I have
in the world'. In 1754 Potter writes to Wilkes: 'At dinner
yesterday we read over your parody. He [Pitt] bid me tell you
that he found with great concern you was as wicked and
agreeable as ever.' That parody was evidently 'Veni Creator,
or the Maid's Prayer,' which begins:

Creator Pego, by whose aid
Thy humble suppliant was made;
O source of bliss and god of love,
Shed thy influence from above. . . .
Come, and awhile vouchsafe to dwell
In my dark unfrequented cell.

This and two other short pieces, 'The Universal Prayer' and
'The Dying Lover to his Prick,' were set in type at Great
George Street, together with ninety-four lines of *An Essay on
Woman*. Wilkes's plan was not to publish the poems, but to
print twelve copies for his friends—men who had sung merry

catches with him in the clubrooms of the Sublime Society of Beef Steaks above Covent Garden Theatre, or shared in the erotic revels of Medmenham Abbey, the Buckinghamshire retreat of Sir Francis Dashwood. Wilkes dedicated *An Essay on Woman* to a person some of them knew well, Fanny Murray, a courtesan then living in retirement on her large earnings. (It was written of Fanny's chief rival, Kitty Fisher, 'An hundred buys her for a night'—guineas, that is; perhaps £2,500 now.) He had a frontispiece engraved 'representing a penis by a scale of ten inches' (so the official records state) and associated it with an imputation in Latin linking a late bishop and a living courtier. He worked into the poem a hit at Bute, though a mild one:

> Then in the scale of various pricks, 'tis plain,
> Godlike erect, Bute stands the foremost man.
> And all the question (wrangle e'er so long)
> Is only this: If heaven placed him wrong.

To pure minds it was shocking enough that the poem shamelessly mocked Pope's attempt to 'vindicate the ways of God to man'—

> Presumptuous prick! the reason wouldst thou find
> Why form'd so weak, so little, and so blind?

For some it was equally shocking that there were footnotes ascribed to William Warburton, Bishop of Gloucester, parodying the pedantic commentary with which he had burdened an edition of Pope's poems. The fun of this was heightened for those who knew that Potter (now dead) had been Mrs Warburton's lover. One 'Warburton' note discusses whether Pope ever made 'an Essay on Woman', and says, 'As for my own abilities for such a work, modesty commands my silence.' Another note, commenting on man's preference for 'clean girls', manages to mock the Scots, and has the true Wilkesian touch:

This first (for lewdness is only the second) great virtue of cleanliness ought of all things to be attended to. It is shocking to find how much it is neglected, especially in the northern part of this island. The face, the neck, the hands, I own, are not only clean, but of a whiteness which would rival Leda's lover. All the rest, alas! is hid in mysterious sluttishness. The nobler parts are never in this island washed by the women: they are left to be lathered by the men.

Wilkes went for the summer to Paris; but not merely to be entertained by clean girls. As a king-defying Englishman he was caressed, too, by Diderot and other *philosophes*, and reported, 'The most sensible people here think that the French are on the eve of some great revolution.' There were twenty-six years to go.

The ministerial plot by which in Wilkes's absence a copy of *An Essay on Woman* was obtained from one of his printers by bribery, and then used in the Lords to blacken his name, provides a fine early example of English political hypocrisy. One minor role was played by a man Wilkes described as 'that babe of grace, that *gude chield* of the prudish kirk of Scotland, the Earl of March'. This nobleman, a notorious rake, the future Old Q, 4th Duke of Queensberry, was a Lord of the Bedchamber—one of the unedifying appointees of Bute who were thriving in the service of George III. A major role was played by His Majesty's Secretary of State, John Montagu, 4th Earl of Sandwich. He was one of the Medmenham Abbey 'monks', a lover of bawdy songs, a noted lecher, and a former customer of the expensive Fanny Murray herself. He and Wilkes had shared many merry evenings at Medmenham and at Beef Steak dinners. Early in that year, when Sandwich had briefly been ambassador-designate to Spain, Wilkes had written for the amusement of the Beef Steaks a set of mock royal instructions from 'Our Sublime Court of St Paul, Covent Garden'—a tribute to Sandwich's lechery:

> . . . It is beneath Your Lordship to measure swords with the men, and we do most expressly restrain you to make all your *thrusts* at the women with the little short rapier which you always carry about you. . . . To Your Lordship is committed the care of the English standard. . . . Bear it, my lord, nobly erect. . . . Plant your victorious standard in the citadel of every fair donna whom you beseech or besiege. . . .

Sandwich rarely needed to beseech or besiege. Eight years later, when he became First Lord of the Admiralty, the *General Evening Post* said:

> L--d S------h has had more applications made to him for places and appointments, in the little time he has been at the head of the A-------y, than any other person who ever sat there; and mostly, it is said, from young ladies of his former acquaintance, in favour of their brothers, cousins or other relations, on the claim of past acts of friendship.

Scores of letters among Sandwich's papers prove the justice of this paragraph; and some of the ladies were offering future acts of friendship.

Sandwich took what he called 'a forward part' against Wilkes. One justification for bringing the *Essay* before the Lords was that a Lord Spiritual, Warburton, was named in it. When shown the poem, he called Wilkes 'a diabolical monster', and joined the plot despite a fear that he might be laughed at—'what there is of ridicule in the offence may possibly affect some hearers more than the impiety and the blasphemy'. His own purity, at least of doctrine, had been questioned; and a few months later Churchill wrote in *The Duellist* that the bishop had

> lived with sinners,
> Herded with infidels for dinners;
> With such an emphasis and grace
> Blasphemed, that Potter kept not pace.

Far more comical than Warburton was the sight of Sandwich, with pretended horror and disgust, quoting from an obscene poem. One peer begged him to stop, but others cried 'Go on!' The book was condemned as 'scandalous, obscene, impious, wicked and blasphemous'—and a breach of privilege. The operation contributed to a private amusement of Horace Walpole's, his 'Sketch of a New Method of Writing History':

> 'Wilkes has written a blasphemous and indecent poem.'
> 'Who told you so?' said the king.
> 'Parson Kidgell told it to Lord March, and he told Lord

Bute and me,' said Lord Sandwich; 'and I have heard him repeat it.'

'Where?' said the king.

'At our club at the top of Covent Garden Theatre,' said Lord Sandwich.

'And so have I,' said Lord Le Despencer, 'at our Abbey of Medmenham, where we used to practise all kinds of impiety and indecency.'

'This will do,' said the king.

'I will betray and impeach my friend,' said Lord Sandwich. '. . . I will cant.'

'Do so,' said Bishop Warburton.

Sandwich was thrown out of the Sublime Society of Beef Steaks, where a few months before he had sat as chairman under a canopy inscribed in gold with the words Beef and Liberty. And when at a performance of *The Beggar's Opera* Macheath spoke the line, 'That Jemmy Twitcher should peach me, I own surprises me,' the audience took the point with a roar, and Sandwich was Jemmy Twitcher to the end of his days.

The Despencer that Walpole mentions was Dashwood under a newly acquired title. He was another reproach to the virtuous king. At the age of fifty-five, through Bute's friendship, he had become Chancellor of the Exchequer—although, Wilkes wrote, he had been 'puzzling all his life over tavern bills'—and he lingered on in a court sinecure until 1781. Even his steward, pimp, poet and buffoon, Paul Whitehead, was awarded the sinecure of Deputy Wardrobe Keeper.

The world at large had had some hints of the delights of Medmenham in a delicately censored article by Wilkes in *The Public Advertiser:*

. . . There is one remarkable temple in the gardens at West Wycombe, dedicated to -----, the Egyptian hieroglyphic for ****. To this object His Lordship's devotion is undoubtedly sincere, though I believe now not fervent, nor do I take him to be often prostrate, or indeed in any way very regular in his ejaculations. . . . As to the temple . . . the entrance to it is the same entrance by which we all come into the world. . . . It is reported that, on a late visit to his Chancellor, Lord Bute particularly admired this building.

The article, unsigned of course, told of an attempt by Le Despencer in 1762 to buy him and Churchill over to the government's side. On a hilltop Le Despencer had built a church topped by a 'magnificent gilt ball . . . the best Globe Tavern I was ever in'.

I admire likewise the silence and secrecy which reign in that great globe, undisturbed but by his jolly songs, very unfit for the profane ears of the world below. . . . It is whispered that a negotiation was here *entamée* by the noble lord himself with Messrs Wilkes and Churchill. . . . If from perverseness neither of those gentlemen then yielded to his wise reasons nor to his dazzling offers, they were both delighted with his divine milk punch.

Bribery and prosecution were two ways of dealing with a troublesome writer. A third, more chancy, was to challenge him to a duel. One mocking passage in *The North Briton* had involved Wilkes in a bloodless duel with Lord Talbot, the king's Lord Steward. Now, during a Commons debate in which No. 45 was condemned as a seditious libel, Wilkes received another challenge. It came from Samuel Martin, a Treasury secretary who had betrayed the Duke of Newcastle's secrets to Bute and had then gone into Bute's service. In *The North Briton* Wilkes called Martin 'the most treacherous, base, selfish, mean, abject, lowlived and dirty fellow that ever *wriggled* himself into a secretaryship'. Now Martin said, looking at Wilkes, that anyone who could write such anonymous abuse was 'a cowardly rascal'. Next morning Wilkes sent him a note:

I whisper in your ear that every passage in *The North Briton* in which you have been named . . . was written by—
Your humble servant, John Wilkes

A duel with pistols followed in Hyde Park. Wilkes was hit just below the navel. Soon his challenger was nicknamed Target Martin, for he was reported to have been practising for many months.

47

Lying gravely wounded in Great George Street, Wilkes had the satisfaction of knowing that the *Essay on Woman* affair had not harmed him among the shouters of 'Wilkes and Liberty'. When on parliament's orders the public hangman tried to burn a copy of No. 45 on a heap of faggots in front of the Royal Exchange, a crowd of Wilkites turned the ritual into a violent farce, belabouring constables with the faggots, and rescuing No. 45 from a solitary pro-court alderman who lit it. And the mob built its own fire to burn what had become universal symbols of satire on Bute and the princess—a boot and a petticoat.

Soon Wilkes slipped away to France, having been stripped of his MP's privilege. He promised to 'feed the papers from time to time with gall and vinegar', but devoted more energy to his pleasures. At home 'Wilkes and Liberty' was not forgotten, however: the court's unpopularity made sure of that. This was well demonstrated in 1765 at the pillorying of John Williams, who had been jailed for selling Wilkes's *North Briton* reprint. At his shop at 38 Fleet Street, Williams had also sold some of the most virulent anti-Bute caricatures, a fact that probably contributed to the decision to put him in the pillory. This punishment was most often used for perjurors and sodomites, who would helplessly face an hour's barrage of rotten eggs and fruit, dead cats, and such quantities of filth that they sometimes died. But when a man was pilloried in a popular cause, he could expect an hour of glory. The street became the scene of a drama of good and evil.

The day chosen for Williams's pillorying happened to be February 14. His supporters rejoiced in the fact that this was the forty-fifth day of the year. They contrived to have him brought to the pillory in Palace Yard, Westminster, in hackney carriage No. 45. The whole scene was displayed to the nation in a print with hardly a touch of caricature: John Williams on his pillory stage—the crowd cheering him—two King's Messengers with their silver greyhound badges standing by discomfited—and an improvised gibbet of two ladders, from which hang a jackboot, a Scotch bonnet, and an axe (for beheading the boot as a final gesture). Some verses beneath the picture say:

> But where's the petticoat, my lads?
> The Boot should have its mate. . . .

> When wicked M[iniste]rs of St[at]e
> To fleece the land combined,
> As guardian of our liberties
> The *Press* was first designed.

> But now the scum is uppermost,
> The truth must not be spoke,
> The laws are topsy-turvy turned
> And justice is a joke.

The crowd round the pillory was not a mere rabble. A collection for John Williams came to £200: enough to pay a printer's wages for four years.

Williams's triumph inspired a daring pamphlet, *The Petition of an Englishman*, addressed to Bute, in which the petitioner asks to be admitted to the Order of the Pillory and even seeks the honour of more exquisite punishments:

> Squeeze out therefore the eyes that presume to pry into your mysteries and intrigues of state or LUST. Slit be the nose that dares to smell a RAT. Wring off the ears and root up the tongues that listen to or whisper the words Liberty and Laws. . . . And let Fulvia, with her bodkin, pierce through again the tongue of Cicero.

This pamphlet was believed to be the work of John Horne (later Horne Tooke), vicar of Brentford—that rare eighteenth-century thing, a radical Church of England parson. It had to be anonymous because of its most audacious part, an engraving, 'A *true* and *accurate* plan of some part of Kew Green,' with explanations.

In the background: 'The P.D. [princess dowager] of Wales's house and gardens.'

Middle foreground: 'The house in which Lord Bute's family resides.'

Left foreground: 'A house built for Lord Bute (to study in), and where none of his family resides, and kept for him by one C-----, a German, who is brother to the Ps. of W.'s woman, but now housekeeper to Lord Bute. By means of which

49

lucrative post he is at present become a man of considerable property and fortune.'

The pamphlet points out that there is no access from the family garden to the princess's grounds, but a tree-shaded walk leads to them from Bute's separate house. Even when this plan and commentary were published over-the-counter by a reformist monthly, *The Political Register*, and with the title 'A View of Lord Bute's Erections at Kew', no action was taken.

Despite an undertaking by Bute and the king in 1763 to have no further communication, Bute exercised power for some time 'behind the curtain'. The two were certainly exchanging letters through the princess three years later.

George III to Bute, 3 May 1766: I have reason to suspect that my sister watches when I deliver any letters to my mother. . . . She has also said that during the great confusion in the winter, De Marche used frequently . . . to bring letters from you on the days I went to my mother. All this . . . shows how cautious we must be.

But soon Bute was thrown into agony. The king, lurching about in search of security, made Pitt, the 'blackest of hearts', prime minister. It was at about this time that the princess had a dream and told it to her women. It was passed on to Horace Walpole. Psychologists will see various meanings in it:

'The princess dowager dreamed that . . . the window was open, and the moon, level to it, shook with a tremulous motion before her eyes, to her great disquiet. She bade Lord Bute try to fix it. Extending his arms to stop its motion, it burst in his hand into ten thousand fiery splinters; on which, turning to the princess, he said reproachfully, "See, madam, to what you have brought me!" '

4

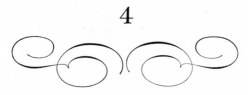

A Set of Prostitutes

WHEN GEORGE III had been on the throne less than eight years, and had changed prime ministers five times, it was possible to believe that England rather than France was 'on the eve of some great revolution'. Times were hard, government was chaotic, and pliable friends of the court were seen to prosper. Shouts far more dangerous than 'Wilkes and liberty' began to be heard—shouts such as 'Damn the king, damn the government, damn the parliament!'

The king's cause was not helped by the man now serving as prime minister, Augustus Henry Fitzroy, 3rd Duke of Grafton. His wealth and title descended from one of Charles II's bastards. He also inherited that king's dark complexion (he was nicknamed Black Harry), and his enthusiasm for women and horses. The high and uneasy position in which Grafton found himself at the age of thirty-two did not curb his self-indulgence. Separated from his wife, he was living flauntingly with a woman of wide fame, Nancy Parsons, who called herself Mrs Hoghton—'the Duke of Grafton's Mrs Hoghton, the Duke of Dorset's Mrs Hoghton, everybody's Mrs Hoghton', said Horace Walpole. She and Grafton inspired Junius, the savage anonymous polemicist of the day, to write verse:

> Can Apollo resist or a poet refuse
> When Harry and Nan solicit the muse:
> A statesman who makes a whole nation his care
> And a nymph who is almost as chaste as she's fair.

Dear Spousy had led such a damnable life
He determined to keep any whore but his wife.
So Harry's affairs, like those of the state,
Have been pretty well handled and tickled of late!

From fourteen to forty our provident Nan
Had devoted her life to the study of man,
And thought it a natural change of her station
From riding St George to ride over a nation.

A woman 'riding St George' is in the superior position. And
here one may quote from the journal of Lord Glenbervie, son-
in-law of Grafton's colleague Lord North: 'She possessed . . .
peculiar merits in the exercise of those endearments in which
she had had so much practice. . . . Would tell some of her
intimate friends that in the early part of her life she had once
earned, in single guineas, one hundred in one day.'

Secret service had wasted the national wealth,
But now—'tis the price of the Minister's health:
An expense which the Treasury well may afford—
She who serves him in bed should be paid at the Board.

Then there is Thomas Bradshaw, one of Grafton's Treasury
secretaries, a man Junius was to lash for years as an unctuous
pimp, 'the cream-coloured parasite':

So lucky was Harry that nothing could mend
His choice of a mistress but that of a friend:
A friend so obliging, and yet so sincere,
With pleasure in one eye, in t'other a tear.

The friend holds the candle; the lovers debate;
And among them, God knows how they settle the state.
Was there ever a nation so governed before,
By a jockey and gambler; a p--p; and a wh---?

A man in Grafton's high station was expected to maintain
some decorum. He offended time and again; particularly one
night when he took Nancy to the opera, that display-case of
high society, when his own wife was there, and paid no
attention to anyone but Nancy. Junius commented in one of

52

the many letters he addressed to Grafton in *The Public Advertiser:*

> To a mind like yours, my lord, such an outrage to your wife, such a triumph over decency, such an insult to the company, must have afforded the highest gratification when all the ordinary resources of pleasure were exhausted.

In another letter Junius felicitates Grafton because his royal ancestors 'left no distressing examples of virtue, even to their legitimate posterity'.

> Charles I lived and died a hypocrite. Charles II was a hypocrite of another sort, and should have died upon the same scaffold. At the distance of a century we see their different characteristics happily revived in Your Grace.

Walpole, a friend of Grafton's wife, is gentler: 'His whole conduct is childish, insolent, inconstant and absurd . . . thinking the world should be postponed to a whore and a horserace.'

The government that Grafton was meant to be directing was the 'tessellated pavement without cement', as Edmund Burke called it, which had been put together under Pitt. It was tessellated in accordance with George III's insistence on breaking all parties. The cement was missing because Pitt had withdrawn into near-madness. The result was confusion, but when uncourtly citizens seethed, George III complained of 'outrageous licentiousness . . . raised by wicked and disappointed men', for he himself was never to blame.

When a general election was held in the spring of 1768, the wicked advocates of a more representative Commons could hardly hope for a change. *The Political Register*, published by John Almon, one of the most active opposition journalists (his office in Piccadilly was also a 'gossiping shop' where MPs and others exchanged information), printed a dialogue of cynical voters in which one man says:

> Now, sir, as your money, and my money, and the money of every man in the kingdom, has flowed in such torrents into the pockets of ministers, placemen and pensioners, why, in God's name, should not these ministers, etc., be allowed to

open some counter-channels through which the money may flow back, if not in torrents, at least in gentle streams . . . ? Especially as the former channels are always kept open; the latter are opened only once in seven years.

This was the election for which Wilkes came home, seizing the chance to become a hero again, his one hope of solvency. When he was elected for Middlesex, one of the few constituencies in which some thousands of 'the middling and lower set' had a vote, the celebration kept London awake for two nights. Every prudent householder lit up his windows. An American observer, Benjamin Franklin, wrote to a friend, 'Even the small cross-streets, lanes, courts and other out-of-the-way places were all in a blaze of lights, and the principal streets all night long, as the mobs went round again after 2 o'clock and obliged people who had extinguished their candles to light them again. Those who refused had all their windows destroyed.' This was the traditional way for the common man to make his voice heard. Bute's windows, of course, were shattered. Ballads were 'sung or roared in every street'. Fine ladies and gentlemen were forced to shout 'Wilkes and Liberty'. Some of the mob shouted 'Wilkes and no king'. And the mystic number 45 was chalked everywhere—not only in London. Franklin, travelling to Winchester, saw '45' on every door for fifteen miles, and on many doors the rest of the way.

In Buckingham House, George III sat up through the second night, indignant at the victory of 'this audacious criminal'; and said (so George Grenville, one of his former prime ministers, was informed) that he wished the mob would come there, for then he would be justified in 'giving proper orders to the guards'. Six weeks later, when the new MP for Middlesex was sitting in the King's Bench Prison in Southwark awaiting sentence for No. 45 and *An Essay on Woman*, the king's guards fired on a crowd turbulently demonstrating outside. Seven people were killed, some of them uninvolved local residents. This 'massacre of St George's Fields' brought a warm message from the king: '. . . His Majesty highly approves of the conduct both of the officers and

men. . . . Every possible regard shall be shown to them. . . .'
At best, it was not a tactful thing to say when the town was
already inflamed.

There was great alarm. Horne Tooke, denouncing the
shootings at a public meeting, said a magistrate at the scene
had told him 'it was better to kill twenty or thirty today than
to have a hundred to kill tomorrow'. William Beckford, the
powerful City of London MP, said in the Commons, 'It seems
as if there is a plan of ruling by a military force, both here
and in America,'

Such was the setting of the famous duel between the
government and the Middlesex voters, who were told by the
ministerial majority that Wilkes could not sit in the Commons, yet kept on returning him. At the fourth round the
government produced, from one of Bute's pocket boroughs,
a champion to oppose Wilkes: Henry Lawes Luttrell, the
twenty-six-year-old son of a dissolute Irish peer. Wilkes by
now had a remarkable organization that could turn crowds on
and off, distribute thousands of handbills, feed friendly newspapers, and send out to the Brentford hustings vast parades
of carriages, bands and marchers with blue flags, cockades and
ribbons bearing the holy words Wilkes and Liberty, Magna
Carta, Bill of Rights. Luttrell got 296 votes against 1,143 for
the man in jail. The Commons declared that Luttrell should
nevertheless have the seat. The House showed, Walpole
quipped, that it could be 'bribed to contradict arithmetic'.

Wilkes sat at ease in prison. Admirers serenaded him—

> Of all the jails in England
>   The King's Bench is the best,
> For when a patriot's weary
>   He there may sit at rest:
>   And to Wilkes we all will go, will go, will go,
>   And to Wilkes we all will go.

He had to serve twenty-two months, but in the King's Bench a
gentleman had a room of his own and need not be solitary.
Gifts flowed in—some of them from Americans, who saw
themselves as engaged in the same struggle as Wilkes. Women
brought gifts, and themselves. One of these was Mrs John

Barnard of Berkeley Square, daughter-in-law of a great City
alderman. She writes to Wilkes after one visit, 'Everything
you do is charming in my eyes. . . . So delighted with everything you said and did. I hope you like the currant jelly.' He
inspires her to acts of political warfare. At Christie's salerooms
she encounters Le Despencer, 'the High Priest of the *Re-
nowned Abbey*', and says in his hearing, 'What a pity it is that
such old goats should be suffered to corrupt the morals of
young fellows of spirit.' 'Perhaps,' she tells Wilkes, 'this was
going a little too far.' Another day she sees 'that pert little
thing' Luttrell in Pall Mall.

> 'Good God!' says I, as loud and as quick as possible. 'Is that
> thing Luttrell? I know my Lord Irnham, his reputed father,
> well. It is impossible that *that* thing could spring from his
> loins.'

It was not revealed until after the election that the 'nourishing
torrents' had flowed so freely for eight years that the royal
fountain was dry. The king had to ask the Commons to vote
£513,000 to pay accumulated debts on the Civil List. Why was
he in such difficulty, despite much-publicized economies in
his palaces? The cost of maintaining the royal family had in
fact gone up a little. But secret and special services, those
items made up largely of political rewards, had absorbed
(according to one surviving Treasury account) £630,000,
despite George III's professions of purity. That was by no
means all; pensions, for example, had gone up by one-half.
Such facts, however, were not given to parliament. (A year
later, some misleading and untruthful figures were presented.)
In the Commons, Edmund Burke called it 'a downright
mockery' that they were asked to vote the money without seeing any accounts. 'They whom we treat as the mob are to pay,'
he said. 'There is not the meanest person in the kingdom who
does not feel the taxes.' The Burke of 1769, though no friend
to Wilkites, said things that were forgotten by the Burke
of the 1790s, who feared revolution and had a pension. 'Who
are the representatives of the mob?' he asked. 'Let us not
forget from what original we sprung. . . . It is they who have
made us of consequence.'

A Set of Prostitutes

An attack that must have been more painful to the government came from George Grenville, who during two years as prime minister had distributed some of the money. Although 'the influence of the Crown' (the polite phrase for rewards) was dangerous and in part 'irregular and unconstitutional', he argued, it was necessary to government. But then this dry, unrhetorical man gave warning:

> That influence is infinitely increasing. . . . If it is extending itself everywhere, no wonder it spreads dissatisfaction among the people! . . . When neither the government, nor the parliament, nor the magistracy enjoys that necessary share of respect and reverence from the people by which the constitution can alone be preserved, it is in the power of enterprising men to turn you out of doors in a moment. Let gentlemen consider whether we are advancing towards that extremity or not.

The notion of revolution was not merely a shout in the street.

The opposition found 135 MPs to vote for production of accounts, but on the side that had had the money, 248 said No. *The Political Register* printed a mock King's Speech:

> You know that last winter there was only half a million of which I could not give an account. You had it among you; and that is enough to satisfy any reasonable man.

The arts of 'influence' had been brought to a routine, in this time of weak ministers, by a group of middle-ranking men, mainly at the Treasury. It did not escape notice that some of them had been raised up by Bute. The most important was Charles Jenkinson, Bute's ex-secretary, who quite early was advising the king how to 'make his reign easy' by dominating the Commons. Another was John Robinson, who began as the political agent of Bute's son-in-law, the much-hated Sir James Lowther, and became the grand manager of political douceurs.

When caricature after caricature showed a sinister Bute and princess still commanding a childlike, blindfold or witless George III, courtiers could tell themselves how wrong the satirists were. But in spirit they were right. The king listened to nobody who wished to free him from the Butian ideas instilled in him a dozen years before. At Christmas 1769, *The Public Advertiser*, which went to the palace, printed a 'Letter to the King' by the mysterious Junius (since proved to have been Philip Francis, an official in the War Office). It went beyond anything in Wilkes's *North Briton*.

> It is the misfortune of your life, and originally the cause of every reproach and distress which has attended your government, that you should never have been acquainted with the language of truth until you heard it in the complaints of your people.

Junius dares to warn the king that he may involve his country in 'a fatal struggle'. To whom can he turn if his English people rebel? The Irish 'have been uniformly plundered and oppressed'. The Americans 'consider you as united with your servants against America, and know how to distinguish the sovereign and a venal parliament on one side, from the real sentiments of the English people on the other'. The king cannot even count fully on his army, says Junius, adding in a footnote: 'The private men have fourpence a day to subsist on; and five hundred lashes if they desert. Under this punishment they frequently expire. With these encouragements, it is supposed they may be depended upon whenever a certain person thinks it necessary to butcher his *fellow subjects*.' Junius closes with an appeal:

> Come forward to your people. Lay aside the wretched formalities of a king, and speak to your subjects with the spirit of a man and in the language of a gentleman. Tell them you have been fatally deceived. . . . The prince who imitates [the Stuarts'] conduct should be warned by their example; and while he plumes himself upon the security of his title to the crown, should remember that as it was acquired by one revolution, it may be lost by another.

The Public Advertiser, which already led the field with daily sales of 3,000, that day printed 4,800. Instantly other papers and journals reprinted the Junius letter. If the government did not prosecute, the press would seem untouchable.

A Set of Prostitutes

But there was a difficulty. The paper's proprietor, Henry Sampson Woodfall, had to be tried within the City of London, which was vehemently anti-court. A City jury would hardly be shocked at Junius's words, although he was hinting at civil war, and might well acquit Woodfall. Therefore Lord Mansfield—whose title was Lord Chief Justice, but who played the role of a cabinet minister—enunciated a surprising piece of law: that when Woodfall was alleged to have 'unlawfully, wickedly and maliciously aspersed, scandalized and vilified' the king, those were 'mere formal words . . . with which the jury were not to concern themselves'. Whatever they thought of the alleged libel, they must say 'guilty' if Woodfall were merely proved to have published it. The jury outflanked Mansfield by finding Woodfall 'guilty of printing and publishing only'. The prosecution fell into its own legal pit. Woodfall and several other proprietors went unpunished.

The war of words was now being carried to the foot of the king's throne in St James's Palace. Citizens moved by dangerous longings for a freer parliament were holding public meetings and bringing him petitions. They came not only from the City, but the boldest were from there. One spoke of 'desperate attempts' to destroy the constitution; of ministers who had 'prostituted Your Majesty's sacred name and authority to justify, applaud and recommend their own bloody actions', had imposed 'numberless unconstitutional regulations and taxations' on America, and were 'wresting from the people the last sacred right we had left, the right of election'.

All this they have been able to effect by corruption; by a scandalous misapplication and embezzlement of the public treasure, and a shameful prostitution of public honours and employments. . . .

The king treated the petitioners with scorn. As soon as they had spoken, he turned his back on them—a rebuke known as rumping. A caricature on the incident gives the petitioners some comic remarks: 'By my shoul, we have a very good front view of the backside of his face. . . . I fear he will answer our petition the backward way. . . . An ill wind for us.'

59

Within a few weeks, William Beckford, now lord mayor, led a procession of sixty carriages to St James's with a remonstrance, written by Horne Tooke, calling upon the king to dismiss his 'evil ministers', and denouncing the 'secret and malign influence' which had 'defeated every good and suggested every bad intention' in parliament. Next day Horne Tooke gave the readers of the Wilkite *Middlesex Journal* this glimpse into the throne-room:

As they were withdrawing, His Majesty instantly turned round to his courtiers and *burst out a-laughing.*
Nero fiddled whilst Rome was burning.

A day later he said this had offended some people, so he printed a saucy correction: 'Nero did not fiddle while Rome was burning.' This inspired *The Oxford Magazine*, one of several Whiggish gentlemen's publications that were now using caricatures, to picture George III as a fiddling Nero and his mother as the sinful Agrippina. London is in flames, and the king says, 'What a charming blaze! This shall make them know I am their master.' But more often the king is a trivial figure. The inventor Pinchbeck had been indulging the king's pleasure in mechanics by showing him how to make buttons. A caricature shows him holding a card of buttons and saying to the petitioners, 'Do not you see that I have been employed in business of much more consequence?' 'What a genius!' says a courtier. 'Why, he was born a button-maker.'

Pitt, restored in mind and back in opposition, tried to justify his ministry of 1766 by saying, 'I was credulous, I was duped, I was deceived.' On the very day that Beckford presented his remonstrance, Pitt (now Lord Chatham) said in the Lords, 'I will trust no sovereign in the world with the means of purchasing the liberties of the people. . . . Does he mean . . . to procure a parliament, like an infamous packed jury, ready to acquit his ministers at all adventures?. . . There are many men to impeach . . . and, by God's blessing, I will arraign and impeach them.' Lord North, who had become George III's prime minister, hit back next day in the

A Set of Prostitutes

Commons: 'I assert that to say that this parliament is corrupt is false. . . . I defy the gentlemen to impeach. Let them appoint a day.'

But how could they find a majority? It was stalemate. A caricature gave this dialogue between the king and his seven-year-old son George:

—Papa, I want some paper to make a kite.
—Take some of these petitions and remonstrances, they are fit for nothing else.

The Political Register offered a 'Specimen of a New Glossary' in which these were some of the items:

The father of his people—One who is totally deaf to their prayers.
A Member of Parliament—One who gets into the House by bribery, and there sells his country for a place or pension.
The freeholders of England—The scum of the earth.
A libeller—One who speaks necessary truths.

North argued in the Commons that mercenary libellers were the source of all the trouble:

Slander and defamation are become the food and raiment of printers and booksellers. It is the credulity of the people, wrought upon by flagitious libellers, that has excited this outrageous opposition to government. . . . The first thing we lay our hands on in the morning is a libel; the last thing we put out of our hands in the evening is a libel. . . . Libels, lampoons and satires constitute all the writing, printing and reading of our time.

To a politician in trouble, no time seems so wicked as the present. North almost wished for the days of *The North Briton:*

The press had not then overflowed the land with its black gall. Political writers had some shame left. They had some reverence for the crown, some respect for the name of majesty.

Kings, Lords and Wicked Libellers

But juries were refusing to convict, said Edmund Burke. Libellers were 'secure in the protection of the people'. And why? 'The ministers are the grand criminals.'

We owe our knowledge of these and other speeches to news-writers who crouched behind the clock in the public gallery, taking shorthand notes in defiance of a routine Commons resolution declaring any reporting to be a breach of privilege. Sometimes the hardpressed reporters only stored what they could in their memories, or worked from friendly MPs' briefings, and pieced out speeches more coherent than the originals. By 1771 some papers were daring to throw aside the longstanding fiction that they were reporting debates in 'a great assembly' or 'the Robin Hood Society'. They even began to name MPs in full, and unflatteringly. This brought a showdown, masterminded by Wilkes, in which furious George III and unhappy North were led into sending the lord mayor to the Tower—amid riots in which the king was violently abused and North was near to being killed—for refusing to hand over the printers of the defiant newspapers. *The Middlesex Journal* said:

> It matters not where a set of prostitutes may assemble. . . . Though they should sit at Westminster, they are not a parliament if they sit and act in defiance of the inclinations of the people. . . . The people would by these publications . . . see who were worthy to be returned to parliament, when we shall have an assembly fit to be so called.

If the point were yielded, the king told North, the authority of the Commons would be 'totally annihilated'. But the last thing North wanted was to provide dramatic causes to the violent forces outside parliament. By the next session the king had been persuaded to turn a blind eye to the news-writers. Not for the first or last time, organized mass demonstrations gained a point from a government in trouble.

But this battle of the newspapers proved to be the Wilkites' last great fling. Wilkes split his own leadership with squabbles about money. In parliament, the Whigs too were split, having no prospect of office to bind them. There was a mood, said

A Set of Prostitutes

Burke, of 'sullen languor'. *The Political Register* tried not to despair:

> The age, indeed, is truly vicious; selfishness prevails; corruption stalks forth at noonday, and patriotism is fled; our virgins put manhood to the blush; our wives riot in debauchery; kept-mistresses are caressed; players and common strumpets set the fashions; our senators nod over cards and dice . . . and are dead to every sense of feeling—but the touch of gold. Yet, ye patriotic few, despair not. . . . Be ready at a moment's warning to assert your rights. Too long have we been galled by the yoke of a detestable aristocracy; but the world shall see we can easily shake it off.

The 'patriotic few' had organized a Bill of Rights Society to campaign for a fair distribution of seats, household suffrage and a secret ballot. None of them would live to see even the first step toward a fulfilment of those dreams. The yoke was not easy to shake off.

5

This King had a Brother

IN HIS DOMESTIC LIFE the king gave his enemies few openings. The decorum of Buckingham House, Kew and Windsor made an elevating contrast with the careless or desperate profligacy of so much of the aristocracy. At worst, critics could sneer that this pure king gave high posts to licentious men. Satirists might make jibes at George's parsimony, gracelessness and philistinism, and at Charlotte's annual childbearing; but for many of the rising middle class these faults were not far from virtues. George's court was almost the only one in Europe in which the monarch had no mistress, and nobody could imagine Charlotte taking a variety of lovers, like Catherine of Russia, or even one lover, as George's young sister Caroline Matilda, Queen of Denmark, did at this time.

Before long there would be a return to royal form in England: George's sons, and some of his daughters, would create scandal enough. Meanwhile there were his brothers. The most scandalous was the youngest, Henry Duke of Cumberland, a small flaxen-haired young man, 'pert, insolent, senseless, and not unwillingly brutal', says Horace Walpole, whose niece was married to Henry's brother. The affairs of this duke have a continuing interest because they were the cause of the passing of the Royal Marriage Act, which still governs the matrimonial decisions of the family.

At the age of twenty-one, after a confined upbringing under the eyes of the Princess Dowager, the duke, says Walpole, 'sallied into a life of brothels and drunkenness'. He also ranged higher than brothels. Great ladies were not inaccessible.

This King had a Brother

'If you see a female enter a public place with a bold *knock-me-down* air,' says *The London Magazine* of March 1770, 'set her down for a person of quality. . . . A lady may soon perhaps intrigue, and game, and swear, and smoke tobacco, more openly than her husband does at present.' Princes, however pert and senseless, were eagerly pursued. In July 1770 the duke was accused in the Court of King's Bench at Westminster Hall of criminal conversation (adultery) with the wife of Lord Grosvenor.

Never before had a prince been sued for adultery. The case gave the public some comical glimpses of amorous letter-writing and intrigue as conducted by their betters. It served to disillusion anyone who wished to believe that royal blood necessarily conferred wisdom or, indeed, a veneer of grace. It also cast a shadow on the court itself, for it was revealed that a go-between in the intrigue was Lady Grosvenor's sister, Carrie Vernon, a Maid of Honour to the Queen. None of this deterred Lord Grosvenor, even though he had received his title from George III, as cupbearer at his coronation. Grosvenor had enormous wealth, flowing from his family's development since 1730 of streets and squares of fashionable houses in Mayfair; but he wanted more. He sued for £100,000.

Letters exchanged by Lady Grosvenor and the duke were read out. 'To the lady's honour be it said,' comments Walpole, 'that bating a few oaths, which sounded more masculine than tender, the advantage in grammar, spelling and style was all in her favour.' The duke's letters were published without punctuation, but perhaps he owed this to the malice of journalists. Here is the duke, aged twenty-three, writing to his love from a warship off Weymouth, where as nominal Admiral of the Blue he was engaged in naval exercises:

My dear little angel
. . . I then prayed for you my dearest love kissed your dearest little hair and lay down and dreamt of you had you on the dear little couch ten thousand times in my arms kissing you and telling you how much I loved and adored you and you seemed pleased but alas when I woke I found it all dillusion nobody by me but myself at sea. . . .

This instantly inspired 'A R---l Love Song in the Modern C---t Style':

> God bless my dearest little dear—
> The wind is not quite fair—
> From Portland Road I write this here—
> God bless your little hair.
> > *Doodle doodle doo.*
>
> All on the couch last night I lay,
> I dreamt what now I sing—
> I held you fast and kissed away,
> Ay—just like anything.
> > *Doodle doodle doo.*
>
> Oh! then me thought *dear you* did lie
> Within my arms—but soon
> The dream went off and there was I
> Just by myself alone.
> > *Doodle doodle doo.*
>
> God bless my *dearest little dear*,
> God bless your *little mouth*. . . .

In this letter the duke says he has ordered the squadron to be anchored so that he can send 'dispatches': letters to her. She answers:

> O my dearest soul, I've just received two of the dearest letters in the world from you. . . . How kind it was of you to say you had letters of consequence to write when it was only to poor me. . . . God bless you my dearest dear life, I shall ever love you.

She plots to stay on in London when Lord Grosvenor travels to the family home in Cheshire, Eaton Hall:

> 'I've already complained I've got a pain in my side. . . . At the end of five or six weeks I'll grow very ill and send for Fordyce the apothecary and make him send me a quantity of nasty draughts which I'll throw out of the window. Only think how wicked I am!

In London the husband is a nuisance: he dislikes her fashionable friends. Lady Harrington calls; 'I longed to see her but dared not, as he was at home.' Grosvenor was justified here, for Lady Harrington was one of the most notorious women of the time. *The Town and Country Magazine*, that industrious guide to eighteenth-century scandal, calls her 'The Stable-yard Messalina' and says, 'The world have ascribed to her a subordination of lovers from a monarch down to a hairdresser' (the monarch being probably Stanislas of Poland). As for life at Eaton Hall—in another letter Lady Grosvenor describes her husband, a great racing man who three times won the Epsom Derby:

> He will sit for half an hour with his eyes fixed on a table or chair, and then apply to Tom or anybody that is by, 'Do you know what mare such a filly was out of? . . . By God, I have got the best stud in England, nobody will have any horses to run but me very soon.' Then if anybody else that don't understand that subject offers to mention anything else, he is as cross as anything for half an hour, and then fast asleep. . . . I'll tell you how I pass my time. I get up about 8 or I'm afraid 9, breakfast at 10, then walk or ride, dine at 3, stupefy or play at stupefied cards after tea with anybody that drops in (he never plays). . . . We sup soon after 9, and in bed before 11, where I always dream of you, my dearest friend. I hope soon to have a letter from Carrie, with some writing from you in milk.

The duke also sent messages in lemon. And the lovers had many happy meetings. Lady Grosvenor would go to her sister in St James's Palace, and then walk with her through a courtyard 'and in at the Duke of Cumberland's back door'— for he lived nearby in Pall Mall. Then there was an obliging widow, Mary Reda, who kept a milliner's shop in Pall Mall and let out discreet upstairs rooms to the best people. Once, too, Madame Reda gave the lovers the use of a room at Covent Garden Opera House. A third helper was an earl's daughter who styled herself countess, claiming to be the widow of a Count Dönhoff of Poland. She let them meet at her house in Cavendish Square. She was an odd friend: more than once she left them in a room together, then wandered in a little later and found to her surprise (she said) that they were in an intimate posture. Walpole touched on these matters in a merry ballad:

> . . . This king had a brother as wise as himself,
> A chattering, gossiping, puppet-like elf,
> Who had tutors so learn'd, and was brought up so well,
> That he wrote fine love-letters—and almost could spell.
>> *Derry down—*
>
> He debauched a fair lady—or she debauched him;
> They were caught twice or thrice in a ticklish trim
> By a modest young countess who could not conceive
> They would do what she left them alone to achieve
> > *Up and down.*
>
> A milliner too, who was prudish and grave,
> Who had wares for to sell, and a soul for to save,
> To the opera house her commodities carried,
> For a shop is too public for dames that are married
> > *Up and down.*
>
> She collected the fact from a number of hints,
> For the lady was big, and her elbows left prints;
> Madame Reda besides, as she carried 'em tea,
> Heard her ladyship laugh, and the duke cry hee-hee
> > *Up and down.*

But soon Lord Grosvenor began to receive little notes signed 'Jack Sprat' (whose identity emerged later):

. . . place yourself at king's garden door at a little before 8 and you will see her and her little sister go with him to his own back door. . . .

. . . continually playing fine pranks under your nose . . . Kensington Palace in the morning (where no servant is allowed to follow) is the constant practice.

Perhaps Grosvenor hesitated to storm the duke's house or Kensington Palace. But a third note came as Lady Grosvenor was travelling between London and Cheshire:

This King had a Brother

. . . if you have not a mind you will take no notice perhaps of a certain person that is gone in disguise and lies at every inn where she does. . . .

The duke was so fond of his dearest love that when she travelled back and forth he would stay at the same inns, at St Albans, Towcester, Coventry and Whitchurch, dressed as a farmer, 'Squire Morgan' or 'Squire Jones', with a black wig to hide his flaxen Hanoverian hair. 'He sometimes appeared as a young squire disordered in his senses,' said Grosvenor's counsel, 'and used to be called at the inns The Fool.' This was useful if he was noticed scurrying along a passage toward Lady Grosvenor's room.

The affair ended at the White Hart, St Albans. A Grosvenor butler broke open Lady Grosvenor's room and found her with her breasts bare, and the duke trying to button up his waistcoat. ('Indeed,' says Walpole, 'there was none of that proof which my Lady Townshend once said there was in another case. . . . "Lord, child, she was all over proof!" ') The duke 'stood very much confused, like a statue.' Then he had an idea. He ran out and said, 'I'll take my Bible oath I was not in my Lady Grosvenor's room.'

In a caricature of the trial, a spectator says, 'It was a pity to disturb them when they were going to prince-making.'

The only question for the jury was what damages to give. 'They could not charge His Royal Highness with intriguing merely for the sake of intrigue,' said Grosvenor's counsel, 'as the incoherency of his letters plainly proved him to be really a lover.' However, there was evidence that Grosvenor had kept various women, of a humble kind. One, above a staymaker's in Jermyn Street, had had a child by him, for which he consoled her with £20. Lord Mansfield urged the jury not to levy a large sum 'as a punishment'. Grosvenor got £10,000. With costs, the duke owed £13,000.

Four months later, George III wrote to North, 'He has taken no one step to raise the money and now has applied to me.' He told North to find it at the Treasury, for otherwise Grosvenor would raise the question in the Lords, 'which would at this licentious time occasion disagreeable reflections on the

69

rest of his [the duke's] family. . . . I ought as little as possible to appear. . . .' Later that day the king gave his brother a sharp lecture which, he told North, 'may be of some use in his future conduct'.

The licentious time was already casting reflections on the king. *The Whisperer*, a savage weekly, wrote of 'the r---- idiot, alias *Bible oath*, alias *dear little hair*, alias *Squire Jones*, alias *Squire Morgan*, I mean the FOOL (and it is shrewdly suspected there are more *fools* than one in the same family)'. Again: 'Adultery, debauchery and divorces are now more frequent than in the days of Charles II.'

More painful for the duke were some hints dropped in *The Town and Country Magazine*. 'Jealousy, it is plain, operated on Jack Sprat (alias the Countess D--h-ff),' it said; and named the countess among the duke's 'variety of mistresses (some of whom he has afterwards placed in the more useful station of procuresses)'.

Almost exactly a year after the king had lectured him, the duke struck what the king called a 'cruel blow'. He wrote from Dover before dawn on 3 November 1771 to announce that he was sailing to Calais on honeymoon, having been married for a month to a young widow, Mrs Anne Horton. He had hit on a new alias: 'To avoid suspicion I have taken the name of Thomas Johnson Esqr.' The bride's friends made sure, however, that within a few days the news was in the London papers.

'What was the astonishment of mankind, what the mortification of the king . . . and what the triumph of Wilkes,' writes Walpole, 'when it came out that this new Princess of the Blood was own sister of the famous Colonel Luttrell . . . !' Walpole describes her: 'Extremely pretty . . . very well made, with the most amorous eyes in the world, and eyelashes a yard long. Coquette beyond measure, artful as Cleopatra, and completely mistress of all her passions and projects. Indeed, eyelashes three-quarters of a yard shorter would have served to conquer such a head as she has turned.' Walpole wrote in his ballad:

King and queen when they heard how th'undutiful whelp
Had disgraced the great houses of Mecky and Guelp,

Swore and cried, cursed and fainted, and calling for Bute,
'Of your Luttrell-connection,' cried George, 'see the fruit!
. . . I'd as lief he had married the daughter of Wilkes.'

It was very true that the king was furious; but not particularly because of the Luttrell connection. Any non-royal
bride was unthinkable. The instant he got Henry's letter, he
wrote ('so agitated') to his mother about 'the abominable
step he has taken . . . his inevitable ruin . . . a disgrace to the
whole family'. To Henry he wrote demanding that the
marriage must not be announced; and when the news was published, he told the duke to deny it. 'The story has been too
industriously spread by her family,' he wrote to his other surviving brother, William Duke of Gloucester. '. . . But if he
does not avow her, people will by degrees grow doubtful.' In
any country, he added, it was dishonourable for a prince to
marry a subject; 'here where the crown is but too little respected it must be big with the greatest mischiefs—civil wars
would by such measures again be common'. There was a
terrible irony in this for William (then lying dangerously
ill in the south of France): he himself had been secretly
married for five years to an illegitimate daughter of Horace
Walpole's brother Edward—a woman even more questionable
in origin—and had not dared tell the king.

There were ironies as well against George III himself in his
certainty about what was dishonourable. The mothers of many
English sovereigns—most recently Queen Mary and Queen
Anne—had been commoners. George III's own great-grand-
mother, George I's queen, was the daughter of a decidedly
non-royal Frenchwoman. And then George III was for-
getting that he himself had desperately desired to marry an
English girl, Sarah Lennox. His passion for her began when she
was fifteen and he was twenty-one. 'She is everything I can
form to myself lovely,' he wrote in anguish to Bute. 'I am
daily grown unhappy, sleep has left me.' He asked Bute to
'consent to my raising her to a throne' or at any rate 'devise
any method for my keeping my love'. But George's mother
could not think of a Hanoverian prince, though English-born,
marrying anyone but a princess found in her Berlin Almanack.

Besides, Sarah's eldest sister was the wife of Henry Fox, who at that time, 1759, was very far from being in Bute's political camp. A marriage might make Fox the future power behind the throne. Bute gave a flat No.

And yet two years later, in 1761, in the first springtime of George's reign, he still wanted to marry Sarah, showed every sign of love, asked her cousin Susan to tell Sarah he thought nobody 'so fit' to be his queen, and asked Sarah to 'believe that I have the strongest attachment'. (Attachment: the word Bute used of himself and the princess.) But at their St James's drawing-room meetings the young king and Sarah were being watched 'as a cat does a mouse' (said Sarah) by Bute's wife and others; and Bute had emissaries in the little dukedom of Mecklenburgh-Strelitz arranging a marriage with a princess on whom the report was, *pas tout à fait une beauté*. When Sarah next came to court, George, miserable and shamefaced, managed a remark about the weather. His mother and Bute had overruled the king.

In 1771, the deep-hidden wound only served to make him violent against other breakers of the code. The king's anger, which was no secret, brought a savage commentary from the *London Evening Post:*

> It is pleasant to hear the King's Friends (as they call them-selves) . . . complaining of *seduction* in the marriage of the Duke of Cumberland. . . . Who will believe there was any *seduction* in the case? . . . It would be more agreeable to truth to ascribe it to the natural depravity of the family.

The paper goes on to speak of a series of 'misalliances', beginning with Prince Frederick and the mistress he had when his bride arrived. Next comes what is apparently the earliest mention in print of George's alleged love for the Fair Quaker, a shopkeeper's daughter in St James's Market, midway between George's two residences in the 1750s.

> What *seduction* was there in the misalliance with the fair Quaker of St James's Market? . . . Modesty, or some other cause, has secreted the mellifluous, tender, soothing, sighing, loving letters to Abigail. . . . How often did he go round St James's Market—muffled up, not disguised, in a

greatcoat—to get a sight of the fair Abigail at the dining-room window?

This paper's deliberately strained use of the word 'misalliance' perhaps helped to inspire later stories of a secret marriage to the Quaker girl, with whom George was probably smitten at the time he confessed to Bute his fascination with 'those divine creatures'.

Then comes Sarah, who in 1762 married a man called Bunbury:

> What *seduction* was there in the misalliance with Lady Sarah Bunbury, which so alarmed Lord Bute and the Princess of Wales that they called in a princess of the House of Mecklenburgh?

And finally there is George III's brother William:

> What *seduction* was there in the misalliance between the Duke of Gloucester and Lady Waldegrave, the daughter of Mrs Clements, who kept a milliner's shop in Pall Mall, and whose father sold brooms upon the moors in Yorkshire?

The daughter of Edward Walpole and Mrs Clements was Lady Waldegrave when William married her because Walpole had launched her in society and had married her to George III's boyhood governor, Earl Waldegrave—who left her a widow in 1763.

The *London Evening Post* then turns to Anne Horton's profligate father, and suggests that Lord Mansfield might 'exert himself in discovering who *seduced* Hellfire Davis (now a noted prostitute upon the town), and there is no doubt Simon Lord Irnham might be of great service'. In *The Public Advertiser*, Junius enlarges on the Hellfire Davis story, calls Irnham 'this hoary lecher', and dares to counsel the Duke of Cumberland: 'Whenever you want a divorce, you need only leave your spouse alone for an hour or two with *** ******'— which can only mean 'her father'. More seriously, Junius wishes the duke 'did not stand quite so near to the regency'. The duke was next in line for a regency after Gloucester and the princess dowager; she was dying of cancer; and six years earlier the king had been so alarmingly ill that a Regency Act was passed. 'We have now,' says Junius, 'a better reason than ever to pray for the long life of the best of princes.'

Emissaries were sent to the newspapers to ask them to stop commenting so cruelly. 'The little runners of the Buckingham House junto,' says the *London Evening Post*, 'are endeavouring to excite compassion for the deplorable situation of the royal mind. . . . They say, *The king is quite unhappy.* . . . Will he be pleased to recollect how many persons he has made unhappy since he came to the throne? When he *feels* for his people, they will *feel* for him.'

The king was not helped by the tone his brother Henry took. 'If it can in the smallest degree contribute to your felicity,' he said in one letter, 'call my wife by any name which you think political necessity requires.' According to the *London Evening Post*, she was offered £10,000 and a £4,000-a-year pension to renounce the title of duchess. The paper invented a letter of refusal that well reflects her love of social glory:

> My ambition leads to a larger compass; and six shining footmen calling out, 'The D----ss of C--------d's carriage here!' at any of the public places will give me more heartfelt satisfaction than all the *partis carrés* I should ever have at B--------m House.

She used the title from the start. She and the duke were barred from court, and he was even forbidden to see his mother before she died.

As parliament assembled early in 1772, the king's next move was revealed. 'I have children who must know what they have to expect if they would follow so infamous an example,' he had written to the unhappy Gloucester (who was to confess his own crime a few months later). The king insisted on the passing of a law that no previous king had found necessary: a law requiring all descendants of George II, except those deriving from princesses married into foreign houses, to seek the sovereign's permission before marrying. Foreseeing a parliamentary fuss, Lord North persuaded the king to add a saving clause by which a person refused permission might at the age of twenty-five apply to the privy council, and marry at twenty-six if parliament did not object. Anyone who assisted at an unapproved wedding would face the medieval punishment of premunire: forfeiture of all possessions, and imprisonment at the king's pleasure.

The proposal was hotly attacked as an extension of the royal prerogative. MP after MP pointed to the bill's illogicality and injustice. Why the magical age of twenty-five, or twenty-five-plus-one? A prince could rule the realm at eighteen, and could then choose a bride but forbid the choices of older men. A newspaper offered a mocking justification:

> Quoth Dick to Tom, 'This act appears
>   Absurd, as I'm alive:
> To take the crown at eighteen years,
>   The wife at twenty-five . . .'
> Quoth Tom to Dick, 'Thou art a fool
>   And little know'st of life.
> Alas! 'Tis easier far to rule
>   A kingdom than a wife.'

What was an improper marriage? The bill did not define it, said one MP, 'but every king upon his arrival at the throne is (I suppose instinctively) endued with a power of distinguishing it. If they mean a marriage with a native [Englishwoman] is improper, let them say so.'

A rollicking speech came from Colonel Barré, a follower of Pitt. 'Do you imagine that any man arrived at the age of maturity, much less a spirited young prince, will submit with patience to the loss of the rights of man, that power enjoyed by the meanest subject . . . which entitles all but idiots and lunatics to choose a helpmeet? Is it the intention of the minister to make us insinuate that our royal family are but idiots and lunatics?' Barré looked forward, with a touch of prophecy, to the next generation (George III's heir was then nine): 'A young man, probably handsome, in full vigour—you won't allow him to marry, you won't give him a little paddock for his own feeding. . . . If you yourself was married to a handsome woman, and I the Prince of Wales, found in bed with the handsome woman, do you imagine any twelve men in the kingdom would find a verdict against me?'

Another prophetic hint came from a rising man of twenty-three, Charles James Fox, who within a dozen years would have a great deal to do with an amorous Prince of Wales. In 1772 Fox was a follower of North, but he boldly assailed the bill. It was 'very probable', he said, that the Prince of Wales would 'marry a woman without the consent of his father, and live with her as his wife notwithstanding the act of parliament'. He was right; but the rest of his prophecy—of a situation that might lead to civil war—was not quite fulfilled. 'As the lady would not suffer in her reputation,' he said, 'and would be thought his legal wife by the greatest part of the world, when he came to the throne he would marry her again. And in that case the children he had by her during the life of his father would be illegitimate by act of parliament but legitimate in the eyes of all the rest of the world.'

The bill could not be said to preserve the dignity of the crown, said Fox, 'for the king of England may marry an apple-girl, and at the same time prevent his heir from making the most proper match. Then where is the dignity of the crown?' And it is piquant to find him saying, obviously with his cousin Sarah Lennox in mind, that he can see no inconvenience ever arising from a prince marrying a subject: 'Nay, I will go further—I believe he could not do better, for there are much greater evils may arise from foreign connections.' People objected, said Fox, that if a subject became queen, there would be partiality to her relations. 'We will suppose,' he replied—prophetically again—'that a future king should have a mistress. Is it not probable he will be as partial to her friends as to his wife's?'

Fox was by no means the only one on North's side who dared to oppose the bill. In one division, on an amendment to make the act lapse three years after George III's death, the opposition lost by only 132–150, even though the king had written to North, 'I do expect every nerve to be strained to carry the bill through. . . . I have a right to expect a hearty support from everyone in my service, and shall remember defaulters.' These were not idle words. After one division

This King had a Brother

George III told North that if two royal equerries, Colonels Burgoyne and Harcourt, had abstained, he would have dismissed them. Two days later the king asked for a list of 'abstainers and deserters' as a guide 'for my conduct in the Drawing-room tomorrow' (offenders were dauntingly treated to royal snubs). He told North, 'I hope every engine will be employed'—that is, rewards as well as threats.

'The whole kingdom is set in motion,' said Colonel Barré. 'Members who seldom honour these walls with their presence are pressed into service. I have no doubt but we shall soon feel the effects of such an extraordinary effort in the arrears of the Civil List.' He congratulated supporters of the bill on 'the fine harvest which lies before them'; and with his one eye fixed upon North (for he had lost the other at Quebec), he said, 'As even a ministerial member the other day said, I should not be surprised to see the majority of the house, if ordered by a certain noble person, attempt to come hither upon their heads.'

Even so, North managed to get the bill through only by a majority of 168–115. A last satirical thrust came from Sir Joseph Mawbey, a Southwark brewer. He moved to 'correct' the title of the act by inserting the words, 'An act for enlarging and extending the prerogative of the crown, and for the encouragement of adultery and fornication.'

John Almon's *Political Register* said, 'The kings of this limited monarchy are erected into family tyrants,' and alleged:

> The Royal Marriage Bill has been passed at the expense of two British baronies, five Irish ditto, one advancement from ditto to an Irish earldom, one blue ribbon [the Garter, for North], three red ones [the Bath], one baronetage, three reversionary patent places, £25,000 in occasional gratuities, besides innumerable promises of lottery tickets.

The power of an agitated king prevailed; and to what end? His heir, at least one other son, and perhaps a daughter, married in defiance of the Royal Marriage Act. The daughters spent the best years of their lives in bitter frustration. Only four of the king's many children had legitimate offspring (otherwise there might now have been hundreds of people subject to the act, instead of a few dozen). Only once in later reigns has marriage with a commoner caused a real crisis: but the act was no help, for (as Fox saw) it could not have barred Edward VIII from marrying even an apple-girl.

6

The Die is now Cast

A CIVIL WAR is not a laughing matter. George III's attempt to impose his will on his fellow-Britons in America inspired satire that was mordant rather than merry. As early as January 1766, *The Public Advertiser* printed a modest proposal that a force of 2,000 Highlanders should be raised for a quick punitive action:

> I would propose that all the capitals of the several provinces should be burnt to the ground, and that they cut the throats of all the inhabitants, men, women and children, and scalp them, to serve as an example; that all the shipping should be destroyed. . . . No man in his wits, after such terrible military execution, will refuse to purchase stamped paper. . . .

This piece, tinged with prophecy, is credited to Benjamin Franklin, who was busy in London using every opinion-moulding technique. The following month he appeared before a Commons committee on which Whig MPs had been primed with questions to help his case against the Stamp Act:

> *Q* What was the temper of America towards Great Britain before the year 1763?
> *A* The best in the world. . . . They were governed by this country at the expense only of a little pen, ink and paper. . . .
> *Q* And what is their temper now?
> *A* Oh, very much altered. . . .

Q What is your opinion of a future tax, imposed on the same principle with that of the Stamp Act? How would the Americans receive it?

A Just as they do this. They would not pay it. . . . Their opinion is that when aids to the crown are wanted, they are to be asked of the several assemblies, according to the old established usage—who will, as they have always done, grant them freely. And that their money ought not to be given away, without their consent, by persons at a distance. . . .

Franklin designed a prophetic print, 'Magna Britannia—The Colonies Reduced', showing the colonies as limbs hacked off Britannia's body. He had it reproduced by the hundred, postcard-size—and not only for sending messages, as George Townshend had done. Just before the deciding Commons debate, Franklin hired a man to put one in every MP's hand. The Whigs were temporarily in power, so the court did not govern the Treasury. The Stamp Act was repealed 'in the teeth of all the old mercenary Swiss of state . . . the whole embattled legion of veteran pensioners', as Burke later put it.

Soon, under a ministry more to the king's liking, new taxes begot new resistance. This time troops were sent to Boston. What would follow? In January 1769, Franklin presented in *The Public Advertiser* a mock ministerial balance-sheet for a war against the Americans. Satire failed to equal the coming reality. On the basis of 'a war of ten years, in which 25,000 of land forces only are to be kept up', he estimated a total cost to Britain, including loss of trade and every other possible item, of £108,500,000. As it turned out, the mere increase in national debt exceeded that sum.

The mock balance-sheet also assumed 'that after they are reduced, they shall be in the most perfect good humour with us . . . be as fond of us and of our fashions as ever they were, and that it will be therefore quite unnecessary to keep up an equal or indeed any army to continue and secure the subjection we have reduced them to'. Here was the final salutary argument. In the Commons a week later, Pitt's follower, Colonel Barré, who knew America, put the same point:

The Die is now Cast

A passionate governor may wish to see America chained down like a conquered province; but can any man believe that would heal the wound, that that would restore order?

This argument was ignored as stubbornly as all the other arguments by the king and by men such as Charles Jenkinson who influenced his thinking. The possibility that he might lose America did enter George III's mind, but then his fervour only grew hotter. We see the all-or-nothing thinking that was nurtured under Bute. We even see Bute's phrases. 'The die is now cast,' says the king in 1774. 'The colonies must either submit or triumph.' Anyone who urges a compromise is dismissed as absurd. 'It is to no purpose making objections,' Lord North told subordinates (according to John Almon). 'The king means to try the question with America.'

What the king wanted to be given was evidence that the colonists were a craven rabble. There were plenty of men to oblige him, and convince themselves. 'The good of this act,' said North, instructing the Commons to close the port of Boston, 'is that four or five frigates will do the business without any military force.' A year later the gallant Lord Sandwich outdid this with a speech that sounds like another piece of Franklin satire:

> Suppose the colonies do abound in men, what does that signify? They are raw, undisciplined, cowardly men. I wish instead of forty or fifty thousand of these brave fellows, they would produce in the field at least two hundred thousand— the more the better, the easier would be the conquest. If they did not run away, they would starve themselves into compliance with our measures.

Sandwich's nonsense was being nourished by letters to him from ardent officers. Major John Pitcairn of the Marines, two months before leading his men into action at Lexington and Concord: 'Vigorous measures will soon put an end to this rebellion. . . . When this army is ordered to act against them, they will soon be convinced that they are very insignificant.' (He is 'hurt and mortified', however, to find he has been sent a great many men shorter than five-foot-six.) And a little later:

81

'One active campaign, a smart action, and burning two or three of their towns, will set everything to rights . . . convince these foolish, bad people that England is in earnest.' (But cheap rum has been killing his men—'will destroy more of us than the Yankies will'.)

When the news of Lexington and Concord reached London (after thirty-nine days), the stock market fell; and George III wrote, once again, 'The die is cast. . . .' Sandwich sent him Pitcairn's letters, and was rewarded with the comment, 'I am of his opinion that when once those rebels have felt a smart blow, they will submit.' (Pitcairn was dead at Bunker Hill.) Burning two or three towns seemed a good idea, and Sandwich wrote to Admiral Samuel Graves that bomb-vessels were on the way for that purpose. 'We must have no further delicacies,' said Sandwich. 'You may be blamed for doing too little, but can never be censured for doing too much.' Graves was not inspired by this royal hint, and the king ordered him home. Sandwich thought this unjust, but (he told John Robinson) he was 'not so indiscreet as to opiniate (*sic*) this matter after the impression I perceive it has made at the fountainhead'. If the king wanted total war, Sandwich was not the man to be awkward.

From the City of London there came a new remonstrance:

> . . . We desire to repeat again that the power contended for over the colonies, under the specious name of dignity, is to all intents and purposes despotism; that the exercise of despotic power in any part of the empire is inconsistent with the character and safety of this country. . . .

Trade would be ruined, taxes would go up, there was 'nothing now to expect from America but gazettes of blood'.

> If anything could add to the alarm of these events, it is Your Majesty's having declared your confidence in the wisdom of men, a majority of whom are notoriously bribed to betray their constituents and their country.

In the Commons, the Whigs had lost heart. Horace Walpole called them 'the most timid set of time-serving triflers that ever existed'. Did the king say the opposition had encouraged the Americans? 'You might as soon light a fire with a wet dish-clout.' In the country, North was practising news-management. John Almon wrote after the war:

> The ministry resorted to the same methods to deceive the nation which had been so successfully practised by their predecessors . . . hiring a number of writers, hiring a number of newspapers, and printing an immense number of pamphlets which were sent free of postage and expense to every part of the kingdom.

Almon mentioned the 'hired pens' of, among others, Samuel Johnson, who denounced the Americans in *Taxation no Tyranny*—a work from which John Wesley borrowed freely for a penny pamphlet to still the Christian doubts of humbler folk. The country began to be told, too, of the king's quiet virtues. 'A Sketch of Their Majesties' domestic Life at Kew during the summer Season' describes how they rise at 6, have breakfast with their five elder children, and so forth. The king's private life is 'no less exemplary than it is truly amiable.' Moreover, 'he exercises his troops himself . . . has the Articles of War at his fingers' ends . . . takes the models of all the celebrated fortifications, knows the soundings of the chief harbours in Europe, and the strong and weak sides of most fortified towns . . . can name every ship in his navy, and he keeps lists of the commanders. . . . His Majesty feeds chiefly on vegetables and drinks little wine.'

Of the newspapermen who took North's money, the most colourful was the editor of *The Morning Post*, Henry Bate—another worldly man of the cloth, chaplain to Lord Lyttelton, that Lyttelton known as 'the Wicked'. A satirist wrote of Bate:

> A canonical buck, vociferous bully,
> A duellist, boxer, gambler and cully,
> A student at law, collector of news,
> A preacher in churches, an actor in stews:
> If vices like these recommend to the great,
> Then who is so fit for a bishop as B--e?

Bate was an inventive publicist. One November day in

1776 Horace Walpole was astonished to see thirty or forty men 'like hussars, in yellow with blue waistcoats and breeches, and high caps', marching down Piccadilly playing drums and trumpets. 'On their caps was written The Morning Post, and they distributed handbills. . . . Are not we quite distracted, reprobate, absurd, beyond all people that ever lived?' At this time Walpole felt the world was out of its senses: the war seemed to heighten the follies of London society. Young gentlemen were gaming desperately. When a peer's son, ruined, shot himself, Walpole wrote, 'What a distracted nation!' and then (alluding to a Dr Battie, proprietor of a madhouse), 'I do not wonder Dr Battie died worth £100,000. Will anybody be worth a shilling but mad-doctors?'

Henry Bate was not the man to die mad or broke. All through the war he was propagating official half-truths and lies, and violently abusing the opposition. (In 1780 he went so far against the Duke of Richmond that he was sent to jail for libel.) The arrangement was, as North put it later, that in return for £200 a year and 'hopes of preferment' in the church, Bate would 'keep a newspaper open for all writings in favour of Government'. In 1781, North told Bate that his promised reward in the church would take the form of £3,250 towards buying a good living (a thing as purchasable as a parliamentary seat or a regiment). But then the king disallowed the payment: he was not scrupulous about promises when a man had ceased to be useful. Bate bobbed up in charge of another paper, *The Morning Herald*, subsidized by the Prince of Wales in opposition to the king. Eventually he became not a bishop but a baronet.

Once the shooting began, the unbought papers had to watch what they said. Wilkes might speak in the Commons (to which he had been readmitted) of the 'unjust, ruinous, felonious and murderous war' and even say that every soldier killed 'has been murdered by Administration'; but newspapers must beware of such words. Four of them were fined £100 for having printed, eighteen months earlier, an announcement by Horne Tooke that the reformist Constitutional Society was collecting money for the relief of the widows, orphans and aged parents of our beloved American fellow-subjects, who, faithful to the character of Englishmen, preferring death to slavery, were, for that reason only, inhumanly murdered by the king's troops at or near Lexington and Concord.

When Horne Tooke himself was brought before Lord Mansfield on 4 July 1777, he argued: 'What might be fairly deemed a libel in 1777, could not in 1775, before the Americans were proscribed or declared rebels.' He was being prosecuted 'at the request of the most corrupt House of Commons that ever disgraced this or any other country'. He was fined and sentenced to a year in jail.

Newspapers and journals, however, got away with printing the Declaration of Independence, softening its long list of George III's offences only by using blanks for the king's name. They also printed a letter from Franklin to Viscount Howe denouncing British atrocities, declaring that the British would not be able 'to forgive the people you have so heavily injured' (a thought likely to puzzle George III), predicting that the war would be the ruin of Britain, and asking Howe to remember 'the tears of joy that wet my cheek when at your good sister's in London you once gave me expectations that a reconciliation might soon take place'.

The prosperity of these newspapers depended on their readers. Year after year they show that the spirit of opposition was strong in the land, although powerless until disaster was undeniable. The content of political caricatures strikingly confirms this: of the hundreds of prints issued on the subject of the war, only *three* anti-American ones survive. Many British prints were pirated in America—by Paul Revere among others. The popular printshops were loftily attacked by the subsidized *Whitehall Evening Post:* 'They collect the idle and the profligate, by means of which the foot-passengers are driven into the horse-road, and lose their handkerchiefs.' The ordinary man is appealed to in prints showing the hard fate of sixpence-a-day soldiers, or depicting a ragged family, amid a scene of ruin, singing 'Oh, I wish that the wars were all over.' Washington and even the naval raider Paul Jones are heroes; North and Sandwich are villains. George III is shown as early as 1775 driving to destruction in a carriage drawn by horses named Obstinacy and Pride. In 1778, the John Williams who had been the hero of a pillory in 1765 shows the king in conference with Bute and Mansfield:

BUTE: Be bloody, bold and resolute—be firm—fear nothing.
MANSFIELD: Kill them or they will kill you.
GEORGE: Sic volo. I am firm. Hem! Who's afraid? Eh?

By 1779, a chamberpot is being emptied over the king's head, and his crown is falling.

Verse lampoons were equally daring. In 1776 a scare story about a republican plot to kidnap the king on his way to parliament and pack him off to Hanover inspired *An Elegiac Epistle from an Unfortunate Elector of Germany*. The king speaks (the blanks are not hard to fill in):

> No more that st-ffn-cked, f-t, l-th-rg-c thing,
> That pl-mp unm--n-ng image of a ----;
> Now worn by fasting and dissolved in tears,
> The waning grandeur of my form appears . . .
> Not titled jockeys mounted for a race;
> Not hungry Scotsmen gaping for a place;
> Not British soldiers baulked of all supply
> E'er looked so dwindled and so lean as I.

He recalls the day he was seized:

> No acclamations sounded in the air—
> The vulgar stared, and I returned the stare . . .
> Not even my hireling shouters now were heard,
> Though paid full well . . .
> See the mad populace in swarms appear,
> Inspired at once by liberty and beer.

His captors treat him with great indignity. He is thrust into a cart full of 'all the filth of some vile jakes'.

> I sunk like lead and floundered to the chin.
> There did I lie and soak at least an hour.

Now the exiled king addresses an appeal to Pinchbeck, the inventor who had amused him with buttonmaking:

The Die is now Cast

Couldst thou not make thy ---- a pair of wings?
. . . With cautious art, like Daedalus I'll rise,
A royal buzzard through the middle skies;
Safe o'er the seas my skilful flight pursue
And light at Windsor Castle or at Kew . . .
Again, as at the vagrant Ch-rl-s' return,
These cursed republicans we'll hang or burn.

The king's actual state of mind at this time, and for years
to come, was well summed up by 'Hem! Who's Afraid?' He
wrote to John Robinson: 'It has been a very comfortable gift
of Divine Providence to me that when difficulties arise, my
spirits also increase.' Unlike the spirits of Lord North, who
very early lost belief in the war but could not bring himself to
give up the sweets of office. In October 1776 he was trying to
draft an inspiring King's Speech, and we find one Treasury
secretary, Grey Cooper, writing to another, Samuel Martin
(Wilkes's old enemy), 'The beginning is certainly *not neat*, and
the close is *certainly bald*. We must end with something of a
tirade, though expressed in quiet words.' A quiet tirade, to
prepare the nation for a hard war against a rude rabble.

Just then, the woman whom George had loved, Lady Sarah,
was writing to her friend Lady Susan:

You talk of the time when we used to *fancy great things*. I
am sure I can thank God very sincerely I am not queen. . . .
If I had loved & liked him, & not had interest enough to
prevent this war, I should certainly go mad . . . such a
shameful war.

Parliament was being kept in order—at a price. Only eight
years after the king had got his debt of £513,000 paid off, he
came forward with a demand for a further £618,000, plus a
grant henceforth of an extra £100,000 a year. Once again a
disillusioned ex-premier spoke against the court. Grafton
said: 'That very influence of the crown which could settle and
unsettle administrations at pleasure was the great cause of the
deficiency'.

Earl Talbot, the Lord Steward, diverted peers' minds from

87

political realities by a recital of distress in the royal household
the king's coal-merchant had £6,000 due to him and 'was
ready to turn His Majesty off', six quarters' wages were due
to menial servants, and the king's peace of mind was broken
by 'stories of distress and wretchedness'. In a burst of frank-
ness, Talbot said it was difficult to reduce the roll of salaries
'when the profits are enjoyed by persons of a certain rank, and
services performed by another. . . . One of the turnspits in
His Majesty's kitchen was, and I believe still is, a member of
the other House'—that is, a loyal MP rewarded with a
sinecure.

The king got his money, but not without a public protest
from fourteen Whig peers. The incurring of this new debt was
'a criminal act', they said; they could not vote 'great sums out
of the property of Your Majesty's subjects' to create 'an undue
influence in parliament'; the money would be 'a treacherous
gift . . . to the crown itself, as it will enable the ministers to
carry on those delusive systems which . . . must lead to the
ruin of this once great empire'.

Year after year, the portly shortsighted Lord North amiably,
vacillatingly, lucratively, plausibly, sleepily, despondingly,
abjectly directed a war he did not believe in—or ostensibly
directed it, for the role of prime minister was in fact performed
by a trio not thought of in the constitution: George III,
Jenkinson and Robinson.

In June 1779, when North had been trying to resign for
eighteen months, the king wrote to him: 'I have heard Lord
North frequently drop that the advantages to be gained by
this contest could never repay the expense' (one did not *say*
unwelcome things to the king, but *dropped* them) 'but this is
only weighing such events in the scale of a tradesman behind
his counter. Independence is their object . . . the West Indies
must follow them. . . . Ireland would soon follow the same
plan . . . then this island . . . would be a poor island indeed.'

North, however, had to face the Commons. Five days later,
Edmund Burke pointed at him and said, 'I could make a
motion—the impeachment of the minister.' France was in the
war; the country was alarmed. The following week, the king
showed that he was aware he might need to justify himself: he

summoned his Cabinet and addressed them for nearly an hour. 'He had the satisfaction to find, upon the strictest examination of his conduct,' one minister recorded, 'that there was no one action of his life that he could blame himself for, but his . . . consenting to the repeal of the Stamp Act. . . . It was to the repeal he imputed all the subsequent misfortunes.' He was resolved 'to part with his life' rather than give up the colonies.

A pamphlet was on sale forecasting Charles I's fate for the king:

> Be weakly right, but obstinately wrong.
> Be all the bigot martyr was before
> (A blessing for the nation yet in store!).
> See other Hampdens, other Cromwells rise,
> And modern Tea Acts mimic ship-supplies . . .
> One revolution raised you to the Crown;
> Another revolution may—dethrone.

The new Hampdens were talking, not of revolution, but of something almost as disturbing: 'radical reformation' of parliament. Such talk seemed dangerous to Edmund Burke and the Whigs' timid chief, Lord Rockingham. Burke presented instead, early in 1780, a plan for 'economic reform'—a trimming of the court's power by reducing the number of sinecures and pensions.

Burke in 1780 was no flatterer of courts. Britain was a limited monarchy, he said in a Commons speech full of passionate wit, but she maintained a cumbrous Gothic establishment. 'When the reason of old establishments is gone, it is absurd to preserve nothing but the burthen of them. This is . . . to burn precious oil in the tomb; it is to offer meat and drink to the dead.' But like Old Sarum, that supremely rotten borough ('its sole manufacture is in members of parliament'), the royal palaces had a political use: 'For the purposes of influence, and for those purposes only, are retained half at least of the household establishments.'

Burke recalled what Talbot had said in 1777 about the turnspit-MP:

The king's domestic servants were all undone, his tradesmen remained unpaid and went bankrupt—*because the turnspit in the king's kitchen was a member of parliament.* His Majesty's slumbers were interrupted, his pillow was stuffed with thorns, and his peace of mind entirely broken—*because the turnspit in the king's kitchen was a member of parliament.* . . . All the wheels of government at home and abroad were stopped—*because*— etc.

A whole list of 'gently ripening hot-houses' for useful MPs came under Burke's lash. When he explained why he would not go so far as to dismiss the king's attendant lords, he spoke of both king and lords in terms that were to be quoted against him with relish a dozen years later:

> Kings are naturally lovers of low company. They are so elevated above all the rest of mankind that they must look upon all their subjects as on a level. . . . It must indeed be admitted that many of the nobility are as perfectly willing to act the part of flatterers, tale-bearers, parasites, pimps and buffoons as any of the lowest and vilest of mankind can possibly be. . . .

For the sake of the king, to protect him from parasites of a lower kind, fit nobles must however be found: 'Though they are not much the better for a court, a court will be much the better for them.'

There was none of Burke's jesting tone in a weekly paper, *The Scourge*, that appeared at this time. It called the king 'a dastardly, mulish tyrant' and said:

> We have known you, sir, upon the arrival of dispatches from that seat of blood which have contained an account of the slaughter of thousands of the bravest men upon earth, immediately burst out in a fit of laughter and express a peculiar kind of joy and satisfaction at the butchery of mankind.

Certainly the king was exhilarated by warfare. When the news came, for example, that Ticonderoga was retaken, he ran to the queen shouting, 'I have beat them! Beat all the Americans!'

The Die is now Cast

The Scourge called North and his followers 'Right Honourable and Honourable TRAITORS'. The next week it reported 'threats and terrors of a prosecution held forth to the booksellers and vendors and to the publisher'. It was silenced after four months—but not before addressing North as 'the notorious plunderer of the people, corrupter of parliaments, state criminal and public traitor', and asking:

> Shall a highwayman or a pickpocket be hanged at Tyburn for taking the paltry sum of a few shillings or pounds, and such a parricide as Your Lordship, who has robbed a whole nation for years, and ruined a mighty empire, not only escape punishment but be *honoured* and *rewarded?*

At the same date Horace Walpole wrote 'A Merry Song about Murder':

> There once was a very great fool
>   Who fancied all subjects were slaves;
> Who endeavoured at absolute rule
>   By the help of a parcel of knaves.
> Now *cutting of throats* was his joy
>   And making red rivers of blood;
> A *fine button* his favourite toy,
>   Though his *habits* were not very good.
>   *Toroddle, toroddle, toroll.*
>
> Swords, hatchets and knives he prepared
>   To slaughter his people like sheep.
> Man, woman and child he ne'er spared,
>   Which made even savages weep.
> Then like a great lubberly calf
>   On his marrow-bones down he did fall:
> 'I have killed of my people but half;
>   Lord, help me to murder them all!'
>   *Toroddle, toroddle, toroll.* . . .

This is among Walpole's memoirs, marked 'For the *London Courant*'—a paper of John Almon's; and though it cannot be found in the scattered issues that survive, it is clear that Walpole (no radical) thought it printable.

The Commons in the spring of 1780 pained the king more than any verses might do. John Dunning moved his famous motion 'That the influence of the crown has increased, is increasing, and ought to be diminished.' All the arts of that very influence could not prevent the motion from being passed by 233 votes to 215. George III began preparing for an election 'to stem off the strides that are making to anarchy'—an election into which he threw every penny he could spare. Dunning and all other reformers would have been delighted to discover that since 1777 the king had been putting aside (as a supplement to all other political sums) £1,000 a month from his Privy Purse, to buy parliamentary seats. Just before the 1780 election he sent Robinson a £14,000 instalment, making more than £30,000 in all, in a sealed box from Windsor Castle, and wrote, 'I thought this the most secret way of doing it.'

And if peers, in defiance of the law, used every art to influence elections in their boroughs, why should not a king do so in his own parish? He told Robinson he would 'get my tradesmen encouraged to appear' for the government candidate at Windsor, and he welcomed a hint from Robinson that he should put six houses 'in different names of my servants, so that it will create six votes' (we must be grateful to the king for spelling everything out).

The opposition candidate at Windsor was Admiral Keppel, who had suffered from Sandwich's incompetence and perfidy at the Admiralty. Keppel was defeated—'but though all the royal bakers, and brewers, and butchers voted against him,' Walpole wrote to a friend, 'you must not imagine it was by mandate . . . for His Majesty himself told the admiral that he hoped he would carry his election. How saucy in his own servants to thwart his wishes!'

Elsewhere too, the old methods kept most of North's seats safe. Borough managers knew that a government in trouble would pay well. North's brother, the Bishop of Worcester, served as go-between for the sale of a seat in that city for £1,500. In some constituencies, however, much larger sums were not enough. North badly wanted to win seats in Westminster, the City of London and Surrey, with their large rolls of voters, so that he could claim to have public support.

Robinson poured more than £4,000 of the taxpayers' money into Surrey, £4,000 into the City, and more than £8,000 into Westminster—and still failed.

Westminster, to which Charles James Fox had transferred from a pocket borough to demonstrate that he was a Man of the People, had a radical reformist organization, the Westminster Association. It called for equalized electoral districts, salaried MPs, annual elections and the secret ballot; and for adult male suffrage: 'A portion of the soil, a portion of its produce, may be wanting to many, but every man has an interest in his life, his liberty, his kindred and his country.' There is an echo here of the seventeenth-century Levellers' cry that 'the poorest he that is in England' has a right to be heard. Fox was saying, privately, that the influence of the crown in parliament ought to be, not diminished, but 'entirely destroyed'. When he won at Westminster, supporters carried him in a tumultuous parade, hissing and groaning as they passed St James's Palace and ministers' houses. One of the toasts drunk at a victory banquet was 'The cause of universal liberty throughout the world.' Such was the mood that the American rebellion had created, and which was to inspire idealists in France only nine years later.

Ministers showed signs of looking to their future. *The London Courant* said in September 1780:

> The most sanguine admirers of His Majesty say that the American war has been and is still *his hobby-horse;* and the ministers, whenever they are censured for the folly and absurdity of any particular measure . . . constantly excuse themselves with saying that 'His Majesty is his own Minister'.

But a king alone cannot maintain a war. Fox in the Commons in May 1781 pictured North speaking to MPs at his levee:

> Without the American war I shall have no places, no emoluments to bestow, not a single loan to negotiate; nor shall I be able to retain this poor situation of mine that I have long held thus disinterestedly. Put an end to the American war, and you undo all.

Such motives, however, could not long survive the day six months later when North got the news of Cornwallis's surrender at Yorktown and paced up and down his room exclaiming wildly, 'O God! It's all over!' Somehow he had to write, the next day, on the king's orders, a King's Speech saying it was not all over. (Even a year earlier he had been so perplexed that he wrote to Robinson, 'I cannot tell what to do about the speech—I have lost my understanding—') North's majorities faded away as the truth took command of more MPs' minds; but not of the king's mind. When North quit at last in the spring of 1782, the king drafted an abdication statement saying he was being prevented from carrying on the war by a 'sudden change of sentiment' in the Commons. He was ready to hand the crown to his nineteen-year-old son and sail to Germany. At the last minute he swallowed a Whig coalition, with Fox as Foreign Secretary—Fox, who in the Commons had been picturing North expiating his crimes 'on the public scaffold'.

Next the king had to swallow the independence of America. Everyone was to blame but himself. He was in the hands of 'a desperate faction', the victim of 'knavery and indolence' and 'every sort of chicanery'. In March 1783 he again prepared an abdication speech justifying himself at great length, and hinting that thoughts of a royal coup had occurred to him:

> The oath I took at my coronation prevents my exceeding the powers vested in me, or submitting to be a cipher in the trammels of any self-created band.

The closing phrases might have come straight from the Butian days of twenty years before, mixed metaphor and all.

Lord Thurlow, the Lord Chancellor, told the king it would be easy to go to Hanover, but very hard to come back. Yet how could he live with the political monster that was rising from the chaos—a coalition between Fox and that erstwhile candidate for the axe, North? It was hinted to the king that the monster might destroy itself. He stayed; but wrote, 'My sorrow may prove fatal to my health if I remain long in this thraldom.' He told an old courtier, Lord Hertford, 'that every morning he wished himself eighty, or ninety, or dead.' Not the

American disaster, but the disaster to himself, tormented him. When he signed terms granting what he had said he would never grant, he told North, 'This completes the downfall of the lustre of this empire. . . . Religion and public spirit are quite absorbed by vice and dissipation. . . . I am innocent of the evils that have occurred.'

7

The Virgin Minister

THE KING was not long in his thraldom. The Fox–North coalition had dubious foundations; a combination of backstairs intrigue, lies, lures, caricatures, public distrust and unconstitutional royal pressure overturned it. William Pitt, the twenty-four-year-old Immaculate Boy, son of a famous father, became prime minister. Among his makers were those ageing King's Friends (unwounded by their war), Jenkinson, now known as Daddy Jenky, and Robinson, nicknamed the Political Ratcatcher for his crafty use of palace-flavoured baits to tempt North's followers to rat. The make-or-break issue was a bill of Fox's to control the East India Company in its highhanded private empire-building. The king was ready to do almost anything to escape from being 'dictated to by Mr Fox'. In the most unconstitutional of the measures he used, the king's agent was the 2nd Earl Temple, a son of George Grenville and thus Pitt's first cousin. Temple told peers behind the scenes that the king would treat as his enemy every man who voted for Fox's bill. The peers threw out the bill. The Commons, not yet quite restored to obedience, condemned Temple's action as 'a high crime and misdemeanour', and he feared he would be impeached. Pitt, uttering the lie of the day, declared that the charge against Temple was 'the lie of the day'. (Within a year, Temple was made a marquess). The Commons did not protest for long. The king had shown, only nine months after deciding to abdicate, that his power was not dead.

The Virgin Minister

PITT AND PREROGATIVE FOREVER!
Bless the Lords of the Bedchamber!
Back Stairs and Secret Influence forever!
. . . Oh, Billy's a sharp one, though he looks as
if sugar wouldn't melt in his mouth!

So read a satirical 'proclamation' in *The Morning Herald*, the paper that Henry Bate, late of *The Morning Post*, was editing in support of Fox and with subsidies from the Prince of Wales, who in the Hanoverian tradition was at war with his father.

Yet Pitt was able to present himself as the untainted newcomer who was saving the country and the king from an unprincipled alliance of the old Ins and the old Outs. Moreover, Pitt was pledged to enact the parliamentary reforms for which so many citizens longed. It was hard for North and Fox to claim political purity. When Pitt went to the country in the spring of 1784, they were assailed with abuse, and nowhere so much as in the Westminster contest, where Fox was fighting for re-election. North was one of Fox's problems. A Pittite handbill said:

> You will undoubtedly remember that Mr Fox is the man who formed the *disgraceful coalition* with *Lord North*, who was the author of the *accursed American war* and of all your late heavy taxes.

A satirical print by the artist Thomas Rowlandson went further. It said the accursed war was 'fomented by Opposition and misconducted by a timid Minister'. That became the official line. Fox and North had to carry the king's load of guilt. *The Public Advertiser* (no longer anti-court) carried some verses written from the point of view of a lady in the Commons gallery. She saw Fox speaking:

> I own to my shame I was ravished to hear him,
> In praise of himself and a man who *slept* near him;
> A joss of a figure that seemed a mere lubber,
> A mass of unwholesome, inanimate blubber;
> But Deborah gave me a jog on the knee,
> 'You've heard of Lord N---h, my dear—well—*that is he*—

The curse of our nation, the noted blood-spiller,
Who paid for it all with a joke from Joe Miller.'*

Fox could hardly protest about such descriptions of his ally,
for he had been saying worse things about him not long
before. Fox's enemies delightedly jogged the electors' memories with a clever compilation, *The Beauties and Deformities of
Fox, North and Burke*, which had an enormous sale. In 1779, it
recorded, Fox had called North 'a lump of deformity and
disease, of folly and wickedness, of ignorance and temerity',
and, still more embarrassing, had said:

What! Enter into an alliance with those very ministers who
have betrayed their country, who have . . . prostituted the
public wealth, who have prostituted . . . the glory of the
nation! The idea is too monstrous to be admitted for a
moment.

North had indeed made overtures to Fox, having been advised by Robinson in 1778, 'If you get Charles Fox, it may do
for a while, but otherwise you are at your last gasp.' Robinson
was the last person to publish that advice now; or to point out
that to join with North to shore him up then was different
from joining him in 1783.

A greater problem for Fox was his own reputation. He was
an obsessive gamester, and usually in debt. More than once
the fashionable world of St James's had watched the bailiffs
carting away his furniture from his lodgings. He had long ago
lost most of his father's ill-gotten money, and since 1781 his
chief income had been a one-twelfth share in the profits of
a faro bank at Brooks's Club, plus six guineas an hour when
he dealt.

One anti-Fox handbill is in the form of a warning to house-
holders from Bow Street police station that canvassers for 'a
certain candidate' have been stealing silver spoons and will
'carry off whatever they can lay their hands on'. It adds:

The above people are a set of shabby, ill-looking fellows,
and are set on by a *short, black, swarthy kind of a person*,
who has lately been *turned out of his master's service* for
attempting to rob him of *half a crown*.

Joe Miller's Jests, first published 1739.

Here we see the more serious charge that Fox had tried to encroach on royal power. He gave colour to this charge by joining in toasts to 'the Majesty of the People' at his meetings. Nicknames calculated to frighten timid citizens were thrown at him: The Man of the Mob, General Blackbeard, the Black Protector.

North himself, knowing what royal power had achieved between 1770 and 1782, had reached the conclusion (as he wrote to Fox) that 'the appearance of power is all that a king of this country can have'. But he could not say that to the country. And all Fox's reform talk could be attacked as a ruse to seize on the nation's wealth. One handbill sardonically lists reasons for voting for Fox:

. . . Because Mr Fox's family have never robbed the public of £370,000, as is maliciously asserted. . . .

Because Mr Fox, when he came into office, did not hire the public papers by giving each of the printers drafts on the Treasury for £500.

Because Mr Fox, had he continued in office, agreed to pay off only £50,000 of his debts in the course of the year.

Because Mr Fox did not drive Mrs Robinson in a phaeton through the public streets, by way of insulting his electors.

Fox had indeed been openly the lover, two years earlier, of the actress 'Perdita' Robinson after she had been discarded by the Prince of Wales; and this satirist might have said that *she* was seen to be driving *him* in her phaeton, which was considered shameful. Many other men had enjoyed her; so the wit George Selwyn remarked, 'Who should the Man of the People live with, but the Woman of the People?' By 1784 Fox was associating with another demi-mondaine, the woman he was to marry, Elizabeth Bridget Armitstead, who had also been honoured with the eager lust of the young prince.

Mrs Armitstead is mentioned scurrilously in a paragraph in the Pitt-subsidized *Morning Post* about Fox's anger over caricatures:

An eminent orator is extremely indignant at certain exhibitions in the print-shops, particularly that where he is represented as suffering *flagellation* at the cart's tail; though he has no great objection to receive the same discipline from the *delicate* hands of the charming A--------d.

Two days later the same paper accuses Fox's friends of attacking the caricature shop of S. W. Fores at No. 3 Piccadilly:

> On Friday night some well-dressed men broke the windows of Mr Fores, printseller, in Piccadilly. . . . A few days before, two of Mr Fox's intimate friends called at Mr Fores's shop and informed him of the probability of some such vengeance if he did not remove the obnoxious prints.

This was the least of the violence during the forty days of the Westminster poll. It was a hot contest, for if Pitt defeated the Man of the People at Westminster, with its voters' roll of perhaps 13,000 of all ranks, he could claim that public opinion was firmly behind him. The Treasury was spending, this time, £9,200 against Fox; and he had long purses on his side—the prince's among others. Both sides hired gangs of strong men to protect their voters and their parades from attack, and to terrorize their opponents. Battles were frequent round the hustings, which stood on the west side of Covent Garden market piazza. More than one man was killed.

Fox's chief opponent was Admiral Lord Hood, whose gangs were mainly seamen. Fox's were mainly Irish sedan-chair men and Irish coal-heavers, whom their organizer, Colonel George Hanger, described whimsically as 'those gallant troops of high rank and distinguished fame, the Knights of the Strap and the Black Diamond Knights'. And he adds, in his memoirs, 'I trust I shall live to taste many a good pot more of brown stout with them'—a tribute to a sturdy Irish habit. This Hanger, a raffish but endearing crony of the Prince of Wales, describes the qualities needed by a gentleman helping either side in a Westminster election:

> He must help a porter up with his load, shake hands with a fishwoman, pull his hat off to an oyster-wench, kiss a ballad-singer, and be familiar with a beggar. If, in addition to these amiable qualities, he is a tolerable good boxer, can play a good stick, and in the evening drink a pail-full of all

sorts of liquors in going the rounds to solicit voters at their various clubs, then, indeed, he is a most highly finished and useful agent. In all the above accomplishments and sciences, except drinking, which I never was fond of, I have the vanity to believe that I arrived nearer to perfection than any of my rivals.

Another accomplishment was at least as useful: a talent for writing political songs. Ballads were weapons on both sides, and not only in London. *The Morning Herald* reported that 'ministers have actually sent down three coachloads of *ballad-singers* to Yorkshire. They are hired at a fixed salary.' A covered wagon full of ballads and pamphlets went with them. In Westminster, the Foxites' balladeer was Captain Charles Morris, soon to be famous as a bawdy entertainer in the prince's circle, and as the laureate of the Sublime Society of Beef Steaks (he sang there for the last time in 1832 at the age of eighty-six). The Pittites fumed at Morris because he had been wooed from their cause after writing a song against the Fox–North coalition.

Morris went straight for the weak point of Pitt the Immaculate: that he had got into power by devious means, and with the help of Jenkinson, that heir of Bute (the Thane):

> They say that his judgment is mellow and pure
>> And his principles virtue's own type, sir;
> I believe, from my soul, he's a son of a whore,
>> And his judgment more rotten than ripe, sir . . .

> It's true, h' has a pretty good gift of the gab
>> And was taught by his dad on a stool, sir;
> But though at a speech he's a bit of a dab,
>> In the state he's a bit of a tool, sir . . .

> Though reason united a North and a Fox,
>> The world of this junction complain, sir:
> But what's that to *his*, who joined (with a pox!)
>> To the cabinet pimp of the Thane, sir!
> Who sold to a high-flying Jacobite gang
>> The credit of Chatham's great name, sir!

That, pleased, we might hear the Young Puppet harangue
While Jenkinson plays the old game, sir!

The song ends with a toast:

'Britannia! and *may he ne'er stand at her head*
Who never can stand at her tail, sir!'

This is one of many jibes at the bachelor Pitt's remarkable lack of interest in women. Opposition papers printed epigrams on the subject:

'For Pitt, so young,' cries Ned, 'just twenty-five,
    Why don't the women make a fuss?'
'A fuss for him!' quoth Nell. 'Why, man alive,
    He never sure *stands up* for us.'

Fox was abused, and far more rudely, as a sly, shabby, lecherous rogue, a Falstaff leading his prince astray. He is pictured among his 'best friends' at a house in King's Place, a Westminster byway that contained the most expensive brothels. The prince is with him, and a bawd is saying, 'He introduced His R---- H------- to my house.' This print is by Thomas Rowlandson, who produced a series of anti-Fox caricatures full of lewd innuendoes. His chief target was Fox's most glamorous canvasser, the twenty-six-year-old Georgiana, Duchess of Devonshire. Rowlandson depicts a fox kissing the duchess's bared breast. He makes play with a slang phrase for making love—to give a woman 'a brush'—and at the end of the contest he shows Fox saying goodbye to the duchess and her sister Henrietta:

Ladies, for your friendship and good will
My bushy tail is at your service still.

Fox is seated on an ass, his brush hangs over the front of his saddle, and the duchess caresses it, saying, 'For sure no Fox had e'er so fine a tail.' All this was not sheer invention. Fox was certainly one of the duchess's lovers. His black brows inspired her to call him The Eyebrow. A year later he was reproaching her for not parting from the duke to live with him.

Prints by Rowlandson and others also show the duchess, with a FOX rosette in her hat or at her breast, kissing and embracing butchers. Some prints, now lost, seem to have gone further. One newspaper said, 'The duchess is much enamoured with the prints which condescend to notice Her Grace in such a variety of canvassing positions. Strict orders are given to buy all that come out'—meaning she tried to suppress them. There are songs, too, that went very far:

> When Devon's high duchess the *thing* takes in hand
> What man can refuse at her quarters to stand?
> Then haste for the Man of the People to poll,
> And tickle the duchess's—*tol de rol lol*.

> Ye tinkers, ye tailors, ye cobblers and all,
> Haste away, leave the kettle, the shopboard and stall,
> For who for the Man of the People won't poll
> To touch a fair duchess's—*tol de rol lol?*

'I am unhappy beyond measure here, and abused for nothing,' the duchess wrote to a friend. 'Yet as it is begun I must go on with it.' The abuse certainly deterred some of the duchess's friends from joining her in her almost daily canvassing skirmishes from Devonshire House in Piccadilly, in a carriage decorated (like her footmen, and the horses themselves) with Fox rosettes, foxtail emblems, and ribbons in Fox's blue-and-buff colours.

It was true that Fox was desperate for any sort of help. There were three contenders for two seats, and early in the poll he was running last. Fox to his 'darling Liz', 7 April: 'Worse and worse. . . . There is very little chance indeed.' Next day: 'I have serious thoughts, if I am beat here, of not coming into parliament at all.' Next day: 'We have certainly a chance, but a small one. . . . Oh, how I do long to see my Liz!'

Each side accused the other of collecting dubious votes.

> A group of dames with borrowed names
>   And dressed in men's apparel
> Polled twice-told o'er, and roundly swore
>   That Fox should wear the laurel. . . .
> And many said, among the dead
>   There'd been a resurrection.

The duchess was accused of handing out golden sovereigns, or of using a less direct form of bribery:

'I'll lay you five guineas,' says a celebrated canvasser, 'and stake the money in your own hands, that you will not vote for Mr Fox.' 'Done,' says the independent elector of Westminster. Thus one more vote is procured for the Man of the People.

(Each vote, of course, was open. The ballot came eighty-eight years on.)

When George III saw that Fox was gaining, he wrote to Pitt that it 'could only be by bad votes'; and so the king ordered that 'similar means must be adopted against him'. Within Westminster there lived numerous people employed by or dependent on St James's Palace and Buckingham House. 'Yesterday,' a Foxite newspaper reported, 'the *household troops* of St James's, from the Page of the Back Stairs to the scullion in the kitchen, were mustered.' Another paragraph spoke of 'stable boys and helpers, a Great Lady's [the queen's] musical band of foreigners, lodgers of all descriptions' and even 'convicted felons discharged from the ballast lighters' (prison hulks). It was further reported that 'no less than four hundred' guardsmen were marched to the polling station in Covent Garden. It was hard for a soldier to vote the wrong way. In the eighteenth-century Brigade of Guards, as another paragraph pointed out, it was customary to give privates leave 'to work at their respective trades', a privilege that might be worth thirty shillings a week to them; but their officers could easily say No.

Again and again the Foxites attacked the revival of royal prerogative. A handbill said:

Shall we, the people, be governed by the king only? No!
Shall we, the people, be governed by the king and Bedchamber Lords only? No! no!
Huzza! Fox for ever!

Pitt is never forgotten:

The Virgin Minister

Billy blustered and vapoured and gave himself airs;
He spoke for the people and swore he was theirs,
Till Jenkinson ushered him up the back-stairs—
    Oh, the back-stairs of St James's,
    And oh, the St James's back-stairs . . .

Then as Billy stands up for prerogative strong,
If the father was right, sure the son must be wrong,
So let every Englishman join in my song—
    Success to the Whigs of old England!
    Success to the old English Whigs!

And John Wilkes, who, a self-styled exhausted volcano at the
age of fifty-six, had gone over from Fox to Pitt, is the subject
of an anti-prerogative song:

    Johnny Wilkes, Johnny Wilkes
    Thou boldest of bilks,
What a different song you now sing!
    For your dear Forty-five,
    'Tis *prerogative*,
And your blasphemy—*God Save the King!*

Was not a court-supporting Wilkes a stranger sight than a Fox
joined with a North? A caricature showed Wilkes and the
king embracing, with the legend: 'When Piety and Blasphemy
agree/Can there a stranger coalition be?'

Lord Hood held his lead, but Fox moved into second place
and eventually had a margin of 231. He was able to write to
Liz Armitstead about more things than politics: 'It may
sound ridiculous, but it is true that I feel every day how much
more I love you than even *I* knew. You are *all* to me. . . .
Pray, pray do not abuse your power.'

Fox's impending victory unnerved *The Morning Post*. One
day it managed to put the entire blame on the renegade
Captain Morris: 'Had he not basely changed his principles,
and employed his wit and convivial talents for the unsub-
stantial prospects and promises of a despised and degraded
faction, Mr Fox would have been at this time at least a
thousand behind-hand. . . . Her Grace and the captain have
tickled the butchers and bakers out of their sober senses.' And

a few days later: 'While Her Grace was squeezing and fingering the butchers, Captain M----s was amusing their female connections with his great parts at every alehouse and ginshop in Westminster . . . singing and drinking with forty half-naked whores and rogues of the lowest description.'

Lord North, who had been *The Morning Post's* hero so long as he was serving the king, was reviled. His political marriage to Fox was pictured by this paper in a charming scene:

'My dear Boreas,' says Carlo Khan one day to his beloved spouse, 'our mutual affections have gained us many enemies, but let us kiss and be friends—and a fig for the world.' Boreas then held out his chuckle head, while the dear bewitching black Carlo Khan mumbled his spouse's delicious blubber lips, and clasping the lovely creature by the middle —so! so! so!—they sunk down in ecstatic bliss.

Fox had a great victory parade, passing Carlton House, which had become the Prince of Wales's home and therefore a Whig shrine. The prince flaunted his support for his father's enemy, swelling the parade with his state carriage and twenty-four gentlemen of his household and displaying laurel and a Fox favour in his hat. Fox rode in a triumphal chair. There were brass bands, trumpeters, and a squad of twenty-four butchers making their own special marching music with marrowbones and cleavers. Flags proclaimed The Whig Cause, The Rights of the Commons, The Man of the People. Everywhere fluttered foxtails and buff-and-blue ribbons. At the corner of Cockspur Street and Pall Mall, marchers and Fox's loyal Irish chair-men could drink beer from barrels provided by baldheaded, open-necked Sam House, the egalitarian keeper of a Wardour Street public house. 'The night,' says *The Gazetteer*, 'was spent with unusual exhilaration.'

Next day, George III drove from St James's Palace to open the new parliament, with the pleasing knowledge that dozens of Fox–North MPs had been swept away. As the king passed the garden of Carlton House, however, there was a sight to pain him. Nine marquees stood on his son's vast lawn: a fête was being held to celebrate Fox's personal success, his consolation for his rout in the country. Among the prince's six hundred guests, a notable figure was Lord North. The scene was recorded by a Tory MP, Nathaniel Wraxall:

> Lord North, dressed, like every other individual invited, in his new livery of blue and buff, beheld himself surrounded by those very persons who, scarcely fifteen months earlier, affected to regard him as an object of national execration, deserving capital punishment. They now crowded round him to admire the sallies of his wit.

Did his sallies extend to *The Morning Post?* That very day it called him 'the man who has brought all the ruin upon the country', accused him of 'plunder and peculation', and asked (as Fox had once done), 'How long shall the just indignation of an insulted people cry for vengeance?' It is hard to be harrowed with pity for North; and hard to respect *The Morning Post.*

The Whigs, robbed of power so soon after the king's American disaster, were bitter. A caricature entitled 'The First Levee' showed Pittite MPs queueing to kiss the king's arse. A little later there was one inspired by a venerable English phrase: it showed the sun shining from the same royal part.

Josiah Wedgwood, the Whiggish potter, joined in the attack, if we are to believe a verse collection by friends of Fox, the *Probationary Odes,* in which Pittite ministers and courtiers are imagined to be making their claims for the post of Poet Laureate, vacant in 1785. The ode of Pitt's Lord Chancellor, the blunt-spoken Edward Thurlow, reads in part:

> Lo! Wedgwood too waves his Pitt-pots on high!
> Lo! he points where the bottoms yet dry
>   The visage immaculate bear.
> Be Wedgwood d-mned, and double-d-mned his ware. . . .

And there is this footnote to 'Pitt-pots':

> I am told that a scoundrel of a potter, Mr Wedgwood, is making ten thousand vile utensils with a figure of **Mr Pitt** in the bottom; round the head is to be a motto,
>
> > We will spit
> > On Mr Pitt,

And *other such* d-mned rhymes, suited to the uses of the
different utensils.

Pitt's virginity never ceased to be a target. Fox's friends
amused themselves with epigrams:

> 'Tis true, indeed, we oft abuse him
> Because he bends to no man,
> But slander's self dares not accuse him
> Of stiffness to a woman.

A pretended journal of Pitt's colleague and drinking companion, the unprincipled Scotsman Henry Dundas, has Pitt
shying away from the fashionable brothel of Charlotte Hayes
in Berkeley Street:

> Took Pitt to town in my chariot—drove to Berkeley Street
> —got Pitt to the door, but he would not come in—lounged
> an hour with Charlotte—promised her a company in one of
> the new regiments for a disbanded private of the Horse
> Guards. . . .

Charles Morris delighted Fox and Carlton House with a new
song, 'The Virgin Minister':

> Come then, be silent
> And join in my ballad.
> A better you never saw
> Pinned on a wall.
> Oh, the subject won't hurt
> Any lady's nice palate,
> Because it ne'er meddles
> With ladies at all.
> It is all of a sweet pretty
> Well-spoken gentleman,
> Come to delude this
> Lewd world and its wife:
> Oh, by c--t, he's so chaste
> He won't trust his p---le, man,
> Out of his hand
> To save Venus's life.

The Virgin Minister

Troth, and it's right
    That the tool of a Minister
Ne'er should be managed
    By hands but his own:
Then, though his labour's
    By dexter or sinister,
Still, it's all one
    While he's working alone. . . .

But mark what he did
    For to get to his station:
He told a damned lie
    In the ear of the king.
Then a shite on his name,
    For I'm all for the nation,
So don't bother me
    With the name of the thing.
His taxes now prove
    His great love for the people,
So wisely they're managed
    To starve the poor souls.
Sure the praise of the man
    Should be rung in each steeple
That would rob them of daylight,
    Of candles and coals. . . .

A month after the election, Pitt had introduced new taxes on,
among other things, windows and candles.

Then what's all this nonsense
    And humbug about him,
His purity, chastity,
    Virtue and pride?
Troth, in Ireland we would
    Be all apt to doubt him:
A man with virginity
    Is all my *backside*.
Oh, burn your men-maids
    And each f--g---g pretender
In stoical coldness
    And pitiful art!

Then a toast to Fox:

> Here's the lad, my brave boys,
>   With the nature that's tender,
> And touched by the passions
>   That honour the heart!

Yet Pitt was secure. One of the *Probationary Odes* admitted this (and provided a glimpse of the ever-fidgetty king at his levee):

> Sooner our gracious king
> From heel to heel shall cease to swing;
> Sooner that brilliant eye shall leave its socket;
> Sooner that hand desert the breeches pocket,
> Than constant George consent his friends to quit
> And break his plighted faith to Jenkinson and Pitt!

Fox, it was true, had a royal patron now; a Whig court at Carlton House; but the Prince of Wales was becoming a questionable blessing.

8

The Greatest Buck in Town

QUEEN VICTORIA'S eldest uncle began his long amorous
life in an age when a poor man could become rich, a great man
could repair (or multiply) his fortune, and a talented girl could
live like (or become) a duchess, by indulging a prince's desires.
Ambition excuses many things, and sometimes it takes comical
forms, as the prince learned long before he was of an age for
panders. 'Lord Bath does not hobble up the back stairs for
nothing. Oh, he is an excellent courtier,' Horace Walpole wrote
to another excellent courtier, Lord Hertford, when George III's
heir was not yet twenty months old. 'The Prince of Wales
shoots him with plaything arrows; he falls down dead; and the
child kisses him to life again. Melancholy ambition—!' for
Bath was eighty years old.

The prince was only seventeen when he was put into the
skilled hands of Perdita Robinson. The affair was arranged by
a twenty-two-year-old friend of the prince, Lord Malden, heir
to the Earl of Essex, who had been keeping her. She was a
much-admired actress (hence her name), had been set up by
Malden in a house in Clarges Street, and drove about in a silk-
lined carriage he had given her, 'the admiration of all the
charioteering circles of St James's', with an enwreathed
cypher on its side to resemble a titled person's coat of arms.
Perdita loved to be besieged by admirers, and perhaps Malden
got tired of this.

Her *petits soupers* were select and elegant; her levees
crowded; her box at the opera (which was fitted up . . .

exactly in the style of Her Majesty's of France) was surrounded by distinguished beaux.

So say *The Memoirs of Perdita*, a journalist's account which
claims that many intimate details were furnished 'by one who
has for several years been her confidant, and to whose pen she
has been indebted for much newspaper panegyric'. Perdita
certainly cultivated the newspapers, and even wrote for them
when in decline. The widening social role of the newspapers in
the late 1770s is indicated by the statement in this account that
envious rivals of Perdita fed the papers with abuse of her,
which was *'well paid for* (sometimes in cash, and when that
run low, with personal favours)'.

As Florizel [so the prince was quickly nicknamed] approached to manhood, every female heart was upon the
rack . . . *maids* of *professed honour*, as well as ladies of no
honour at all, threw out their lure for the royal bird; and
the contest was warm among the most distinguished of the
Cyprian corps.

Perdita, with Malden's help, won. The prince had not long
before been describing himself, to a girl he loved at court, as
'too subject to give loose or vent to his passions of every
kind . . . rather too fond of wine and women'. Perdita became a passion. The *Memoirs* tell the story in many ripe and
inventive passages, from the first assignation, when Florizel,
'who never failed the woman he scarce wished for, the most
homely of his mother's train . . . had extended in his arms the
charming longing Perdita, yielding, defenceless' and yet
'wanted power to seize the trembling prey', and 'not even the
application of Perdita's soft hand could possibly rouse the
languid godhead'.

What a delight it must be, but sometimes what an in-
hibiting delight, to have the power to act out what other men
dream of! What excuse for failure can a prince give himself?
One need not be astonished that he early became a heavy
drinker, and passed his life compulsively betraying every
mistress.

His second night with Perdita, all was well—'that glorious
night, the first of all my joys, the blessedest of my life, trem-

bling and fainting I approached your chamber', and so an alleged letter from the prince goes on; and indeed that is not unlike his lifelong epistolary style.

Days, weeks and months ran on in this intercourse of pleasure, and Perdita was now the envy of every female heart: her chariot, her phaeton, her dress, her everything, was equally the subject of censure and imitation.

The censure was sometimes cruel. A sixpenny illustrated broadside appeared with a 'Florizel and Perdita' song to be sung to the tune of 'O Polly is a sad slut':

> A tender prince, ah well-a-day!
>   Of years not yet a score
> Had late his poor heart stol'n away
>   By one of's many more:
>
> As many more (at least) she is,
>   And might have been the mother
> (You'd say it, if you saw her phiz)
>   Perhaps of such another.

Perdita admitted to being only four years older than the prince, but perhaps she had mislaid a few years.

> Her cheeks were vermeiled o'er with red,
>   Her breast enamelled white,
> And nodding feathers decked her head—
>   A piece for candlelight.
>
> Sometimes she'd play the tragic queen,
>   Sometimes the peasant poor.
> Sometimes she'd step behind the scene
>   And there she'd play the w----.
>
> Two thousand pounds, a princely sight!
>   For doing just no more
> Than what is acted every night
>   By every sister w----.
>
> She never played her part so well
>   In all her life before,
> Yet some, as well as Florizel,
>   Know how she plays the w----.

Her husband too, a puny imp,
Will often guard the door
And humbly play Sir Peter Pimp
While she performs the w----.

Perdita is pictured standing amid boxes labelled 'carmine, dentifrice, whitewash, perfume, pomatum'. She holds out an *Essay on Man* to the prince. To one side stands a man labelled 'Sir Peter Pimp'—the husband, Thomas Robinson, said to have been an attorney's clerk. He appears in a bad light in several accounts. One pamphlet tells of one of Malden's predecessors with Perdita, the Wicked Lord Lyttelton: 'They were continually together . . . and the husband trudged after them. . . . They were frequently in a carriage with the blinds up [drawn], and Mr R------- a mile or two behind on horseback.'

Within a year the prince's passion cooled, and the fault was not all on Perdita's side. After his eighteenth birthday in August 1780, the prince was given an adult establishment, with equerries and so forth, although still kept at Buckingham House by his jealous father. According to Horace Walpole, who got his information from the Duke of Gloucester, and from his lifelong friend, Lord Hertford, the Lord Chamberlain, 'As soon as the king went to bed, the prince and his brother Prince Frederick went to their mistresses or to brothels.' In 1781, to divide the two, Frederick, the future Duke of York, was sent off to Germany, where for six years he revelled and studied other military arts. The prince did not mend. Two of his mentors in debauchery and insolence were the king's younger brother, the Duke of Cumberland, hero of the Grosvenor case, and the duke's shameless Luttrell wife. The prince's conduct made 'the greatest noise', says Walpole.

The prince drank hard, swore publicly in the [palace] drawing-room, and talked there irreligiously and indecently in the openest manner (both which were the style of the Duchess of Cumberland). He passed the nights in the lowest debaucheries, at the same time bragging of intrigues with women of quality, whom he named publicly. Both the prince and the duke [Cumberland] talked of the king in the grossest terms, even in his hearing.

114

Walpole blames the king for having tried to keep the prince 'locked up in the palace of piety'. In 1781 the king must have felt vindicated. The prince was being blackmailed by Perdita. She was threatening to publish sheaves of the prince's letters. He had promised her £20,000 when he came of age; he had also written outrageous things about the king and others. Moreover, she was a married woman, and had not Lord Grosvenor got £10,000 out of another prince?

Lord Malden found himself spending most of the summer in negotiations to settle how much she should be paid. She insisted that she was not *selling* the letters; but she had found (so women always said in such cases) that she had incurred great debts by living in the manner to which her lover was accustomed. This got her £5,000—'undoubtedly an enormous sum,' the king wrote to Lord North, distracting him from the American war with a request for the money. 'I am happy at being able to say that I never was personally engaged in such a transaction, which perhaps makes me feel this the stronger.' A Florizel-and-Perdita pamphlet dared to say of the righteous king:

> The mischiefs which have been experienced by this unhappy country during the reign of the best of princes are all to be attributed to His Majesty's want of knowledge of the world. He is the most pious, the most virtuous, most domestic sovereign that ever reigned; but perhaps it had been better for his subjects had he been as early acquainted with masquerades and brothels as his brothers and his sons.

The prince also gave Perdita a £600-a-year pension. One cannot help suspecting that when Fox took her up the following year, having superseded Colonel Tarleton of American fame, her money was an attraction. 'Charles *lives* with Mrs Robinson, goes to Sadler's Wells with her,' his cousin, Lady Sarah Lennox, the king's old love, wrote to a friend; and *The Morning Herald* commented on his riding in her carriage: 'The lady gives the gentleman the airing, and not, as usual, the gentleman the lady.'

But before long Fox had passed on to Mrs Armitstead.

According to *The Town and Country Magazine*, she was the daughter of a man who got 'a very decent livelihood' in the shoe trade, but turned Methodist and went broke. She was 'tall and genteel, with a beautiful face and captivating eyes', and a notable bawd, Mrs Goadby, introduced her to the ever-active Lord Lyttelton. Then the Duke of Ancaster kept her in 'a genteel house near Portman Square'. One succeeding lover was the Duke of Grafton. In 1779 came a leading Whig peer, the young Earl of Derby (who had thrown out his wife because of her amours with, among others, Grafton). The prince kept Mrs Armitstead for only a brief period, but remained fond of her. It is touching to find Fox writing to her in 1798, when the prince had been pestering her: 'I am not afraid of my angel's doing anything wrong. . . . But I collected from what you said that his way of persuading you is to tell you inventions about me. . . . The next time I have seen my Liz . . . she has had one of those *coldish* looks that make things so *mis.*' Such was the gentleman prince's technique.

Letters might be hushed up, but the prince could be seen in action. Scarcely veiled paragraphs in the newspapers spread the news of his wickedness through the country; satirical verses, with blanks that anyone could fill in, added details. When he was not yet twenty-one. *The Devil Divorced* appeared. The devil speaks:

> First on my list a man of rank appears,
> Far versed in wickedness above his years.
> The ------ of -----, if I can ought foretell,
> Will most assuredly come down to hell.
> Whenever vice or lewdness lead the way,
> With what officious zeal doth he obey!
> Him no ambition moves to seek renown;
> To be esteemed the *greatest buck* in town
> Appears to be his wish and sole delight.
> Full many times at twelve o'clock at night
> I've known him drunk, with half a dozen more,
> Kick up a row, break lamps, perhaps a door,
> And to conclude the night, to bilk his w---e.

A footnote to 'whore' says, 'And to thrash the wretch too, or a watchman, might have been added. The latter he thinks a most excellent joke—' and it tells of the prince and his friends attacking a watchman in Pall Mall 'on their return from one of the nunneries in the vicinity', and ending up paying bribes to avoid appearing at Bow Street.

Then there is Lord Malden, in a passage containing an expressive bit of slang:

> With him Lord ------ I shall here expect,
> His wipe-[arse], sycophant, and pimp direct;
> Scorning in shabbiness to be outdone,
> He'll pimp for [George], then take his *buttered bun*.

Should such a man die young? Malden seems to have been more likeable than these verses suggest. He was certainly durable. In his eightieth year he married a singer as his second wife; who lived until 1882, just one hundred years after these verses were written.

The prince, in these early years, was several times very ill after debauches. He was, says Walpole, 'deeply afflicted with the scrofulous humour which the Princess of Wales [George III's mother] had brought into the blood, and which the king kept down in himself by the most rigorous hermitical abstinence'. This 'humour' is now believed to have been porphyria, the erratic inherited malady which in the king appears to have contributed to his attacks of madness. As a result of the prince's heavy drinking, 'the humour showed itself in blotches all over his face'—which is indeed a symptom of porphyria.

More things than wine can touch a reveller's health. Another *Devil Divorced* footnote says that after the prince had taken into keeping a French dancer at the opera, 'a certain disorder broke out'. Elsewhere it is alleged that his Windsor apothecary sent in a bill of £947 (which palace officials cut to £300) 'for medicines and about two months attendance', which aroused 'shrewd suspicions that he had not so often sacrificed at the Cytherean shrine without carrying *fire* from the *altar*'. Soon caricatures of the prince began to show bottles of venereal nostrums, Velnos Vegetable Syrup or Leake's Pills, at his bedside.

The king 'had the comfort of finding,' says Walpole, 'that with so depraved and licentious a life, his son was not likely to acquire popularity'. People did expect an appearance of good behaviour from a Prince of Wales, and more so by the 1780s than in the days of George III's rackety father. This comfort for the king was a political comfort when Fox and the prince openly became each other's champions. Courtiers and Pitt himself did not discourage the king's belief that Fox was the cause of the prince's bad behaviour. In the palace drawing-room the king publicly snubbed the prince, 'speaking to people on each side of me & then missing me,' he told his brother Frederick, '& then if he does honour me with a word, 'tis either merely " 'tis very hot" or "very cold" ': the usual treatment given to any out-of-favour politician.

Politics drew the prince into the society, and sometimes the arms, of a number of Whig ladies. One was Lady Melbourne. She was devoted to the Earl of Egremont (who is regarded as the true father of Queen Victoria's first prime minister), but she pleased the prince sufficiently to get her husband made a Gentleman of his Bedchamber, a post he held for a great many years. Then there was the Duchess of Devonshire, whom the prince wooed ardently enough, says Wraxall, to 'excite some emotion' in the usually torpid duke. Perhaps he saw a caricature inspired by a new craze: it shows duchess and prince standing face to face in the basket of a balloon.

> PRINCE: It rises majestically.
> DUCHESS: Yes, I feel it.

Gossip said that the prince at least believed that a baby the duchess had in 1785 was his. We shall never be sure, for a bundle of their letters so shocked George V that he burned them in 1913.

According to *The Rambler's Magazine*, a more professional lover, Grace Dalrymple Elliot, was claiming in 1784 to have a baby by the prince, a baby with the flaxen Hanoverian complexion. Among the strollers on the Mall, it says, are 'Dally with her *white-eyebrowed infant*, which she protests is the perfect image of its r---l papa; and Perdita, with her new-enamelled face, displaying her *neat ankles* against the *gummy*

The Diamond Eaters, Horrid Monsters!: A bitter picture of George III not long before madness. With Queen Charlotte and black-browed Lord Chancellor Thurlow he allows plunder showered down by Warren Hastings, then fighting to escape impeachment.

19 *The Wedding Night or the Fashionable Frolic*: The Prince of Wales dances his bride, Mrs Fitzherbert, toward the royal bed, above which we see Danaé receiving her shower of gold. The prince's crony George Hanger plays The Black Joke.

20 *The* [*Royal*] *Nursery or Nine Months After:* Within five months of the Fitzherbert wedding, a caricaturist foresees a baby. On the wall, a Catholic bishop is pictured performing a baptism. Is the little boy meant to suggest some earlier child of the prince's? (See page 120)

21 *Monstrous Craws at a New Coalition Feast:* May 1787; the prince has managed to get more money out of parliament. He joins his parents in devouring John Bull's blood—golden guineas. The 'craws' were inspired for Gilray

22 *Election-Troops bringing in their accounts to the Pay-Table*: After a hard-fought Westminster election in 1788, newspaper editors, soldiers, ballad-singers, illegal voters and club-wielding sailors queue to get their reward from Pitt. (Gillray: see page 10)

23 *The Prospect Before Us*: At the height of the 1788 regency crisis, Pitt is accused of aiming at unlawful power with

4 *Don Dismallo, after an Absence of Sixteen Years, Embracing his Beautiful Vision:* Edmund Burke as a quixotic knight is mocked, a few days after his *Reflections on the French Revolution* appeared, for his rhapsody on Marie Antoinette. His dowdy wife weeps. 'Whoo-oo-oo-oo!' says the owl. (See page 147)

25 *The Hopes of the Party*: A Whig dinner to celebrate the second anniversary of the fall of the Bastille inspired this Gillray accusation of king-killing dreams. Horne Tooke holds George III's legs, Sheridan holds his ears, Fox steels himself to emulate the executioner 'who chopped the calf's-head off a hundred and forty years ago'. Priestley consoles the fuddled king with

26 *Un petit souper à la Parisienne:* It is typical of Gillray's double-edged art that this detailed picture of sans-culotte cannibalism could be taken by sophisticates as a satire on horror stories, and by the naive as a dire warning.

27 Pitt on the shoulders of a fearsome George III rides into battle against reformers-comment in June 1792 on a royal proclamation against seditious writings.

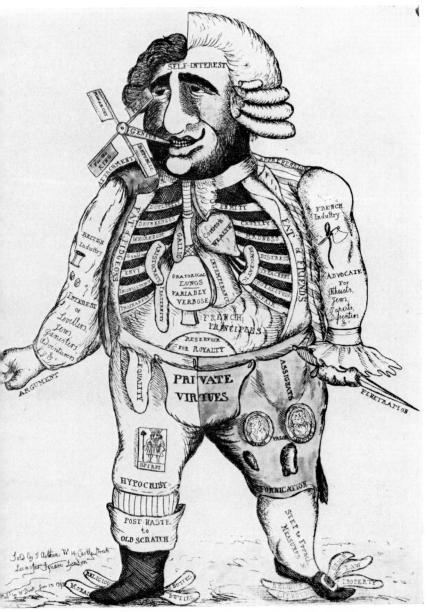

8 *A Right Hon. Democrat Dissected:* January 1793; Fox is striving to keep Britain from going to war. This dissection makes every possible allegation against him. Even the contents of his bladder is 'for royalty'. The medals on his 'fornication' leg are of Perdita and Mrs Armitstead.

29 *Fatigues of the Campaign: May 1793*—the Duke of York's campaign against the French has collapsed. Gillray, back from Flanders, pictures the duke leading a scene of revelry, a plump Dutchwoman on his knee, a tattered

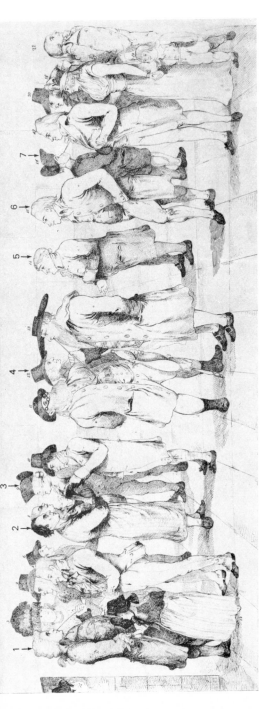

30 *Promenade in the State Side of Newgate:* Prisoners and visiting friends in October 1793. 1, William Holland, printseller, charged with publishing a seditious pamphlet. 2, John Frost, solicitor, serving six months for seditious talk. 3, John Horne Tooke, reformer, a visitor; the following year he was tried for treason. 4, Charles Pigott, radical writer, a visitor; he was to die in another jail. 5, Henry Delahay Symonds, bookseller, serving three years for selling Pigott's *Jockey Club*. 6, James Ridgway, bookseller, serving four years for selling *Jockey Club* and works of Paine. 7, Daniel Isaac Eaton, bookseller, a visitor, between trials for publishing Paine and John Thelwall. This print, sold at Holland's shop, served as a news-picture of the day. (See pages 145, 158–9)

31 *The Night Mare:* In a parody of Henry Fuseli's painting, Pitt as an incubus on John Bull's stomach holds a loaf at the enormous price of 13 pence. A spectral Jacobin, wearing a model guillotine round his neck, says 'Republic, war and

32 *The Republican Attack*: Double-edged comment by Gillray three days after attack on king's coach. Fox and his followers are the attackers. But coachman Pitt is driving over Britannia. One of Pitt's ministers riding behind is Dundas, his drinking crony (bottle in pocket). Note crape-draped loaf. (See page 174)

33 *The Modern Hercules:* Pitt strikes a final blow at John Bull. 'Convention Bill' me[a]
legislation rushed through to suppress the nationwide reform movement, after the att[a]
on the king. This was published by S. W. Fores, usually anti-reformist. (See page 17[•]

one of Dally'. The baby, says Dally, 'is a convincing proof that the P----- has long passed the era of childhood'. But perhaps this was bold By Appointment advertising.

By this time the prince had discovered the only woman who had the power, not to keep him faithful, for he was faithful to nobody, but to live in his memory even until he lay dying forty-six years later. Maria Anne Fitzherbert, a widow of twenty-eight, six years his senior, was the grand-daughter of a baronet and niece to two peers. By the death of two husbands she had acquired some wealth. She had no need to wish for a noble lover to set her up in a 'genteel house' in Mayfair: she bought her own house in Park Street.

And a prince only promised trouble. She was a commoner; more serious, she was a Roman Catholic. Only four years earlier, London had been terrorized by an orgy of rioting touched off by the anti-Catholic campaigning of Lord George Gordon. Besides, a Catholic wife was barred under the Act of Settlement of 1689. But the more Mrs Fitzherbert stood out, the more violently the prince pursued. He faked a suicide attempt to persuade her of his love. He made plans to go abroad with her. She went off to France alone—whether to wait for him, or to evade him, or to raise her value, perhaps she herself was not sure. 'I have settled it with Frederick,' he said to his friend James Harris, a diplomat who became Lord Malmesbury. '. . . Frederick will marry, and the crown will descend to his children.' He also said, 'The king hates me. . . . He always did, from seven years old.'

After a year of passionate letter-writing, he commanded 'my dearest & only belov'd Maria' to return to London, and she obeyed. Fox was in agonies. What a disaster if the royal heir, the hope of the Whigs, should forfeit his crown by marrying in defiance of the Act of Settlement! 'Surely, sir, this is not a matter to be trifled with,' Fox wrote. '. . . Your enemies might take such advantage as I shudder to think of. . . . How impossible it would be for her ever to forgive herself!' The prince answered:

My Dear Charles. . . . Make yourself easy, my dear friend. Believe me, the world will now soon be convinced that there not only is [not], but never was, any ground for these reports which of late have been so malevolently circulated.

'The world will now soon be convinced': a neat way to avoid an outright lie. Four days later, on 15 December 1785, the prince was married to Mrs Fitzherbert at her Park Street house.

No ordinary clergyman would have risked committing a felony, subject to dire punishment, under the Royal Marriage Act. No ordinary clergyman could have been trusted with the knowledge that the prince had forfeited his right to the crown. The prince's friends found the Rev. Robert Burt, a young spendthrift in Fleet Prison for debt, and freed him with £500. He was made chaplain to the prince and vicar of Twickenham. To reinforce his loyalty he had the promise of a bishopric; but unluckily he died long before the prince had power to give him one.

Probably the only other persons at the wedding were a brother and an uncle of Mrs Fitzherbert—felons, too, for serving as witnesses. But soon it was the gossip of the town. 'Oh, but the hubbub you are to hear and to talk of, and except which you are to hear and talk of nothing else!' Walpole wrote to a friend less than two months later. People 'of all ranks' were talking of it in the streets. By spring they could buy a variety of caricatures that pretended to depict the wedding. These were not amusing for Fox, especially as they generally showed him at the ceremony. Nor were they amusing for Mrs Fitzherbert. One caricature of her was entitled 'Tender, Trim and only Thirty', which is hard enough when a woman is only twenty-nine; another was labelled 'The Royal Toast—Fat, Fair and Forty', a phrase that stuck until improved to Fat, Fair and Fifty by the passing of time.

Deeper points were made. 'To be or not to be a queen is the question' said a caricature of Mrs Fitzherbert dragging the prince to church. Then there was the anxiety of a possible secret contender for the royal succession. One print dared to be as explicit as its title was witty: 'His Highness in Fitz.' Soon a printshop gave birth to 'The Royal Nursery, or Nine Months After', in which a Roman Catholic bishop is baptizing the couple's baby. When they went to Brighton, the prince's new summer haunt, they were pictured travelling in a carriage crammed with a cradle and a mass of other nursery material.

Did they have children? Possible evidence was destroyed in more than one bonfire of papers. Certainly the prince showed particular concern for a son who in 1820 was serving as an officer in India. When a relation of Mrs Fitzherbert's, Lord Stourton, pressed her in the 1830s to write on the back of her 1785 marriage certificate, *No issue from this marriage,* 'she smilingly objected on the score of delicacy'.

MPs had an opportunity in April 1787 to throw some light on the caricatures' troubling allegations, which went far beyond any hints the newspapers managed. The prince's Whig friends asked parliament to help him with his already enormous debts. An independent West Country MP, John Rolle, said the House should also 'attend to a question which might affect both church and state'. Three days later, Fox told the House that what so many people had believed to be true was 'a miserable calumny . . . a tale only fit to impose on the lowest order of persons in the streets'. Pressed further, he said on 'direct authority' that the marriage 'never did happen in any way whatsoever'.

One lie requires another. Next morning the prince tenderly took Mrs Fitzherbert's hands in his—this is from Lord Stourton's brother—and said, 'Only conceive, Maria, what Fox did yesterday! He went down to the House and denied that you and I were man and wife!' The prince was an excellent actor, but had put himself in an absurd farce. How could he deny Fox's denial just enough to make Mrs Fitzherbert seem an honest woman? She talked of leaving him. After a day of great agitation, he persuaded a master of words, Sheridan, to utter an artful encomium on Mrs Fitzherbert as a woman 'whose character claimed, and was entitled to, the truest and most general respect'.

A wife, then? Within a few weeks, that constant gadfly, Horne Tooke, published *A Letter to a Friend on the Reported Marriage of His Royal Highness the Prince of Wales.* It began:

You agree entirely with me then that the question will be

121

blinked on both sides, and that a sincere performance of their duty . . . is not reasonably to be expected from either party: that those who are IN, conforming just so far as may be necessary to keep them in, will yet be individually very cautious not to exclude themselves hereafter.

He went on to argue, no doubt in pure malice, for acceptance of the marriage. To match with persons not of royal blood had been 'a common and well-precedented practice of the sovereigns of this realm': in the 230 years from Henry VII to Queen Anne, six out of eleven sovereigns were the issue of such matches, and so was George I, 'the very sovereign under whom the House of Hanover claims'. The Royal Marriage Act had not 'the smallest force of law'; MPs had no right 'to assist a parent to degrade his children to something worse than castration, to the unmanly state . . . of a friar'. As for Mrs Fitzherbert's religion, Horne Tooke asserted that she was ready to conform to the Anglican church (she never did); and in any case, he was much more concerned about the universal flouting of the prohibition against MPs' having places of profit under the king, 'being much more easily contented to trust the sovereign with a papist wife than with a corrupt parliament.'

This pamphlet soon became bafflingly unobtainable in the shops, evidently as a result of some urgent purchasing by Carlton House; but people could not help noticing that neither Ins nor Outs ventured to take any action against the author.

The following year something happened that seemed to confirm the wisdom of the Ins when they blinked the question. The king went mad.

9

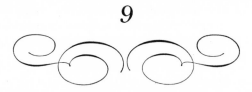

Great anxiety—Fox not well —King better

IT WAS NO SECRET that George III was often hurried, quirkish and puzzling in his everyday behaviour, and especially in his conversation. He fired off half-formed questions punctuated with *What what what? Eh eh eh?*—and frequently answered them himself. Humble cottagers in the Windsor countryside would suddenly find their king demanding to know the price of hogs, or how an apple got inside a dumpling.

Though fine gentlemen might wince or giggle, and though satirists certainly mocked, lesser men could find such behaviour endearing. Caricatures of Farmer George and his homely wife were double-edged, for they pointed a contrast with their luxurious son and his dubious ladies. And unsophisticated people came to disbelieve charges of political craft and chicanery against a man with such simple unkingly ways.

In the late spring of 1788, however, just before his fiftieth birthday, the king gave signs of more than mild eccentricity. After a levee, 'he showed his backside to the attendants, saying he had not the gout,' the Duchess of Devonshire was told a few months later, when there was no longer any point in concealing such small early symptoms. 'He pulled off Sir George Baker's [a doctor's] wig and made him go upon his knees to look at the stars. . . . He told [Benjamin] West the painter he would teach him to mix colours, and throwing some on the ground, mixed them with his foot.'

In July the king's doctors persuaded him to go to Cheltenham to drink the waters. (He had never gone so far from London in all his fifty years.) He did some more odd things, such as trying to run a race with a horse; and held some odd conversations. Once, promenading with the queen, he stepped eagerly up to a Mr Clements.

> KING: Pray, sir, are you the Mr Clements who had an intrigue with Lady Sarah [Lennox] Bunbury when I was in love with her?
>
> CLEMENTS: No, sire, it was my brother.
>
> KING (running back to the queen): I've won my bet! I've won my bet!

But his condition was not yet serious enough to put him beyond satire. That autumn a journal of the Cheltenham tour, *Royal Recollections*, written as if by the king himself, was published anonymously by David Williams, a deist writer, who was busy the same year founding what is now the Royal Literary Fund.

> My health is seriously injured. Twenty-six years of contention and warfare with my people, terminated with such a loss [America], have almost annihilated the habit of sleep. . . . Furious walking, riding and hunting consume my time, and destroy my attendants and horses; but they furnish not peace of mind.

On his first appearance at Cheltenham he is grave and stately

> —but I excel in the arts of familiarity. I have nodded and capered to the band at Windsor until the whole terrace has roared out a boisterous laugh, in which I have heartily joined. Charlotte is not cordial in these condescensions. . . . If we make the people laugh their hearts are always with us. They shall laugh heartily whenever I appear.

Williams puts in a paragraph that shows he was well informed; for in July 1788 one of the king's children, Princess Mary, had a tumour removed from her arm:

> Whence are the complaints of the children? A queen of England privately dressing issues in their arms; and some of

them barbarously mangled for white tumours. Charlotte persists, 'They are not from me.'

We are given some of the king's political thoughts:

I spend as much time in churches, and I hear as much sacred music, as any monarch in Europe. . . . I do not, however, much relish the thoughts of heaven: no distinction of ranks, no privilege of family. None but *levelling* principles take place there. I wish the clergy would review the doctrine. . . .

I love to see a smooth and oily bishop . . . insisting on the meekness, simplicity and disinterestedness recommended by the gospel. It is a solacing proof that the people will bear any contradiction. . . . They would trample to death the daring reformer who would remove their oppressors. . . . On this single pivot rest all the regal and ecclesiastical powers of Europe.

But one king is threatened by something perhaps worse than illness:

The state of France is critical. . . . This d----d philosophy, with its rights of nature, humanity and reason, is the mortal and irreconcilable enemy of power, and princes have a common interest in suppressing it. . . . If a reformation take place in France, it will be on a plan of greater liberty than that of England; we must then follow. . . .

Early in November the British people forgot the unrest in France: the court, and Pitt, could no longer conceal that George III's illness was deranging his mind.

At first some courtiers went to remarkable lengths to make little of the king's malady. They had been equally mad! 'Lord Fauconberg declares all the world saw him in a strait-waist-coat,' the Duchess of Devonshire wrote in her diary, 'and Lord Salisbury says the king has as much sense as he has.'

There was method in their madness, for if the king was beyond hope, Pitt and his followers, except for those who could agilely change sides in time, would be out, and the Whigs, five years after the king had helped to rout them, would be in. A messenger was sent posthaste to Italy to find

Fox, who was travelling with Liz Armitstead. Even before he got back to London on November 24, in nine days' hard driving which shattered his health, a tentative Cabinet list had been drawn up at Devonshire House, the Whigs' head-quarters throughout the crisis.

The Prince of Wales and some of his followers found it hard to look decently sad. A story reached Devonshire House that while the king was raving in his room at Windsor Castle, the prince one night was 'driving his sisters and Lady Charlotte Finch [a court lady] about in a coach at Windsor and breaking the lamps'. Thomas Rowlandson published a caricature, 'Filial Piety', showing the prince bursting into the king's bedroom, followed by the merrily prancing figures of Sheridan and George Hanger, the latter flourishing a bottle. The prince, smiling, says, 'Damme, come along, I'll see if the Old Fellow's —— or not.' The dash could be taken to mean, not 'mad', but 'dead', for the king's life was for a time despaired of.

This appeared the day after Fox's return, and he seems to have taken action to bring Rowlandson, his tormentor of 1784, over to the Whig side. A little later, when Pitt was resisting Fox's claim that the prince had an automatic right to become regent, Rowlandson produced a caricature, 'The Prospect Before Us', in which Pitt holds a paper that reads, 'I think myself as much entitled to be regent as the Prince of Wales.' To point the charge that Pitt is aiming at unjustified power, he has the queen (a fervent supporter of Pitt) in leading-strings, and half a royal crown floats over each of their heads. An onlooker shouts, 'He never meddled with a petticoat before!' Ahead of the queen marches Madame Schwellenberg, her ill-tempered, domineering Mistress of the Robes. She says to the queen, 'Take care to secure the ----- jewels.' This last point suggests that Rowlandson had been briefed on an odd incident recorded by the Duchess of Devonshire on December 2:

The prince went to Windsor as there had been a difficulty in finding the jewels and Privy Purse—the jewels found at last in a place near the window—the prince and Duke of York in presence of the Chancellor . . . sealed them up. The queen, who is wonderfully fond of jewels, flew into an outrageous passion, reproached them, abused them, and they remonstrated and at last got the better.

Courtiers entreated the two princes not to mention this, but of course they did.

By this time not only the royal family but London society and indeed the whole country were split into hostile Tory and Whig camps. Even the royal doctors were at war: they were the oracles who had to say whether the king could ever recover. Those watching the patient in the Whig interest said he could not. The king, who in his quieter moments liked to make jokes, gave the chief Whig doctor, Sir Richard Warren, the nickname Sir Richard Rascal. He also said, 'The Prince of Wales is dead, so women may be honest.' But most of the time he was extremely violent and abusive, talked wild nonsense for hours on end, shouted blasphemies and obscenities that he had never before been heard to utter, and was sometimes tied down on his bed. And some of Pitt's forces began to waver.

Jack Robinson the Ratcatcher, for one, was trying not to make a mistake. One day when the prince and his secretary, Jack Payne, were riding in Hyde Park, Robinson obsequiously kept his hat off from the moment he noticed the prince approaching. 'Damn that fellow!' said the prince to Payne. 'When will he put his hat on?' 'When the king recovers, sir,' said Payne.

Week after week the Whigs were fighting in the Commons against a proposal of Pitt's that the prince should become regent only with severe restrictions. And now Fox's fears about the marriage to Mrs Fitzherbert were justified. On December 10 *The Morning Post* (subsidized by Pitt) printed a few paragraphs which, though they avoided the word 'marriage', were dangerous enough:

. . . That connection, on account of the difference of religious principles, appears to Mr Fox fraught with probable mischiefs. . . . He has now reason to believe that it is of a more *coercive* and *permanent* nature than he was once induced to *imagine,* and ANNOUNCE. . . .

No less a sum than the *annual* allowance of TWENTY THOUSAND POUNDS has been offered to the LADY on condition of her retiring to the Continent—this the lady has *positively refused.*

She even resisted the additional temptation of the title of duchess, says *The Morning Post.*

The prince was so worried that he risked sending Sheridan, three days later, to John Rolle, the MP who had raised the question the year before. Sheridan asked Rolle, in the prince's name, to refrain from raising it again. Rolle would promise nothing: he did not care about the prince's 'smiles or frowns'. This did not make life calmer at Devonshire House, where the mood is revealed in one artless sentence in the diary of Lady 'Bess' Foster, the Duke of Devonshire's mistress: 'Great anxiety on our side—Fox not well—King better.'

A day later the Pittites were 'in great spirits', having won a division by 64. Hostesses were taking great care with their invitation lists, for the least mixture of Whig and Tory was disastrous. Whig ladies were wearing hats with the prince's symbols, triple ostrich feathers and 'Ich Dien'. This was no mere game. Lady Foster records a Devonshire House conversation:

> Sheridan said if they drove us to it there would be a civil war. Grey [the future prime minister] said, 'Then on my soul I should not be for you.' 'Not for us!' said Sheridan. 'No,' says Grey, 'I should be in the parliament army.' 'What, would you not engage in a civil war in a good cause even?' 'Yes, in a good cause, but I don't call this one,' said Grey, 'and the mischief it would cause would be dreadful.'

The fear in Sheridan's mind was that if the prince were limited in his regency—deprived of the power to dispense patronage and create peers—Pitt might try to remain entrenched.

A less imaginary danger was the marriage. Just before Christmas, John Rolle told the Commons he would vote for the prince as regent 'provided it was proved to him that the prince had done nothing to forfeit his claim'. Sheridan, who was living in Mrs Fitzherbert's house to avoid his creditors, reported at Devonshire House that the prince was 'extremely agitated' and 'the most womanish-minded man he ever knew'.

Mrs Fitzherbert, too, was 'in a great fright'. Sheridan, the Whigs' propaganda director, already had *The Morning Herald*, *The General Advertizer* and *The Gazetteer* printing what he wanted. He tried to widen his influence, but subtly. Lady Foster reports: '*The World* is to be bought by our party but in order not to have it appear too clearly it is to be carried on by our paper making a strong attack and *The World* a weak defence.' However, the Treasury outbid Sheridan and made *The World* Pittite for £600 a year.

Further inspired paragraphs about Mrs Fitzherbert appeared in *The Morning Post*. Jack Payne threatened prosecution, but its chief proprietor, John Benjafield, only talked of further disclosures. Something had to be done. The prince sent a second emissary, an odd one: the controller of his kitchen, Louis Weltje, a powerful factotum who dealt smoothly with awkward creditors, outraged husbands and other problems too vulgar for the prince's equerries. Weltje was armed with money. He acquired Benjafield's shares, arranged a £350-a-year pension for him—and soon *The Morning Post* was denouncing the government's 'hired scribblers'.

Pitt countered by adding another paper to his stable of half a dozen. He persuaded John Walter, proprietor of the recently-founded *Times*, to take £300 a year (enough to pay his entire printing costs for five weeks). *The Times* found many ways to snipe at Carlton House. It abused Weltje, a very fat man, as 'a great German toad-eater' and 'the German Man-Mountain Cook of Carlton House' who 'first made his public appearance in this country as a street musician, after which he kept a gingerbread shop'. And it said:

> What a pity a German upstart cannot purchase
> reputations, as well as corrupt newspapers!

An ageing crony of the prince, Lord Clermont, was shot from behind by the prince while snipe-hunting. *The Times* printed a series of malicious items, culminating with:

> Twenty-three grains and a half of No. 4 shot were
> extracted yesterday from Lord Clermont's bum.

The Morning Post had been dealt with, but a new threat

arose. A leading bookseller, James Ridgway, distributed hand-bills announcing a pamphlet that would declare the prince was married to a papist. One handbill was sent to Mrs Fitzherbert and 'alarmed her much', says the Duchess of Devonshire. Sheridan and other Carlton House envoys went round to Ridgway at his shop near St James's Square. The author of the pamphlet, Dr Philip Withers, chaplain to the Dowager Lady Hereford, was summoned from his home in Sloane Square on the edge of town. 'It is a pity, sir,' he was told (he described this in another pamphlet), 'that you have written on the subject . . . just on the point of his being chosen regent.' The pamphlet contained a good deal of other matter—so could he not cut out all reference to Mrs Fitzherbert? He would be handsomely compensated. He refused. Someone blustered about high treason. He smiled. So Carlton House paid Ridgway to suppress the pamphlet. Within a few days, however, Withers was selling a new edition in Sloane Square and in Mayfair.

The pamphlet, *History of the Royal Malady*, is attributed to 'a Page of the Presence', and the opening part gives a lively account, evidently based on inside information, of the king's behaviour. It tells of the day when the court could no longer pretend that nothing was seriously wrong: when the king, out for a drive in Windsor Park, said *There he is*, handed the reins to the queen, and walked over to an oak.

He uncovered and advanced, bowing with the utmost res-pect, and then seizing one of the lower branches, he shook it with the most apparent cordiality and regard. The queen turned pale with astonishment. . . . It was the King of Prussia with whom His Majesty enjoyed this rural interview. Continental politics were the subject.

When the royal carriage was under way again, with the queen, princess royal and two maids of honour sitting in em-barrassed silence, the king suddenly uttered an awful question: 'Charlotte, will you give me leave to **** ***?'

The princess and the junior maid of honour were scarcely able to comprehend the term . . . but the other lady, some-how or somehow, was sensible to the utmost force of the phrase. She blushed. . . .

And after two minutes' further silence, she laughed hysterically.

Every account of the king's madness speaks of his obscene talk. He was liberated from all the restraints he had imposed on himself ever since his painful renunciation of Lady Sarah. In his pamphlet Withers says astutely:

> The royal mind is *inverted*. The ideas of younger life are now floating on the surface of the imagination; and those principles of dignity and decorum, from the practice of which he has been deemed a paragon of virtue and domestic excellence, are now buried. . . . His Majesty can incur no blame. . . . The *songs* and *toasts* of bacchanalians are now as inoffensive to the Deity as the hymns of angels. And it is a consolation.

On his better days the king sang merry catches, played hornpipes on a flute, made his doctors dance with him, and was 'childishly playful, begging romps and making his pages wheel him about the room', says his equerry, Fulke Greville. But he also raged against the queen, said he would not sleep with her again until 1793, and said that his chief physician, the clergyman-doctor Francis Willis, 'that ugly old fumbling fellow', slept with the queen every night.

Nature allowed a man more than one wife, the king told Fulke Greville. In any case, there would soon be an act of parliament to dissolve all marriages: the king harped on this. He did not, however, want to emulate his son. His heart was fixed on one lovely woman, Elizabeth, Countess of Pembroke, a daughter of the 2nd Duke of Marlborough. She was fifty-one; but even sixteen years later, when the king was again pursuing her, she retained her beauty, and she was to live to ninety-four. The king's affection for her appears to have dated from 1761, when at his coronation Lady Pembroke walked at the head of the countesses, and everybody exclaimed at her beauty. In his madness, the king seated himself in his 'chair of coercion' (fixed to a platform so that he could not overturn it), which he called his coronation chair, 'and said that the first time he had seen Eliza, it was from it, over his left shoulder'.

Eliza had become a lady in distress in 1762. Lord Pembroke,

who had served George as a Lord of the Bedchamber since 1756, ran off with a girl called Kitty Hunter and had a son by her. Pembroke named the child Augustus Retnuh Reebkomp —creating the two latter names from Hunter and Pembroke— and placed him in the navy. The king restored Pembroke to favour in 1764, but he never ceased to be unfaithful to Eliza.

The long-suffering wife was from 1783 constantly before the king's eyes as a Lady of the Bedchamber to the queen. In his madness, the king, remembering his Old Testament, said to the queen that he was Ahaseurus, she was Vashti, and Lady Pembroke was his Esther. He also called Lady Pembroke his Queen of Hearts, and wrote on playing-cards, 'O dear Eliza, ever love thy prince.' He kept wanting to be taken for airings to Richmond Park, where she lived, and in preparation for such a trip he stuffed into his pockets a pack of cards and 'two or three pair of stockings, a couple of nightcaps and a pair of drawers'. Even after the king was himself again, his passion continued; he wrote her a loving letter. The Archbishop of Canterbury 'spoke to her seriously on the subject', says another of the queen's ladies, Mrs Harcourt—which implies that Lady Pembroke had perhaps not been entirely without thoughts of becoming the king's mistress. She wrote to the king to say she felt 'like the most affectionate sister'.

To return to Withers's pamphlet: the archbishop appears there, in an imagined dialogue with his brother of York:

CANTERBURY: . . . The truth is, the king was never greatly burdened with sense, and therefore some slight derangement of body has overset him. But what is that to you or me? We are snug for life. . . .

YORK: And so we are, Brother Canterbury. Be so kind as to pull the bell for the page. We have been here half an hour without any refreshment; a bottle of claret will do us good, or do you prefer old hock?

CANTERBURY: Let us have both.

Withers criticizes a phrase in the archbishops' national prayer for George III: 'whom Thou hast been pleased to afflict for our transgressions'. Does the king suffer, he asks, 'for the sins of his transatlantic subjects, who revolted from their allegiance, or for the sins of the people of Britain who endeavoured to reduce them to duty?' Withers makes clear what he thinks: 'It would have been happy if our crimes had provoked the Deity to afflict the prince [king] with madness, and his Minister with blindness, I mean corporeal blindness, twenty years ago.'

Lord North had gone blind. Sometimes the king spoke of him. According to Mrs Papendiek, whose husband was one of his personal attendants, the king said, 'He, poor fellow, has lost his sight, and I my mind. Yet we meant well to the Americans; just to punish them with a few bloody noses, and then make bows for the mutual happiness of the two countries.' Yet having glimpsed the idea that he and North were being punished, the king went on to blame the army, Lord Sandwich, and 'want of unanimity at home' for the loss of America. On this one point his usual beliefs were not inverted. America had been on his mind when his illness began. He said then to Lord Thurlow, 'I, that am born a gentleman, shall never lay my head on my last pillow in peace and quiet so long as I remember the loss of my American colonies.'

At last, on its twenty-second page, Withers's pamphlet comes to Mrs Fitzherbert. She reads *The Morning Post* report of December 10 and bursts into tears. The prince asks whether she thinks he would be so wicked as to drive into exile the woman 'to whom I have been solemnly pledged at the altar'. But the nub of Withers's message is his comment on the 1787 pamphlet of Horne Tooke, 'a man not entirely unknown':

> The Chancellor, the judges and both houses of parliament must relinquish all claim to patriotism and common sense if they permit the assertion of the truth of the marriage to descend unnoticed to posterity. . . . Who can tell what dissensions may arise?. . . *Now* is the time for legal investigation.

All this time the regency argument was dragging on. The Whigs were playing into Pitt's hands by prolonging the fight. Edmund Burke, who rarely made a short speech, talked for hour upon hour, and often so violently that a handbill was stuck up in Whitehall directly parodying the doctors' bulletins on the king:

> The Right Hon. Edmund Burke had last night three hours' sleep; he is calm this morning, but tending towards unquietness.

At last John Rolle referred to Tooke's pamphlet, and appealed to Fox to comment on the charge that his denial of 1787 'was not warranted'. Fox was absent ill, genuinely ill. A little later, when the debate reached a clause to deprive the prince of his powers as regent if he 'shall at any time marry a papist', Rolle moved to insert the words 'or shall at any time be proved to be married, in fact or in law, to a papist'.

Again the ready-tongued Sheridan stood up: 'If any gentleman seriously thought that the matter so darkly hinted at had taken place, it was his duty to state the ground why he thought so, to propose an inquiry, and to probe that inquiry to the bottom'—a challenge followed by some bluster about pamphleteers, seconded with talk from Grey about 'malicious, false, libellous, calumnious' rumours. Rolle remarked that Sheridan had nevertheless not denied or confirmed Fox's 1787 declaration. Sheridan did not rise to this.

And Pitt sidestepped once again. He knew that the debate might well soon be academic; the day before, the king had been well enough to shave himself, with a cut-throat razor. Even more promising, he had this very day, 7 February 1789, employed for the first time in three months his familiar expression, *What what what!* When Walpole heard this news, he wrote coolly, 'I now do believe that the king is coming to *himself*. . . . He is returned to his *what what what* . . . which is coming to his nonsense.'

Pitt left it to his newspapers to goad the Whigs. On February 10 *The Times* said, 'His Holiness the Pope has sent over to a certain lady, who had more husbands than one, a most valuable cross of diamonds and an absolution for all the sins she ever has or ever may commit.' Four days later *The Times* announced:

THE KING IS RECOVERED FROM HIS LATE MELANCHOLY INDISPOSITION. . . .

Great anxiety—Fox not well—King better

When the news came yesterday at two o'clock to the card-room at Brooks's, up starts Surface [Sheridan]: 'Well, what intelligence?' 'Bad news, sir, very bad news. The king is much better.' Down went all the hands of piquet, and one general execration of Willis followed. . . . Alas, poor party! These are sad tidings: no plundering the India Company or the Treasury. . . . The Blue and Buff must all go into mourning.

The chagrin at Brooks's was matched by the delight at the Tory club, White's, which boasted eighty-nine MPs who had been constantly voting for Pitt. The king had recovered just in time, for the Regency Bill was complete. Party hatred rose higher than ever. 'The acrimony is beyond anything you can conceive,' wrote a Pittite minister. 'The ladies are as usual at the head of all animosity.' Whig ladies flaunted their seven-guinea 'Ich Dien' bonnets in the faces of Tory ladies wearing velvet bandeaus embroidered with 'God Save the King'. The Whigs had the mortification of seeing a great outburst of public joy at the king's recovery. On March 10, the day chosen for illuminations in celebration, the streets of the West End were so jammed with happy crowds that carriages bound for balls and banquets were stuck hour after hour, till after midnight.

At the first palace drawing-room, the queen herself wore a 'God Save the King' bandeau. When Fox, Burke, Sheridan and Sir Richard Warren passed by the queen, she would not look at them. She pointedly eyed the heads of the Duchess of Devonshire, her sister Lady Duncannon, and one or two other Whig ladies, for they were almost the only ones without the bandeaus in a great crush of women of both sides. The rush to display loyalty caused an uncourtly tumult. 'One heard nothing but screams & women carrying out in fits,' wrote Lady Duncannon. 'The whole ground was strewed with . . . pearls and diamonds crumbled to pieces.'

Philip Withers was not the man to stop asking questions about the prince's marriage. A relapse could still bring a regency. In a pamphlet addressed to the Bishop of London, Withers quoted the king's proclamation of 1787 against vice and immorality, and proposed that the bishop should take action against 'the WIDOW FITZHERBERT, of Pall Mall, for a loose, disorderly course of life—namely, for fornication with HIS ROYAL HIGHNESS GEORGE, PRINCE OF WALES', and also against the prince, 'for aiding, abetting and comforting the said Widow Fitzherbert in her sinful practices, in direct opposition to the royal will'.

Knowing that the couple passed the night together in Park Street, at Brighton and elsewhere, says Withers, he had declared, like Horne Tooke, that they were married. But then he was warned 'that one Thomas Erskine, a man of terrifying eloquence, and attorney-general to the Prince of Wales, had received instructions to prosecute your unfortunate son, even unto death.' So what must he believe?

> . . . If it be 'treason' to allege that Mrs Fitzherbert
> is married, it is justice to pronounce her a strumpet.

He asks the bishop to summon her; and if he finds her guilty, to chasten her, though mercifully:

> Consider her habit—sanguine and athletic.
> Consider also her age—forty . . . let it be five-and-thirty
> —a perilous age indeed! The maturity of passion. . . . ! [She
> was not yet thirty-three.]
> Consider, also, the temptation. If the lady be a Venus, the
> lover is indisputably an Adonis. . . .
> Remind her that Mary Magdalene—as great a strumpet as
> herself—is now in heaven.

The terrifying Thomas Erskine did not venture to take action against this. But then Withers gave him an opening. In a further pamphlet, *Nemesis*, he said that during her absence in France, Mrs Fitzherbert had lived 'in the greatest familiarity' with the Marquis de Bellois at Plombières, and 'the consequence of this intercourse was a necessity of retiring to Paris'. A footnote here makes the innuendo clear enough: 'Does the author design to insinuate that Plombières was unable to furnish a midwife?' (Perhaps the simple truth was that she had a baby by the prince.) Mrs Fitzherbert's brother Walter Smythe, 'whom she had ill-treated, divulged many of the secrets,' says Withers, 'but he has been lately silenced by a large sum of money'. He further alleges that de Bellois had recently come to London; had demanded repayment of £2,000 Mrs Fitzherbert had borrowed; had refused to give up her letters to him; and had settled for £200. 'That is to say, the lady rated her favours at £1,800—I mean the favours of friendship and familiarity—and cheap enough, considering how dearly England has been obliged to purchase them.'

Erskine prosecuted Withers in the Court of King's Bench for libelling 'Mary Anne Fitzherbert, widow, a good peaceable and worthy subject' by insinuating that she had lived with the marquis 'in a wicked and scandalous intercourse of criminal connection and fornication' and 'had been with child by the said marquis'. By now Withers's pamphlet-writing seems to have become a frenzy. He issued an eighty-six-page account of his one-man fight, concluding with a sharp comment on the description of Mrs Fitzherbert as 'widow': 'This looks like the contrivance of an enemy to pass Your Royal Highness on the world for a WHORE. . . . The affair is too mysterious for my poor understanding.'

Withers boldly told the court, 'The woman who sleeps with the Prince of Wales . . . must be his wife or his mistress.' As Erskine denied the marriage, she must be a mistress 'and neither defamed nor capable of being defamed'. And yet he was fined £50 and sentenced to a year in Newgate jail. He had written of prosecution 'even unto death'; and in that noisome jail he died eight months later.

Before Withers died, he made the acquaintance of the proprietor of *The Times*. John Walter's £300 subsidy got him into trouble. Just after the king's recovery he published this:

> The royal dukes, and the leaders of opposition in general, affect to join with the friends of our amiable sovereign in rejoicing on account of His Majesty's recovery. But the insincerity of their joy is visible. Their late unfeeling conduct will forever tell against them. . . .

For this, and for saying that the prince and the Duke of York had received 'the rebukes of a justly offended father', Walter was prosecuted by Erskine, fined £150 and given two years in

Newgate. What pained him was that although he refused to betray the source of the paragraphs, the government did nothing to help him. 'I was to insert such paragraphs, etc., as were sent me,' he wrote to Jenkinson (now Lord Hawkesbury). 'Two of them are those I now suffer two years imprisonment for . . . in this horrible Bastille.' Eventually he got a £250 bonus from Pitt; and perhaps the government had a hand in having him freed after fifteen months, though this was done at the request of the prince.

It was merciful of the prince to help. In 1789 Walter had attacked him with pamphlets as well. In one, the king is represented as saying (among many other cutting things) to the prince:

> If your understanding had not been influenced by the subtle spells of the bad men about you . . . you would not, during my illness, have been seen intoxicated at an opera—or reeling into a gaming-house—or presiding at petty clubs and convivial associations where your appearance at any time would have been folly, and at this time was a crime.

A merrier Walter pamphlet was *The Death, Dissection, Will and Funeral Procession of Mrs Regency*, in which Fox, Sheridan and a host of Whigs and their ladies walk in mourning to Brooks's Club with many sorrowing followers, such as—

Twenty Paragraph Writers

Two and two, dressed in paper caps, and armed each with a silver pen and a little bottle of gall. They carried four flags on which were displayed the words,

Morning Herald	*Morning Post*
Gazetteer	*General Advertizer*

There are hundreds of bitterly weeping shopkeepers. One of them, Mr Surface's Poulterer, sings:

> Ah, sprightly, witty Congreve Dick,
> Who's probed our pockets to the quick,
> Think what we feel! This regent dart
> Has touched thy tradesmen to the heart.

At Brooks's the prince's followers sing a dirge to the tune of
'Galloping Dreary Dun':

> A prince we have got, and we are his men,
>> Getting drunk night, noon and day.
> To our bumpers, then, boys, we will turn again,
>> With our dice here,
>> And box there,
>>> Rumbling,
>>> Grumbling,
>>> Stamping,
>>> Swearing,
> Sitting up, getting drunk, night, noon and day.
>
> We thought ourselves sure of a regent at least,
>> *Getting drunk*, etc.,
> And that fasting so long, we should soon have a feast,
>> *With our dice*, etc. . . .
>
> Then lay her down gently under this table,
>> *And getting drunk*, etc.
> We'll curse Dr Willis as long as we're able,
>> *With our dice*, etc.

Distrust of the prince, nourished by Pittite papers, by
satirists, and by the facts, certainly heightened the fervour for
the king. And no doubt the joy was all the more heartfelt pre-
cisely because there can hardly be a more disturbing criticism
of the hereditary system than a mad king. For a time it was
good form to forget the king's faults; and nothing resembling
David Williams's Cheltenham *Recollections* was attempted
when the king went to Weymouth to convalesce in the summer of 1789.

The novelist Fanny Burney, one of the queen's attendants,
wrote in her diary:

> Not a child could we meet that had not a bandeau round its
> head, cap or hat of 'God Save the King'; all the bargemen
> wore it in cockades; and even the bathing-women had it in
> large coarse girdles round their waists. It is printed in
> golden letters upon most of the bathing-machines.

There is a print showing the king standing in the sea to his waist—his torso bare—his wig removed, revealing his close-shaven head—while bandsmen stand round him in the sea, playing 'God Save the King'. In the background can be seen (the one touch of satire) two packhorses setting off for London with bundles labelled *News for The Oracle, News for The World*—two subsidized papers that were leading the way with columns of gushing description from Weymouth. There was a demand as never before for loyal gossip. A collection of day-by-day reports, *A Diary of the Royal Tour*, appeared before long in book form. The entry for 14 July 1789 (a day that began fine but became 'extremely wet and disagreeable') reads:

> The Royal Family are every day more and more endearing themselves to the people by their habits of familiarity, condescension and suavity of manners. The *higher orders* of subjects well know the many amiable qualities and virtues of the family; and now the *middle* and *lower orders* speak of them with rapture and a glow of heartfelt expression almost bordering on idolatry.

Although George was hardly suave, and Queen Charlotte was never one to encourage familiarity, there was truth underlying the flattery. People were not kept at a distance. The king's simple confidence in the propriety of his every action permitted him to bathe almost naked in the face of a crowd, which no other king of the time would do. George and Charlotte made a telling contrast with Louis XVI and Marie Antoinette, who on that day of unpredictable weather, secluded in their vast palace at Versailles, learned that the Paris mob had stormed the Bastille.

10

The Hell-begotten Jacobins

A SENSE OF OUTRAGE is at the heart of revolutions. A poor man is more bitter if he daily sees a lucky few childishly squandering great wealth; and especially if that wealth comes partly from poor men's taxes. The events in France made it seem an act of blindness for any prince or peer to persist elsewhere in wanton misbehaviour. And yet in the 1790s in Britain there were few signs of amendment.

'It is to be feared that a revolution in government can alone bring about a revolution in morals,' says a radical journalist, Charles Pigott, in his preface to *The Jockey Club* in 1792. This book, which went through at least six editions in its first year, is a disrespectful guide to the titled prodigals of the age. 'While it continues the custom,' Pigott goes on, 'to annex such servile awe and prostituted reverence to those . . . whose sole merit consists in their birth or titles (the latter, as we shall prove, commonly lavished on the vilest part of the human race) . . . what happy result can be expected?'

Queen Charlotte did not play a Marie Antoinette role, but her older sons and their friends gave the reformers a target. Pigott says of the heir to the throne: 'Sorry are we to observe that the prospect is dreary indeed; or what else could render the present reign tolerable?' Of the prince's companions, he says:

They are the very lees of society; creatures with whom a person of morality, or even common decency, could not associate: the B---ys, Sir John L-de and Mr ------ H----r. . . . Where the h--r to the c---n, on whom the happiness of so many millions is hereafter to depend, affords such testimony of his taste and attachments . . . it becomes [the people] to think seriously for themselves.

The Barrys were a set of Irish brothers known as Newgate, Cripplegate and Hellgate, noted for their profanity, drunkenness, furious driving, cruel japes, and devotion to boxing, cockfighting and every kind of racing. To the credit of the eldest, the 7th Earl of Barrymore, it must be said that he also mounted amateur theatricals. In 1791 the Barrys inspired a new breed of bucks, called Crops because they wore their hair short. The Crops' hair and their negligent clothes had a revolution flavour, but for them it was a fashion without political intent.

Sir John Lade was a nephew of Samuel Johnson's friend, Mrs Thrale, and it was for her that Johnson wrote, when Lade inherited a fortune in 1780, the verses beginning 'Long-expected one-and-twenty':

> Wealth, Sir John, was made to wander:
> Let it wander as it will.
> See the jockey, see the pander—
> Bid them come and take their fill.

That is what Lade quickly did. He was soon in the prince's circle, and shared with the Barrys the honour of teaching the prince to ride in style and to drive his phaetons and carriages with a buckish flourish. In this circle Lade met the woman he married, Letitia Darby or Smith.

According to *The Jockey Club*, a 'warm and tender attachment' of the prince's brother, the Duke of York, for Letitia was one reason for his being sent to Germany in 1783. Years later, the duke told his more famous mistress, Mary Anne Clarke, that when he was sixteen a gentleman of his household smuggled him out of Kew Palace at midnight and took him to Letitia at a house in St James's. 'So fond was she of the duke,' say Mary Anne's memoirs, 'that as she got more into the society of men [a delicate phrase!] she supplied him with money, as the allowance he had from the king . . . would scarce buy His Royal Highness his bats, balls and playthings.'

The Hell-begotten Jacobins

When the duke returned from Germany in 1787, Lade was keeping Letitia. Now the duke did her a good turn. He wrote to her offering 'very handsome terms if she would leave Sir John', says Mary Anne. This was only for the eyes of Lade, who 'kept her on her own terms—*marriage*'. Thus this girl of humble origin became a baronet's wife, and was often out with the royal hunt at Windsor. 'To ride well up to hounds, to be in at the kill—none is ever before her,' says Pigott, 'and in the *noble* art of driving a phaeton four-in-hand . . . she is not excelled by Sir John himself.'

It is not surprising she is a good horsewoman, says Pigott; she was 'brought up under the special care of the late famous but unfortunate Mr J--n R-nn.' A footnote adds that this man 'met with a fatal accident some years ago at a place near Tyburn turnpike'—that is, was hanged. John Rann was a highwayman and a great buck; he introduced the fashion of wearing coloured ribbons or tie-strings at the knees of his breeches, and called himself Sixteen-String Jack. Revelling with his girls at Bagnigge Wells in Clerkenwell, he would say proudly, 'I am Sixteen-String Jack the famous highwayman.' When he came up at Bow Street Court in 1774, his leg-irons were decorated with blue ribbons, he wore a huge bouquet of myrtle and roses, and 'everything he said and did occasioned merriment'. Before he took his last ride to Tyburn, says one account, 'not less than seven girls pined with him' in his Newgate cell; of whom perhaps one was Letitia.

Now, says Pigott, she can be seen 'in *her own box* at the opera, splendidly arrayed, her whole ambition gratified in viewing lords, and dukes, and princes at her side'. Such was the reward of a woman of talent, devoted to 'a strict observance of all the Cyprian rites': 'To raise up those that fall is a generous, noble effort. . . . Indefatigable on these occasions, what miracles has she not achieved!' Making marriages is another of her talents: 'She is now *nobly* connected, being aunt to the young, beautiful widow, the C--nt-ss of B--r-m--e.' In 1792 Letitia's niece Charlotte, daughter of an Irish porter, married the Earl of Barrymore. Nine months later, aged twenty-three, and having run through £300,000, the earl was killed (perhaps accidentally) by his own gun.

Sir John Lade, too, threw away his fortune, as Samuel Johnson foresaw, but though he spent some time in a debtor's prison, he did not die young. During the Regency, the prince gave him a £500-a-year pension (in the name of 'the Rev Dr Tolly'), and he lived on, still pensioned, a stubborn relic of the eighteenth century, into the second year of Queen Victoria.

Then there is Pigott's 'Mr ------ H----r', who is of course the George Hanger we saw at the Westminster hustings. By 1792 he had squandered his share of the fortune of his father, the 1st Lord Coleraine, and had two sources of income: £600 a year as a 'crimp', raising recruits by fair means or foul for the East India Company's private army, and £300 a year as a gentleman in the prince's household. He is always pictured carrying a knobbly cudgel—useful, no doubt, if the prince was in danger of a brawl. Hanger is 'excessively foolish', says Pigott. 'As a certain marksman at a cat or dog with a windgun he defies competition.' His latest mistress is 'none of your flimsy, delicate foreign beauties . . . there is plenty of her, cut and come again'.

Hanger, too, lost favour, and in 1798–9 was in prison for debt. Pride was not among his follies: for a time he was a coal merchant. When the Coleraine title came to him in 1814, he did not use it. In 1824 he was reported to have died 'in a public-house parlour, where he used to smoke his pipe and reign head man over tailors and bricklayers'.

The Jockey Club naturally finds room for 'Her R-y-l H---n-ss the P---c-ss of W--es, commonly miscalled Mrs F---h--b--t'. It repeats many of the points made by Withers; and adds a few words about Mrs Fitzherbert's constant companion, an admiral's daughter, Isabella Pigot, who encourages 'liberal unshackled intercourse between the sexes . . . conferring gratuitous favours on those who enjoy her friendship'.

The book was soon in trouble with the law—not over its remarks about notorious people, however, but over its revolutionary talk:

All reform of government in England, as we have beheld it elsewhere, must begin and end with the people . . . The system is erroneous, and the example of France, we trust in God, will be successful. . . .

If the American Revolution operated as an example upon France, it is natural to imagine, from her vicinity, that the French Revolution will operate at least with equal effect upon us. The people will soon revolt against the influence of corruption. . . .

Is the miserable farce of r---l-y, that p-l-t-c-l h--b-g, to be ever kept up, under such an infinity of discouraging examples, to its present enormous magnitude?

And a comparison of Louis XVI (then a prisoner) and George III:

There is in many instances a striking resemblance in the virtues of these two R-y-l Jockeys . . . no benefit from them having ever reached their subjects.

The Prince of Wales read *The Jockey Club* in September 1792; and wrote an agitated letter to Queen Charlotte. First he passed on the information that 'in the small alehouses in and about London there were a number of French Jacobines who were industriously and strenuously endeavouring to propagate their infernal doctrines by treating the lower classes of people, and by inveighing openly . . . upon the blessings that must come to this country was she alike drenched and deluged with blood'. Then he denounced *The Jockey Club* as 'the most infamous and shocking libellous production that ever disgraced the pen of man'. It propagated 'those *damnable doctrines* of the *hell-begotten Jacobines*' and must be prosecuted 'as a libel upon the king, yourself and the constitution'. He enclosed a copy with passages pencil-marked, and the queen sent it on to the attorney-general. Pigott's name was not on the title-page; but within a fortnight prosecutions were under way against two booksellers, James Ridgway of St. James's and Henry Delahay Symonds of Paternoster Row. The passages quoted above, with others of the same tenor, brought Ridgway two years in Newgate and Symonds (Pigott's publisher) three years.

The prince's fury against damnable French doctrines was not surprising in a royal spendthrift. After setting the attorney-general to work, the prince wrote another letter—to his father, whom he feared—to announce that his creditors were threatening, not for the first time, to send bailiffs to strip Carlton House. Five years earlier, the prince had had to ask his father to get parliament to pay off debts of £160,000, and he had also obtained an extra £60,000 for Carlton House, plus an increase in his annual income to more than £73,000. He had promised to economize. Now he was in debt for a further £400,000—part of which, he confessed, was 'too justly imputable to a want of strict economy.' Indeed, in the nine years since coming of age the prince had cost the country at least £1,300,000. This was equal to an entire year's land tax; and only £500,000 less than the annual cost of the navy.

The French Revolution supplied the prince with an argument in his letter to the king: If his debts were not paid, he would live in complete retirement, but this would be politically most undesirable 'at a moment when a levelling spirit is fermenting throughout Europe'. Ministers tended to support this argument. 'In these times of democratic frenzy,' one of them said, 'it was necessary to support the splendour of courts and princes.' The king made the prince wait for his money, but he got it.

The prince had already broken with Charles James Fox. In 1789 Fox called the revolution 'one of the most glorious events in the history of mankind'. Many Englishmen agreed; but soon the Whigs were split. Edmund Burke had never relished toasts to the Majesty of the People. In the autumn of 1790 Burke published his partly prophetic yet deeply flawed *Reflections on the Revolution in France*. The man who had once inveighed against royal influence and parliamentary corruption now said:

> We know that the British House of Commons, without shutting its doors to any merit in any class, is . . . filled with everything illustrious in rank, in descent, in hereditary and in acquired opulence, in cultivated talents, in military, civil, naval and polite distinction, that the country can afford.

He deprecated annual celebrations of the Revolution of 1688 (a Whig ritual) as 'swallowing down repeated provocatives of cantharides to our love of liberty'. In an often-quoted passage idealizing Marie Antoinette and her court and 'the unbought grace of life', he announced that 'the age of chivalry is gone'.

Philip Francis (the Junius of twenty years before) wrote to Burke, 'All that you say of the queen is pure foppery.' Within a fortnight, caricatures began to appear showing Burke as a new Don Quixote. In 'The Knight of the Woeful Countenance Going to Extirpate the National Assembly', he rides in armour out of the door of his publisher, Dodsley (who was selling thousands of copies a week). Burke is mounted on an ass with a papal crown, and bears a Shield of Aristocracy and Despotism emblazoned with the Bastille and scenes of torture.

Another caricature shows him as 'Don Dismallo' embracing Marie Antoinette, 'his beautiful vision'. 'Thou Adonis of cavaliers! Thou god of chivalry!' says the queen, adding lewdly, 'Give me to grasp thy invincible shillelagh, more powerful than the sword of Rinaldo or that terrible talisman, the truncheon of Marlborough.'

Burke's feeling for the venerable, non-rational, hierarchic elements in society had led him into such a fervid defence of the *ancien régime* that he could say it 'kept alive, even in servitude itself, the spirit of an exalted freedom' and that 'vice itself lost half its evil, by losing all its grossness'. (Louis XVI's cousin, the Duc de Chartres, visiting London in 1783, had proudly shown ladies the buttons on his coat depicting, Walpole records, 'a horse covering a mare, and a dog and bitch equally conjugal'. For Marie Antoinette's polymorphous pursuits there is not room here.) To Burke it seemed that French reasoners were undermining civilization: 'A king is but a man; a queen is but a woman; a woman is but an animal.' Yet he was willing to call the lower orders animals: 'Learning will be cast into the mire and trodden down—' (here came the phrase that radicals were not to forget for a generation) '—under the hoofs of the swinish multitude.'

Soon a favourite underdogs' ballad was 'Burke's Address to the Swinish Multitude':

> Ye vile swinish herd in the sty of taxation,
> What would ye be after, disturbing the nation?
> Give over your grunting—be off!—to your sty!

Nor dare to look out if a king passes by.
Get ye down! down! down! keep ye down!

Do ye know what a king is? By Patrick, I'll tell you!
He has power in his pocket to buy you and sell you,
To make you all soldiers, or keep you at work,
To hang you, and cure you for ham or salt pork!
Get ye down—

The ballad takes note of Burke's 'a king is but a man' passage:

Do you think that a king is no more than a man,
Yet brutish, ye swinish irrational clan?
I swear by his office, his right is divine
To flog you, and feed you, and treat you like swine!
Get ye down—

. . . 'What use do we make of your money?' you say.
Why, the first law of nature—*we take our own pay*—
And next on our friends a few pensions bestow—
And to you we apply when our treasure runs low.
Get ye down—

This jibe at pensions soon hit home, for Burke accepted unannounced pensions from George III worth £3,700 a year.

As soon as Burke's book came out, an ardent republican, Thomas Paine, bought a copy and withdrew to the Angel Inn, in the suburb of Islington, to write a reply. Paine had contributed to one revolution against George III, and hoped to see another. Fifteen years before, this one-time staymaker and exciseman had written *Common Sense*, the pamphlet that did more than any other to push hesitant Americans toward a radical solution. It called George III the Royal Brute, and took a daring rousseauist line: government is at best 'a necessary evil' and 'the palaces of kings are built upon the ruins of the bowers of paradise'. America, kingless and lordless, became a standing example to French and English reformers. Paine's reply to Burke, the first part of the *Rights of Man*, which was on sale within four months, boldly elaborated the charge of political usurpation.

But after all, what is this metaphor called a crown, or
rather, what is monarchy? Is it a thing, or is it a name, or is
it a fraud? Is it 'a contrivance of human wisdom', or of
human craft to obtain money from a nation? . . . It appears
to be a something going much out of fashion.

Paine aims not at Whig gentlemen but at the common man,
the dispossessed and the thinking craftsman. For Burke he has
little but scorn, 'He has discovered a world of windmills' (an
echo here of the Don Quixote caricatures). 'It is painful to behold a man employing his talents to corrupt himself. . . . He
pities the plumage, but forgets the dying bird.' Soon Paine was
far outselling Burke, stirring cutlers in Sheffield and weavers in
Norwich, and infiltrating every village. Working-men's
societies published cheap editions. Within ten years, Paine
claimed, between 400,000 and 500,000 copies were circulated
in Britain and Ireland. Certainly sales must have passed
200,000.

During 1791 opinion wavered uncertainly. When Louis XVI
and Marie Antoinette took flight and were recaptured, the non-
radical Thomas Rowlandson caricatured them unsympatheti-
cally, with the queen screaming, '*Nous sommes tous foutus.*'
But the following month, men of property in Birmingham
stirred up a mob to go on a 'Church and King' rampage against
reformers celebrating July 14, and the houses of the scientist
Joseph Priestley and other dissenters were sacked. Five days
later, James Gillray included Priestley in 'The Hopes of the
Party', a caricature in which George III has his head on the
block and Fox as executioner stands with axe raised, hesi-
tating. It is anti-Whig but subversive. The king says stupidly,
'What what what? What's the matter?'

To picture such a thing, for whatever purpose, became impossible before the next year was out. The turning-point came
in the autumn of 1792. The French routed an invading army
led by George III's brother-in-law, the Duke of Brunswick
(who had promised death to all who opposed him). They proclaimed a republic. In November, as the revolutionary army
advanced, the Paris Convention declared that France would
aid 'all people who wish to recover their liberty'.

And in November in London, with Pitt's backing, the
Association for Preserving Liberty and Property against Republicans and Levellers was founded to fight sedition, stir
magistrates to action, and rouse the nation with penny handbills and tracts.

> The Mounseers, they say, have the world in a string,
> They don't like our nobles, they don't like our king . . .
> They call us already a province of France,
> And come here by hundreds to teach us to dance . . .
> They jaw in their clubs, murder women and priests,
> And then for their fishwives they make civic feasts . . .
> And as all things are equal and all should be free,
> 'If your wife don't suit *you*, sir, perhaps she'll suit *me*' . . .

Alehouses and inns were the natural political clubs of working men and of the self-employed though generally voteless
artisans who often guided their thought. There they shared the
taxed newspapers, distributed radical broadsides, debated
Paine's ideas, and dreamed of a new Britain. In December 1792
the chairman of the anti-leveller association, John Reeves, a
barrister and fiery royalist, sent circulars to all magistrates
warning of the mischief being done by 'newspapers filled with
disloyalty and sedition, the writers of which manifestly appear
by their language to be in the pay of French emissaries who
wish to destroy our excellent constitution'. He urged that 'all
good Englishmen, whether masters of private families, or
keepers of inns, taverns and coffee-houses,' should 'discontinue
and discourage' these newspapers.

The alehouse politicians were also daring to organize a
national network of reform societies. This had to stop. Justices
of the peace, guided by Reeves, posted up warning notices.
Not only big towns had their Jacobins: one of these notices
survives, for example, from the tiny Suffolk parish of Mutford.
It tells alehouse-keepers not to allow 'evil-disposed persons to
form *clubs* and *associations* . . . in which the said persons, by
reading libellous publications and holding seditious dis-
courses, endeavour to render the unwary discontented in their
stations . . . thereby inciting the unthinking multitude to
break out into riots and to produce universal anarchy'. Soon

publicans displayed the words *No Jacobins admitted here* at their doors.

At Sheffield, the unthinking multitude had been celebrating a French victory at Jemappes in the Netherlands by roasting an ox, carrying it through the streets in a parade of 6,000 people, and sharing it among the poor and prisoners. In the parade there was a French tricolor, and a lifesize caricature of Burke riding on a pig. According to a hostile broadside, there were flags demonstrating 'hatred of royalty', and 'infamous labels posted up on the corners of streets, with a finger pointing to the words DEATH OR LIBERTY'. It was a divided city. At its leading Church and King tavern, this toast was drunk: 'May Tom Paine live forever. . . . May he be put in a bag and hung swig-swag over hell's gate till doomsday.'

John Reeves had clever helpers in the anti-levelling work. Hannah More, a religious bluestocking, began a remarkable series of homely tracts with *Village Politics*, which was distributed nationally by the government (twenty-four pages for twopence). A blacksmith and a bricklayer argue:

JACK ANVIL: When this levelling comes about, there will be no 'firmaries, no hospitals, no charity-schools, where so many hundred thousand poor souls learn to read the word of God for nothing. For who is to pay for them? . . . I read my Bible, go to church, and think of a treasure in heaven.

TOM HOD: Aye; but the French have got it in *this* world.

JACK: 'Tis all a lie, Tom . . . 'Tis all murder, and nakedness, and hunger; many of the poor soldiers fight without victuals, and march without clothes. These are your *democrats*, Tom! . . . And this levelling makes people so dismal. These poor French fellows used to be the merriest dogs in the world; but since equality came in, I don't believe a Frenchman has ever laughed. . . . And levelling will rob thee of thy ale. . . .

Tom Hod does not ask why starving French soldiers win battles. He is converted, sings 'The Roast Beef of Old England', promises to 'burn my book'—which can only mean Paine—and mind his own business, as the parson tells him.

When Hannah More began setting up village schools in

backward counties, she ordained for the children's weekday reading 'such coarse works as may fit them for servants', and said, 'I allow of no writing for the poor.' Properly directed reading might keep men in their place. Within a year Hannah and her associates had circulated about two million copies of thirty-six tracts with the help of the government and well-to-do subscribers.

A series of broadsides were produced, too, in which John Bull persuaded Thomas Bull that Britain had best stay as it was. A retort came from a radical Roger Bull in *A Few Words but No Lies:*

> You have heard, no doubt, Thomas, a great deal of different interests, namely, the government interest, the landed interest, the moneyed interest, the mercantile interest, the church interest, and I know not how many interests, but all of them wealthy interests. But never a word of the labouring interest.

If kings and clergymen 'had always made themselves more useful than burdensome,' says Roger, 'they had always been esteemed.'

One John Bull broadside depicts the propagators of Paine as men of some substance. Will Driver, up from the country, sees 'a well-dressed man' writing *No king and Tom Paine forever!* on London Bridge. Will indignantly covers the words with mud, then rubs the man's nose in it. In John Bull's town, a large employer, Ned Powerful, summons his men and says, 'My lads, here is a book for each of you; it is Tom Paine's *Rights of Man;* it equally concerns us all!' He gives them a day off and tells them to read it and let him know what they think. They return with a united verdict: to throw the book in Ned Powerful's fire. Their foreman says, 'What did you take us for? Rascals! Scoundrels! *Frenchmen?*' This broadside is dated 28 December 1792, or ten days after Paine had been sentenced *in absentia* to outlawry for the more dangerous second part of the *Rights of Man.*

Paine had fled to France and was sitting in the National Convention (but was soon to be in danger of the guillotine for being too moderate, a frequent fate of revolutionary thinkers).

The Hell-begotten Jacobins

In the Court of King's Bench, the prosecuted passages were almost all about the monarchy:

> All hereditary government is in its nature tyranny. . . . To inherit a government is to inherit the people as if they were flocks and herds.
>
> Whether the person be wise or foolish, sane or insane, a native or a foreigner, matters not. . . . The people must be hoodwinked and held in superstitious ignorance by some bugbear or other; and what is called the crown answers this purpose.
>
> The farce of monarchy and aristocracy in all countries is following that of chivalry, and Mr Burke is dressing for the funeral.

This and much more was addressed, said the attorney-general, 'to the ignorant, to the credulous, to the desperate'. It was not to his purpose to add that Paine also addressed to them a plan for radical parliamentary reform, and for such visionary notions as birth, marriage and death benefits, child allowances, old-age and ex-service pensions, and a progressive income tax. The attorney-general read to the jury a letter that Paine had written to him from Paris, 'First Year of the Republic':

> . . . Is it possible that you or I can believe, or that reason can make any other man believe, that the capacity of such a man as Mr Guelph, or any of his profligate sons, is necessary to the government of a nation?

This, said the prosecutor, was 'contemptuous, scandalous, false, cruel'; the princes were guilty of 'youthful errors from which even royalty is not exempt'. In a Gillray print on sale at this time, 'Vices Overlooked', inspired by a proclamation against seditious writings, the king and queen represent avarice, the Prince of Wales—a youth of thirty—drunkenness, the Duke of York gambling, and the Duke of Clarence, who had begun his fecund connection with the actress Dorothy Jordan, debauchery. For the defence, Thomas Erskine, the leading Whig barrister, quoted a declaration for radical reform in which Pitt had joined in the brave days of 1782. '*Now* every man is to be cried down for such opinions,' said Erskine. He quoted at length, too, from the 'kings are naturally lovers of low company' passage in Burke's speech of 1780, and argued that Paine, like Burke, must be read in his full context.

Though *Rights of Man* was condemned, Erskine was hailed with applause afterwards as he passed through the streets. Pitt's anti-French tracts and his guided newspapers—he was now subsidizing nine in London—had by no means stifled thoughts of liberty. The day after the trial, Gillray issued a caricature showing Pitt working to panic John Bull with Jacobin terrors:

> . . . The Scotch have caught the itch too, and the wild Irish have begun to pull off their breeches! What will become of us, John? And see, there's five hundred disputing-clubs . . . and twenty thousand bill-stickers with *Ça ira* pasted on the front of their red caps! . . . Down with the book-stalls!—blow up the gin-shops!—cut off the printers' ears! O Lord, John! O Lord! We're all ruined!—they'll murder us and make us into aristocrat pies!

John Bull has both *Vive la Liberté* and *God Save the King* stuck in his hat, and *Rights of Man* and a *Pennyworth of Truth* tract in his pockets. He is puzzled, for he can see nothing but a great flock of gabbling geese.

> . . . But Lord help my silly head, how should such a clod-pole as I be able to see anything right? . . . My business is only to fire when and where Measter orders, and to pay for the gunpowder.—But Measter o' mine (if I may speak a word), where's the use of firing now? What can us two do against all them hundreds of thousands of millions of monsters? Lord, Measter, had not we better try if they won't shake hands with us . . . ?

On the print Gillray says, 'Price 3 shillings—the engraving not having been paid for by the associations for vending twopenny scurrilities.'

Violently anti-French caricatures were more and more common, and some of them were certainly subsidized. One in an old tradition, 'French Happiness, English Misery', by Isaac

The Hell-begotten Jacobins

Cruikshank (father of George), was sold by S. W. Fores of Piccadilly in lots of one hundred 'to those who give them away' at a discount of thirty-six per cent. It shows sans-culottes in such poverty that even their rats are starving, in contrast to the gorging English; and it pretends that the truth of Jemappes was that the French lost 54,090 killed and wounded, against 690. After the execution of Louis XVI in January 1793, prints of his farewell to his family, and of his execution, went out in vast numbers. One entitled 'Massacre of the French King!' was offered at only a guinea a hundred to 'every bookseller, stationer, etc. in England, Scotland and Ireland', and supplies were promised 'at a day's notice, from one to ten thousand copies'.

Pitt was moving to war; it seemed plausible then that an alliance of Britain, Germany and Austria would smash the revolution. Fox challenged him: 'Opinions were never yet driven out of a country by pikes and swords and guns.' And again: 'The people are sovereigns in all countries. . . . They may amend, alter and abolish the form of government under which they live, at pleasure.' This stand lost him a large section of his party. He could gather only forty-four votes in the Commons for a policy of negotiation. War, said George III to Pitt, 'is highly agreeable to me . . . a means of restoring some degree of order to that unprincipled country'.

After Pitt and Henry Dundas, his Cabinet colleague and drinking partner, arrived in the Commons far gone on the day war was declared, the radical *Morning Chronicle* published a series of Epigrammata Bacchanalia by Richard Porson, who is still honoured at Cambridge as a brilliant, though eccentric, professor of Greek.

> In what odd ways we taste misfortune's cup—
> While France throws *down* the gauntlet, Pitt throws *up*.

> PITT: I can't discern the Speaker, Hal; can you?
> DUNDAS: Not see the Speaker! Damn me, I see two.

And when Pitt announced an expedition to Holland:

> The secret's out, and here's the simple matter:
> A war begun in *wine* will end in *water*.

This was prophetic. The expedition was put under the command of the Duke of York, at the insistence of the king and with the warm approval of the Prince of Wales—who wrote to the duke, 'The interest, the honour, THE VERY EXISTENCE OF EVERY PRINCE AT THIS MOMENT IS CONCERNED & DEPENDS ON THE TOTAL ANNIHILATION OF THIS BANDITTI', and so on, together with thoughts about the peril Britain faced from 'the deists, religionists, pedants & politicians which WE ARE CURSED WITH'. The prince added that the Duke of Clarence had made 'a *most incomparable speech* on the slave trade' in the Lords (he defended the trade as highly beneficial to black and white alike). Good wishes, however, could not make the Duke of York a good or even a sober general.

> Kings, lords and courtiers all
> Who wish for freedom's fall,
> This let them learn:
> Let them learn Brunswick's dance
> Which was well taught in France,
> Which was well taught in France
> By freedom's sons.

So said one of the many 'God Save the King' parodies of the day. Like Brunswick, the duke sped forward and then was routed. Gillray, after a behind-the-lines tour in Flanders, published prints of the duke boozing and merrily fondling plump Dutchwomen. By the end of 1793 Pitt was pleading to have the duke replaced. Gillray showed him swaggering tipsily into George III's throne-room with a dismal mockery of French plunder. The king says, 'What! what! Keys of Paris! Keys of Paris! Give us hold! Gad's bobs, it's nothing but *veni* with you, lad, hey? *Veni, vidi?* Ay, ay!' The queen is an avaricious hag—her frequent role now—gleefully holding out her apron for the devil to shovel gold into it. Behind her are rows of moneybags: *Spy money £40,000 pr A.—for flatterers and toadeaters £10,000 pr A.—pin money £50,000*. Gillray was eagerly savaging Fox and his followers as dangerous sans-culottes, and the French as monsters; but in his continuing anti-royal carica-

tures and his frequent attacks on Pitt he well reflected the
country's divided mind.

Charles Morris had a great success with 'Billy's Undone us
by War':

> Oh, dear, what will become of us,
> Dear, dear, what will become of us,
> Oh, dear, what will become of us?
> Billy's so fond of the wars!

... Now see him with rogues and with despots combining.
All work at a stand and all commerce declining.
Ah, soon he will save us the trouble of dining,
To spend all our cash on the wars. . . .

Some of the cash went to Prussia and Austria, which then
gave half their attention to carving up Poland. Pitt raised new
forces for the duke; and in the Commons, Jenkinson's son, a
future prime minister, talked of 'marching to Paris'. He had
twenty years to wait. Morris wrote a harsher song against 'the
Jenky-nursed jackal' Pitt:

> Sending troops to be swamped where they can't draw their
> breath,
> And buying a fresh load of taxes with death.

In parliament, however, Pitt was safe from defeats. The revolution provided a standing argument against reform. The lines
had been drawn. The Commons twice rejected motions by
Fox's colleague Charles Grey for uncorrupt and more frequent elections and for 'a more equal representation of the
people'. It was no use publishing a survey showing that at
both Old Sarum and Marlborough, two MPs were elected by
seven voters; that a simple majority of the 513 English and
Welsh MPs could be obtained from boroughs with a grand
total of 11,075 voters; and that even these purchasable voters
were rarely the deciders, for seventy-one peers and the
Treasury together managed the return of 167 MPs, and ninety-
one commoners (often relations of peers) managed a further
139, making 306 MPs in a convenient number of pockets. The
least reform was repelled as 'an innovation in the constitution';

a constitution which George III prayed would 'remain un-
impaired to the latest posterity'. Grey urged that the correction of abuses was 'the best possible means of preventing
mischief'; Pitt said this was not the time 'to make hazardous
experiments'.

It was no wonder that unpropertied reformers turned more
and more to a national radical movement as their one hope.
Some professional men were with them—often men of a dis-
senting or deist turn of mind, inspired by seventeenth-century
thinkers as well as French *philosophes*. They discovered the
perils of free speech and free association.

An attorney, John Frost, who in 1782 had signed Pitt's
forgotten reform declaration, went to Paris in 1792 to observe
Louis XVI's trial. On his return he said at the Percy Coffee-
house, 'I can see no reason why any man should not be upon
a footing with another,' and added, when asked what he
meant by equality, 'Why, I mean no king.' For this he was
given six months in Newgate. He was also to be pilloried, but
here the common man showed his power. Bills were posted:

> This day at 12 o'clock John Frost
> is to stand on the pillory at
> Charing Cross for supporting the
> rights of the people!!!

And for fear of his being made a hero, the pillorying was can-
celled. Never again, not even in the flag-waving years of the
war against Napoleon, did the authorities venture to punish
seditious words with the pillory.

In September 1793, Charles Pigott of *The Jockey Club* sat
drinking sixpenny glasses of punch in the London Coffee-
house with one Dr William Hudson. They toasted the French
republic, and Hudson said:

> The king, what is he? George Guelph, a German hog-
> butcher, a dealer in human flesh by the carcase. He sells his
> Hanoverian subjects to his British subjects for £30 apiece.

During the American war, Burke had called the German prin-
celings who supplied mercenaries to George III 'traders in
human flesh'. Times had changed: Hudson got two years.

The Hell-begotten Jacobins

There is no clear record of the trial of Pigott for uttering other seditious words on the same occasion; but he died in jail.

For selling Paine (at a date before Paine's conviction) the unhappy James Ridgway was sentenced to a further two years. Paine's writings sent many others to jail, but they continued to be hawked illicitly.

Even to criticize the working of the law became dangerous. William Holland of 50 Oxford Street, one of the leading print-sellers, spent some time in Newgate on a charge of seditious libel for publishing a pamphlet entitled 'Pathetic Particulars of a Poor Boy sentenced to suffer seven Years solitary Confinement in Gloucester Bastille'. One count against him was that the pamphlet was illustrated with a 'scandalous infamous libellous and defamatory etching or print' showing a youth in fetters and a jailor with a whip.

All over the country, the disaffected were being pursued. Henry Dundas, the Home Secretary, offered the large reward of £200 for the discovery of the person who posted handbills on the walls of Norwich saying—

> Tremble, O thou oppressor of the people that reigneth upon the throne. . . . Weep, O ye conductors of this vile and wicked war, ye who grind the face of the poor. . . . Lord Buckingham, who died the other day, had £30,000 yearly for setting his arse in the House of Lords and doing nothing. . . . He who wishes well to the cause of liberty, let him repair to Chapel Field at 5 o'clock this afternoon to begin a glorious revolution.

Parodies of 'God Save the King' became more extreme. American-born Joel Barlow, who had been to Paris with John Frost when the guillotine was in action, wrote 'Citizen Guillotine', which became a broadside:

> Sweet Billy thee shall hail—
> Johnny Reeves at his tail—
>   Pride of our days!
> Placemen swanlike shall sing,
> 'Guillotine, mighty king.'
> Echoes from crowds shall ring
>   With thy just praise. . . .

> Long live great guillotine,
> Who shaves the head so clean
>   Of queen or king;
> Whose power is so great
> That ev'ry tool of state
> Dreadeth his mighty weight,
>   Wonderful thing!!!

English republicans began calling themselves 'citizen'. One of these was Citizen Richard Lee, who sold a variety of daring broadsides at shops called the British Tree of Liberty, in the Haymarket and in Soho. In 'The Happy Reign of George the Last', he says that by acting for themselves they can 'cease to drudge and sweat for courtiers':

> Do we toil while others reap?
> Do we starve while others feast?
> Are we sold and shorn like sheep
> By the despot and the priest?
> Are we born for them alone . . . ?

The reply of *The Antigallican Songster* was:

> Some are born for the court and the city
>   And some for the village and cot;
> But oh! 'twere a dolorous ditty
>   If all became equal in lot. . . .

> 'Rights of Man' makes a very fine sound,
>   Equal riches—a plausible tale.
> But whose labour would then till the ground?
> All would drink, but who'd brew the best ale?

The reform societies indignantly denied that they wanted a levelling of property. However, there was at this time, a quarter-century before Karl Marx was born, much talk of economic justice. The most radical plan of all was offered by Thomas Spence, a frail, shabby, querulous man who came to London from Newcastle on Tyne in 1792 and began printing and selling at a shop he called the Hive of Liberty, in Little Turnstile, Holborn. He dreamed of a paradisal society based on communal parish ownership of land. 'The earth was not made for individuals,' he says. 'Landed property always was acquired either by conquest or encroachment on the common property of mankind.' He recognized that many reformers would not follow him in calling land ownership 'this root of every abuse': 'They have no chance of being kings; but many of them are already, and the rest foolishly and wickedly hope to be sometime or other, landlords.' The importance Spence gave to land was not misdirected, at a time when it was the basis of much wealth and of all claims to political power. But how was the dream to be realized? 'Wealth and property must be wrested from the hands of rapacity and indolence, and divided amongst mankind at large, in proportion as they merit it,' says Spence in his weekly penny paper, *Pig's Meat, or Lessons for the Swinish Multitude*. Sometimes he concedes the probability of civil war; at others he depends on radical reform:

> Awake! Arise! Arm yourselves—with truth, justice, reason. Lay siege to corruption. . . . Claim as your inalienable right, universal suffrage and annual parliaments. And whenever you have the gratification to choose a representative, let him be from among the lower orders of men, and he will know how to sympathize with you.

Spence was soon familiar with Newgate, and even his twelve-year-old son was arrested for selling in the streets halfpenny broadsides of 'The Rights of Man in verse'. But the authorities showed more interest in Daniel Isaac Eaton of Newgate Street, Printer and Bookseller to the Supreme Majesty of the People. Eaton had defiantly issued *Rights of Man* immediately after the Paine verdict, and managed to win from a City jury a verdict of 'publishing, but not with a criminal intention'. This was a rebuff to the government at a time when magistrates and parsons (often the same person) were having Paine hanged and burned in effigy and were rounding up *Rights of Man* vendors and sometimes having them flogged. In February 1794 Eaton came up again at the Old Bailey for publishing in his twopence-a-week paper, *Politics for the People, or Hog's Wash*, a fable told by a leading reformer, John Thelwall, at one of his political lectures.

Thelwall, a former silk mercer, was filling a hall in the Strand
every Wednesday and Friday evening, at sixpence a head.
The charge against Eaton exposed the prosecution to some
ridicule.

> . . . I had a very fine majestic kind of animal, a gamecock
> (*meaning thereby to denote and represent our said Lord the
> King*), a haughty, sanguinary tyrant. . . .

—and so forth, with the parenthetical words inserted by the
prosecution at every mention of the gamecock. The teller of
the fable cannot help admiring the appearance of the gamecock, despite his grasping and warlike ways, 'and above all,
that fine ornamented thing about his head, his crown or
coxcomb, I believe you call it'. But he decides that 'the best
thing one could do, either for cocks and hens, or men and
women, was to rid the world of tyrants. . . . I believe if
guillotines had been in fashion, I should certainly have
guillotined him'. He cuts off the gamecock's head, 'and when
his fine trappings were stripped off, I found he was no better
than a common scratch dunghill pullet'.

The crime was the worse, said the prosecution, because
Politics for the People was sold to 'the lowest class of society'.
Eaton's counsel retorted: 'Whom are politics for, but for the
people? Are politics for placemen and pensioners only?' Besides, why suppose *our* king was meant? Did not a cock represent France? And finally: 'To attack the freedom of the
press . . . is to aim a fatal stroke at liberty itself. . . . Where
that man stands today, you yourselves may stand tomorrow.'
This thought could still touch a London jury: they said Not
Guilty.

Within three months, Pitt struck at the heart of the radical
reform movement: the London Corresponding Society.

The word 'corresponding' was an ominous one. The American and the French Revolutions had come about with the help
of a centrally directed network of corresponding committees.
A still more ominous word was 'convention'. The previous
autumn, delegates from many parts of the country, financed
by the penny-a-week subscriptions of thousands of members,
had held a British Convention at Edinburgh 'to obtain uni-

versal suffrage and annual parliaments'. They called each other Citizen and bandied the phrases *Vive la convention* and *Ça ira*—which helped to get their leaders sentences from the merciless Lord Braxfield of transportation to Botany Bay for up to fourteen years.

The reformers were preparing to hold a bigger convention, in England, when at 6.30 a.m. on 12 May 1794 there was 'a thundering knock' at the door of the London Corresponding Society's secretary, Thomas Hardy. He was a Scots-born master shoemaker, who lived, worked and had his shop at No. 9 Piccadilly, a few doors from Fores's pro-Pitt printshop. He was taken away, together with two sackfuls of his papers and pamphlets—material 'tending to influence the minds of the public in favour of *liberty and equality*', said *The Times*. Those had become frightening words, for Robespierre's terror was at its height. Hardy 'is a tall, thin man', said *The Times;* 'in dress and habit quite a *sans-culotte*'. He found that Horne Tooke and Thelwall were also under arrest, and a number of others followed in the next few days, including the private secretary of Pitt's brother-in-law, the radical Earl Stanhope.

Pitt used the seized papers to justify the suspension of *habeas corpus*. In the Commons he called the corresponding societies 'those great machines of Jacobinism'. To be well or-ganized was a crime. They had 'a deliberate and deep-con-certed plan for actually assembling a convention'. They had circulated pamphlets 'with a share of vigour, cunning and address truly astonishing' (in April they had printed 200,000 copies of a statement of aims). And yet they were 'wretches, outcasts'.

Fox said Pitt was absurd to suggest that the reformers could seriously hope to supplant the government. Grey said, 'This House will never reform itself, or destroy the corruption by which it is supported, by any other means than those of the resolutions of the people, acting on the prudence of this House. . . . This they can only do by meeting in bodies. This was the language of the Minister in 1782; but I do not know what his sentiments are now, for who can know the sentiments of an apostate?'

The Treasury Solicitor was very busy that month. The

London Corresponding Society round-up came when he was dealing with informers' reports on all sorts of disaffection; even the seditious words of Edward Swift, a Windsor old-clothes-man:

> Damn the king and queen, they ought to be put to death the same as the king and queen of France were. . . . Damn and bugger the king and all that belong to him. . . . I would as soon shoot the king as a mad dog. I will go down to Birmingham and bring up a set of rioters and make Windsor worse than ever France was.

Hardy and his associates were brought before Pitt and the Privy Council for questioning. So were other people who might help to incriminate them. One of these was Daniel Isaac Eaton's fourteen-year-old son Harry, who lodged with Thelwall. The government had been told by an agent within the London Corresponding Society that at a supper in Soho after an open-air meeting, Thelwall held up a foaming pot of porter, sliced off the head with a knife, and said, 'This is the way I would have all kings served.' Harry Eaton said he could not remember any such thing; nor the drinking of a toast to 'The lamp-irons in Parliament Street'—lamp-posts, that is, for hanging ministers on. The boy seized the chance to make a speech. He called Pitt 'a traitor to his king and country'; 'by causing unnecessary wars and taxing people to an enormous amount . . . he would make the poor people hate the king'. According to the attorney-general, this exchange followed:

> PITT: Pray, my boy, did you ever see Mr Pitt?
> HARRY: See him, see him! No, no, I would not have these eyes sullied by looking at such a fellow!

The saucy boy knew it was Pitt well enough: his face was constantly on view in the printshops.

Hardy went on trial for his life four months later at the Old Bailey before the Lord Chief Justice, who had taken part in the Privy Council's decision that it could get a conviction for high treason. The attorney-general's opening speech took nine hours: which made Lord Chancellor Thurlow exclaim, 'Then by God there is no treason!' Efforts were made to associate

Hardy with king-killing ideas. Pitt's agent told about the pot of porter and the lamp-irons. A broadside was produced which announced, in the form of a mock theatre bill—

A new and entertaining farce, called
LA GUILLOTINE
or
GEORGE'S HEAD IN THE BASKET!
Dramatis Personae
Numpy the Third, by Mr Gwelp
(Being the last time of his appearing in that character)

—and so forth, with a cast ranging from Burke and John Reeves to the Duke of Brunswick; and with the singing of 'Ca Ira' and 'Bob-Shave Great George Our —' and finally 'a Grand Decapitation of placemen, pensioners and German leeches'.

A song that someone had sent to Hardy was quoted:

The starving wretch who steals for bread
But seldom meets compassion,
And shall a crown preserve the head
Of him who robs a nation? . . .
Proud bishops next we will translate
Among priest-crafted martyrs.
The guillotine on peers shall wait
And knights we'll hang in garters. . . .
The golden age will then revive;
Each man shall be a brother. . . .

But Thomas Erskine, defending, was able to turn the more awkward pieces of evidence away from Hardy. And to campaign for reform was not yet treason. 'A man works hard for thirteen or fourteen hours of the day, the week through,' said a witness from Sheffield, 'and is not able to maintain his family'; the corresponding societies were trying 'to show the people the ground of this'. Such talk did not offend a London jury. Hard times, new taxes, and losses in Flanders helped to make the eight-day trial the occasion of an anti-Pitt demonstration. When the attorney-general emerged each night, a vast crowd greeted him with 'a general hissing and hooting', he wrote years later, which continued all the way down Ludgate Hill; but for Erskine there was cheering and the ritual of removing his horses from his carriage and parading him home.

Hardy was acquitted. Horne Tooke was brought up next. He summoned Pitt himself, and had a great deal of dry fun trying to make Pitt talk about his reformist days. 'He was seized with a total want of recollection!' Tooke wrote in his memoirs. 'With great difficulty, however, he was brought to recollect a meeting at the Thatched House Tavern in May 1782. Mr Tooke asked him what the meeting was but a convention of delegates from different great towns and counties of England, sent by committees? . . . He said he did not recollect how that meeting was composed!'

Tooke was acquitted. So was Thelwall. Pitt dropped the remaining cases. According to Thelwall, 'Eight hundred warrants for high treason were signed and sealed, ready to be executed upon the conviction of Hardy.'

A new mock playbill ('sold by all news-carriers') announced a wonderful illusionist, Signor Pittachio, who makes everyone mad or foolish with a Magical Alarm Bell, distorts everything with Curious Spy-Glasses, sets everyone fighting, conveys the money out of their pockets, makes 'some marvellous experiments upon his own memory', and regrets that 'he has been disappointed of several capital performers whom he had hoped to have brought forward for the purpose of exhibiting feats of activity on *The Tight Rope*'. Pittachio will however finish by 'exhibiting his own person on *The Tight Rope* for the benefit of the Swinish Multitude'.

After two years of fruitless war, Pitt had one consolation: he managed to get the Duke of York removed from his Flanders command. The king reproached Pitt for giving him 'so severe a blow'.

The Prince of Wales had less emotion to spare than formerly for either the Jacobins or his brother. His life was at a crisis.

11

Liberty's Last Squeak

IN HIS FIRST eight years as Mrs Fitzherbert's husband, the prince indulged himself with various women, amateur and professional. Mrs Fitzherbert had the art to survive them. But in 1794 she was ousted by the Countess of Jersey. It was no consolation to Mrs Fitzherbert that the countess was a forty-one-year-old grandmother—three years older than herself, nine years older than the prince; or that the countess did not even possess the generous figure that he usually demanded. 'Which is the woman—the plump dame, or the thin lady?' was the question *The Bon Ton Magazine* asked when the rivalry became public. The thin lady was an old friend. In 1782 the prince was showing 'a great fancy' for her as well as for Lady Melbourne; but Lady Jersey was telling her friends, 'If he is in love with me, I cannot help it.' She did not need to say this for the sake of her husband, the Earl of Jersey, who in that year was described in a satirical pamphlet as 'the pretty-pacing, sweetly-simpering, beauty-blended, odoriferous . . . all-bewitching, all-indulging, all-deluding swain'. In 1794 he was all-indulging to the prince, who rewarded him by making him his Master of the Horse, and by making the Jerseys' son a Lord of the Bedchamber.

Mrs Fitzherbert gave up after many violent quarrels. The prince, of course, could not be in the wrong. 'I really think myself too ill-used,' he wrote to Jack Payne in July 1794. 'God knows what I have done to merit it.' Within a month the Carlton House revolution was noted by S. W. Fores in a print by Isaac Cruikshank, his rising Scots-born caricaturist—'My

Grandmother, alias the Jersey Jig.' The prince lewdly fondles Lady Jersey, a witchlike crone, on his knee, and sings;

> I've kissed and I've prattled with fifty granddames
> And changed them as oft, do ye see,
> But of all the grandmammies that dance on the Steine,
> The widow of Jersey give me.

The earl had so self-effacingly stayed away from the Steine at Brighton and the other places where his wife displayed her triumph that Cruikshank was misled into thinking her a widow. But he was not far out when he showed Mrs Fitzherbert in a tragic attitude, holding a piece of paper inscribed '£6,000 p.a.' and saying, 'Was it for this paltry consideration I sacrificed my—my—my—? for this only I submitted to—to—?' The prince in fact gave her a paltry £3,000 a year; it became £6,000 in 1808.

A greater blow soon followed the parting. By 1794 the prince's debts had passed £600,000. How could John Bull be asked to pay that, on top of the cost of a bogged-down war on behalf of the even more prodigal Bourbons? The prince was told that his only hope was to marry, beget an heir and—as the king put it—'lead a life that would make him appear respectable'.

> . . . The prince he said, 'Good father, if you will find the money,
> You may send for which you please, and she shall be my honey.
> There's Caroline of Brunswick has got a pretty hand, sir.
> Do you but pay my debts, and I'll take it at command, sir.'

> '. . . Johnny Bull, that pays for all, will pay, you need not doubt it.
> Do you prepare to wed, and I'll speak to Pitt about it.'

Caroline, the plump, bouncing, impulsive, chattering, ill-washed twenty-seven-year-old daughter of George III's sister, was the most unlikely of brides to take on the huge task of making the prince respectable. 'With a *steady* man she will do vastly well,' James Harris, the emissary who fetched her from Brunswick, wrote in his diary. Her father's mistress told him that Caroline had not done anything *mauvaise*, but she must be kept *serrée* or else *elle s'égarera*. Harris ventured to warn Caroline 'that anybody who presumed to *love* her was guilty of *high treason*', and she too could be punished with death: 'This startled her.' In the next quarter-century a number of men committed high treason.

Why was she chosen as the prince's bride? Lady Jersey, whose interests were clear enough, was a close friend of Lady Harcourt, one of the queen's ladies, and in great favour with the queen herself. As *The Bon Ton Magazine* pointed out, the dismissal of Mrs Fitzherbert, which pleased the palace, 'was effected solely by the management and address of an *active* countess'. The queen approved the infamous appointment of her son's mistress as a Lady of the Bedchamber to his bride. A woman of stern outward morality is often able to relax rules for her own purposes.

The moment Caroline set foot in England, her Lady of the Bedchamber was putting her in her place: criticizing her clothes and even attempting to sit beside her in her carriage in a position of equal honour. The prince's first words to Harris after Caroline had been presented to him cannot be quoted too often: 'I am not well; pray get me a glass of brandy.' At the wedding more brandy made the prince unsteady on his feet, and yet it failed to save him from looking miserable. The Archbishop of Canterbury paused and looked at him significantly on coming to the question of impediments to marriage; but then united the prince to his second wife. Afterwards the prince said to his brother William, 'Tell Mrs Fitzherbert she is the only woman I shall ever love.'

In one thing the prince did his duty. According to the princess, she conceived the day after the wedding: he was too drunk on the night. One caricature suggested that he performed the royal task with the help of cantharides. Then Caroline had the grief of being attended, mocked, led into errors, and betrayed by her husband's mistress—who was by then three months pregnant, and few thought Lord Jersey the father. Lady Jersey even intercepted Caroline's letters and conveyed select passages to the queen. And the prince was lavishing on Lady Jersey money that the marriage had made available. His income was increased to £138,000, part of which was to go to pay off his debts—now £639,890—in instalments. He also got £57,000 for wedding and other expenses, plus a further £25,000 for Carlton House, where after twelve years he had not finished indulging his whims. From the age of twenty-one to the age of thirty-three the prince had spent more than £1,800,000 (not counting large sums borrowed in Amsterdam and never repaid). This was enough to pay 7,000 labourers generously for the same period.

> O George, great Prince of WHALES,
> Thy swallow never fails,
> > Voracious prince!
> We, all your slaves, agree
> To doat on monarchy.
> Our song shall ever be
> > God save the prince.

This broadside song sardonically commends the prince for forcing the people to pay his debts, in the midst of a war against republicans:

> The prince our champion see!
> Soldiers of liberty,
> > Rest on your arms:
> *He'll* break the magic ring,
> Dispel the charms of *king*,
> For which we're bound to sing
> > God save the prince!

A pamphlet describing 'the peculiar manners and customs of Bull-land' says:

> If any industrious individual is indebted £10, he may be imprisoned for life; but if one whose elevation of rank requires him to be a pattern of virtue and piety runs in debt 70,000 times as much, for the most vicious purposes, the nation is proud to pay the debt for him, and then, by way of reward, doubles his income.

Another peculiar custom is this:

> If any poor famishing Bull-lander knock down a hare as it
> crosses the common path, and satisfies his hunger with it,
> he is liable to a heavy fine or imprisonment—but if a rich
> man break down the hedges of a poor man to do the same
> thing, merely for amusement or mischief, no punishment
> awaits him.

And this:

> If the labouring part of the people find their wages will not
> buy them bread, and consult together how to obtain more—
> to fill out their bellies they are sent to prison.

Charles Pigott, confined to the Giltspur Street Compter
for sedition, compiled a bitter Painite *Political Dictionary* and
wrote in the preface, 'Already I feel the heavy hand of death
upon me . . . entombed within the walls of this English
Bastille.' He has lost faith in the people of England: 'They love
not liberty, why should they possess her?' His dictionary defi-
nition of 'disappointment' is 'the recovery of King George III
in the year 1789', and other definitions are:

> *Debauchery:* . . . The Dunkirk Hero [Duke of York] in a fit
> of intoxication at 3 o'clock in the morning at a brothel, sur-
> rounded by half a dozen prostitutes watching a favourable
> opportunity to pick his pocket.
> *Noose:* A running knot . . . very convenient for the people
> to have by them when summary justice is administered to
> wicked kings and corrupt ministers.
> *War:* Oh, soldiers, soldiers! lay not the flattering unction to
> your souls that you are heroes! You are nothing but mur-
> derers, butchers.

Pigott escaped prosecution for this by dying. Citizen Richard
Lee published a quantity of penny extracts from the dictionary, was arrested, escaped, fled to America—and died there.

Pacifist ideas were not uncommon in print. *The Village
Association*, a kind of radical anthology presented in the form
of a discussion by reformers round an ancient oak, has a
series of pithy sayings:

Human blood is all of one colour.

The best shield against sword and ball is an inch or two of OUT-OF-REACH.

There is less fun in a battle than at a harvest home.

It is the common soldier's blood makes the general a great man.

This book also says, 'Let him that earns the bread—eat,' and it looks coolly at kings:

'Kings must die as well as clowns,' and when they do, some will say, 'Alas! there went one of God's anointed;' whilst others will say, 'Poor man, his main fault was he was good for nothing.' 'He used to have the first cut and all the loaf besides.'

Bread was a dangerous word in 1795. Following a bad harvest, it rose to more than threepence a pound, so that the day's wage of a farm-worker would buy him four pounds of bread. In London beef was a shilling a pound: a carpenter was earning twelve shillings a week. Food riots were frequent. Pitt's house was mobbed. A print was sold showing a tree bearing loaves of bread, and famished men sitting below, saying, 'If you don't *fall*, I must *rise*.' Pitt was shown arrogantly loading John Bull with war and taxes. Gillray produced 'John Bull Ground Down', in which the victim shrieks 'Murder!' as Pitt grinds him in a coffee-mill that is converting him into guineas for Burke, Dundas, the prince and the prince's creditors. From a shining crown comes the voice of George III: 'Grind away grind away grind away Billy! . . . What! what! what! Murder, hey? Why, you poor stupe, is it not for the good of your country? Hey hey?'

The government urged the people to make potato bread. The queen even sent the prince a recipe for it. 'Remarkably good,' she said, and told him that George III had ordained brown bread only at his meals, '& it is to be hoped that this will encourage others to do the same'—which surely raised a laugh round the prince's table.

Hannah More rebuked the rioters in a halfpenny broadside, 'Half a Loaf is Better than no Bread,' in which a loyal country-man says:

Liberty's Last Squeak

And though I've no money, and though I've no lands,
I've a head on my shoulders and a pair of good hands;
So I'll work the whole day, and on Sundays I'll seek
At church how to bear all the wants of the week.
The gentlefolks too will afford us supplies:
They'll subscribe—and they'll give up their puddings and
   pies.

(William Blake was writing: They compel the poor to live
upon a crust of bread by soft mild arts: / They reduce the man
to want, then give with pomp and ceremony.)

The price of bread comes into some verses of a famous
satirist of the time, Peter Pindar, the Devonshire-born Dr
John Wolcot. George III questions his bailiff Frost:

> 'How, how went sheep a score? how corn and hay?'
> 'An't please Your Majesty, a charming price:
> Corn very soon will be as dear as spice.'
> 'Thank God! But say, say, do the poor complain?
> Hey, hey, will wheat be sixpence, Frost, a grain?'
> 'I hope *not*, sire; for great were then my fears
> That Windsor would be pulled about our ears.'
> 'Frost, Frost, no politics—no, no, Frost, no . . .'

The king is on holiday at Weymouth. Pitt comes with news
that the counter-revolutionary Vendée uprising is collapsing.

> Hey, hey—what, what?—beat, beat?—what, beat again?
> Well, well, more money—raise more men, more men.
> But mind, Pitt, hey—mind, huddle up the news.
> *Coin* something, and the growling land amuse:
> Make all the sans-culottes to Paris caper,
> And Rose shall print the vict'ry in his paper.

George Rose was the far from scrupulous Treasury secretary
who guided the subsidized newspapers.

At this time of official Church and King fervour, Peter
Pindar gives his middle-class readers an irreverent picture of
George III:

He breakfasts on the road, gulps tea, bolts toast.
Jokes with the waiter—witty with the host.
Runs to the garden with his morning dues,
Makes mouth at Cloacina's, reads the news.
Now mad for fruit, he scours the garden round,
Knocks every apple that he spies to ground;
Loads every royal pocket. . . .

He buys a load of hay at a bargain price by alleging that it smells bad. But a Dorset pig-farmer won't be tricked:

'Poor, farmer, poor—lean, lousy, very poor—
Sell, sell, hey, sell?' 'Iss, measter, to be zure:
My pigs were made for zale, but what o' that?
Yow caall mun *lean;* now zur, I caall mun *vat.*
Measter, I baant a starling—can't be cort.
Yow think, agosh, to ha' the pigs vor *nort.*'

A one-legged sailor begs for alms:

'Wife and nine children, hey? all, all alive?
No—no—no wonder that you cannot thrive.
Shame, shame, to fill your hut with such a train!
Shame to get brats for *others* to maintain!'

A footnote says: 'Is not this sarcasm as applicable to *thrones* as *hovels?*'

When the king rode in his coach to open parliament that autumn, a hostile crowd hissed and groaned, and shouted 'No Pitt, no war—bread, bread—peace, peace!' Some men also shouted 'Down with George!' and 'No king!' Symbols of despair were displayed: tiny black-draped loaves of bread held up on the ends of sticks. In Parliament Street demonstrators pelted the coach with filth, and smashed some of its panes with stones. A bullet from an airgun allegedly pierced one of the panes. No loyalists in the streets dared turn on the protesters. When the king was returning to Buckingham House, some of the mob were able—despite the alert the guards had had—to halt the coach and open a door. One man claimed at a London Corresponding Society meeting that night that he found the king on the floor, seized him by the collar, and was dragging him out when a troop of guards galloped up. The coach had a further battering while returning to the stables, and boys sold fragments of its panes for sixpence or a shilling.

Were the guards of little effect because many of them sympathized with the people? A radical report of the incident, *Truth and Treason!*, says, 'A number of persons dressed like the Foot Guards when *not* on duty were seen . . . joining in the general uproar. . . . What monstrous ingratitude, to assist in disturbing the peace of so kind a king and master . . . who protects them from being whipped like dogs!' This pamphlet also says:

> Besides other vendors of *democratic* publications about the park, there was a *vile miscreant* near the palace gate with a great bundle of books and papers, crying out, 'The Rights of Man for a penny'.

A guards officer who seized this man was knocked down, and the miscreant was carried about in triumph. Of the few whom the police managed to arrest, one, a printer, spent the next five years in jail for shouting 'No George, no war'.

This riot came three days after the London Corresponding Society had held a vast reform meeting in Copenhagen Fields, Islington. There were three platforms; the LCS claimed 150,000 were present. A speech by John Thelwall reflected the problems that French dissensions created for English reformers. Only three weeks before, a young officer called Buonaparte had used 'a whiff of grapeshot' in Paris to put down demonstrators disillusioned by the way their revolution was going. The republic had produced an embryo emperor. 'I venerate, I esteem, I adore the principles upon which the French Revolution has been established,' said Thelwall; but for six years the French had been 'cutting each other's throats' and losing sight of their first objects.

Thelwall spoke for equality: 'I do not mean equality of property. That is totally impossible in the present state of human intellect and industry. . . . The equality I mean is equality of rights . . . the equality which protects the poor against the insults and oppressions of the rich, as well as the rich against the insults and invasions of the poor.'

In the past, Thelwall had said, 'Property is nothing but human labour.' Now he was watching his words:

Perhaps before twilight information may be lodged at the Privy Council that I am making an inflammatory harangue to persuade you to level property and murder all the proprietors. But I have taken care, by having a shorthand writer at my elbow, that they shall not be able to prove me to have said anything that I do not say.

He urged everyone to avoid violence, which would only help 'the tottering cause of despotism and corruption'. He reiterated the warning in a lecture on the day after the attack on the king, and said, 'Political lectures are not the cause of these disturbances; nor are political associations; but *this* is!' And he held up a halfpenny loaf that weighed only two ounces. (The weight of loaves was varied according to the price of flour.) 'Many of you remember,' he said, 'when a half-penny roll was a breakfast for a man who had not a very extravagant appetite. What will this atom of bread do?'

Pitt used the tumult to justify the swift passage of laws to silence agitation. A conviction for treason became possible for words alone; merely to incite hatred or contempt of the government became a crime; political lectures such as Thelwall's became 'disorderly meetings'; every public meeting required the consent of magistrates. During debate on these measures, the Bishop of Rochester boldly uttered in the Lords what others said less publicly: 'I do not know what the mass of the people have to do with the laws but to obey them.' Without Pitt's new code, he said, 'the guillotine might soon be erected in our streets'. Pitt seems to have been equally alarmed; he said to his friend Wilberforce, 'My head would be off in six months were I to resign.'

Believers in free speech fought back as best they could. Peter Pindar produced *Liberty's Last Squeak*, which includes an elegy for satire:

No more must ye laugh at an ass;
No more run on topers a rig,
Since Pitt gets as drunk as Dundas
And Dundas gets as drunk as a pig.

Liberty's Last Squeak

In 'Ode to an Informer', Pindar says:

> Whoever says that Majesty is *rich*,
> Or calls Dame Schwellenberg a *smuggling b----*,
> Or swears hypocrisy has dwelt in *courts*,
> Blasphemes, speaks treason, and with edge-tools sports. . . .
> Whoever christens but his *dog* Tom Paine
> (And many an itching tongue can scarce refrain),
> The cur and master shall be brought to shame. . . .
> What journeyman will dare to mention *wages?*
> Who talk about the hardships of the poor?
> Off with the villains to their iron cages.

Before the end of the month, truth surpassed satire. A Bloomsbury barber was brought into court for inscribing over his door, *Citizen Ward, Shaver to the Swinish Multitude.* His answer was so good that it was recorded in a print: 'Please your worship, I had advice of counsel. He said I was a great fool for so doing, but your worship would be a greater if you took any notice of it.'

Fox, arguing unavailingly against the new laws, said if grievances could not be discussed, the people had no alternative 'but to use violent means'. Thelwall, at the last mass reform meeting of the 1790s, said, 'Do not be afraid of having your throats cut by the military. . . . When they will not suffer us to reason any longer, why then you know we reasoning beings can no longer advise you what measures to pursue.'

But there was no uprising (except for Ireland in 1798). The corresponding societies dwindled; 1795 was their peak. Working-class radicalism went underground for twenty years.

The disaffected of the realm were very nearly deprived in January 1796 of their 'prince of whales'. He decided to kill himself. Three days after Princess Caroline had given birth to a daughter, a potential successor to the throne, he wrote a will leaving everything he possessed (except one shilling for Caroline), not to his current mistress, Lady Jersey, but to *my Maria Fitzherbert, my wife, the wife of my heart & soul . . . my true & real wife, & who is dearer to me, even millions of times dearer to me, than that life I am now going to resign.* He says, and perhaps believes, that the cause of their parting was that his 'too credulous heart' accepted 'the basest of calumnies' against her (from Lady Jersey?), and 'base, vile and calumnious wretches calumniated me to her'. He asks to be buried with a miniature of her *'placed right upon my heart'*. When Mrs Fitzherbert dies, the sides of their two coffins are to be removed so that the coffins can be soldered together. It was the age of feverish romantic novels.

But the prince lived on, still in the thraldom of Lady Jersey, who was called 'bewitching' by Queen Charlotte and 'the old sorceress' by *The Times*. Someone else called her a sorceress, and to the prince's face. His friend Jack Payne wrote to a friend: 'He cried like a child over me, while I said, "You must escape the clutches of the vile sorceress in *the next room*, or you will be undone." "Stay, stay a little," was the only reply.'

Caricatures showed the prince being escorted to Lady Jersey's bedroom by a servile, candle-bearing Lord Jersey; or, grossly fat as he already was, being carried to her on the back of this gaunt sixty-year-old Master of the Horse. When Princess Caroline wrote to the prince to complain of being neglected and of having to dine with her sinful Lady of the Bedchamber, the prince replied that Lady Jersey was 'a woman who I declared to you on your arrival not to be *my mistress*, as you indecorously term her, but a friend'. To his mother, he called Caroline 'the vilest wretch this world ever was cursed with', and complained of 'her entire want of all principle'.

Politics gave Caroline allies. The government-guided *True Briton* accused the prince's friends of working to blacken the princess's name, and said:

As to the *gentleman* principally concerned, we are afraid he is incorrigible—*a total disregard* to the opinions of the world seems to mark every part of his conduct. . . . We have long looked upon his conduct as favouring the cause of Jacobinism and democracy . . . more than all the speeches of Horne Tooke or all the labours of the Corresponding Society.

The prince was so angry that he misread this as an accusation of Jacobinism. Sending the report to George III, he said, 'Your Majesty will observe the infamous falsity asserted with respect to my political sentiments.' Was the prince less foolish than Marie Antoinette? The blindness of royal profligates is made a byword only if they are overthrown.

Public feeling rose so high that in June 1796 Lady Jersey went into hiding for fear of a mob attack on the house in Pall Mall to which the Jerseys had moved to be near Carlton House. Whenever Caroline went out, she was hailed with applause. The prince instructed Thomas Erskine to prosecute 'every paragraph, every pamphlet, that can be construed into a libel'. And he broadened his efforts to influence the press, with the help of a diligent Irishman in his entourage, John McMahon, the secretary, go-between, gossip-collector, paragraph-monger and pimp who became his Privy Purse. In the course of his visits to the papers, money in hand, to stifle a paragraph here and inspire another there, McMahon learned that a shabby journalist, John Williams, who had served in the entourage of the late Earl of Barrymore, and thus knew a good deal, was about to publish a satire on the prince, *The New Brighton Guide*. McMahon managed 'to turn the edge of his weapon', as he put it to the prince; 'his work will embrace much essential matter'. The result is odd. The heart of the book is a rollicking account of dissipation. The Brighton Pavilion speaks:

> I have seen him inwove with a pestilent crew,
> Who nine-tenths came undone, and the rest to undo!
> . . . His Highness, not knowing my woes or displeasure,
> Renewed the broad catch, and refilled every measure.
> Thus they swilled and reswilled, and repeated their boozings
> Till their shirts became dyed with purpureal oozings.

There is nothing the prince's toad-eaters would not do for him:

> When the munching of immature codlings might gripe him,
> They would tear out the leaves of the psalter to wipe him.
> Yet these summer-fed vermin will fly him, if e'er
> His wintery fortunes should leave his trunk bare.

They post up rude songs:

> And Morris's bawdry's been nailed to my sides . . .
> And I sweat and I writhe when the sensual peruse.

One of their favourites, which lived on, was Morris's 'The Plenipotentiary', which celebrates the delight of London ladies in an envoy from Algiers 'whose bollocks were heavy and hairy'.

After many pages exposing the prince, Williams's book suddenly attacks Princess Caroline. She is 'systematic in the exposure of herself at the opera, and of herself and her child at the windows at Carlton House and the balcony looking into St James's Park, and riding in her carriage with the child at the window, every Sunday only, in Hyde Park' (when the common people were there). People are spreading stories against the prince. One of them, it is suggested, is his brother William, and another 'Mrs Robinson, or the Perdita, or the *lame Sappho*' (illness had crippled her), even though 'she is receiving an annuity of £500 from the bounty of the prince'. Caroline is counselled to be humble like her sister-in-law the Duchess of York, who, while the duke gambled all night at Brooks's, would 'sit in her carriage and wait . . . with the most fascinating resignation'.

All the arts of a dozen McMahons could not have made the prince's life seem worthy. The following year, while Williams was producing a new pamphlet which even managed to eulogize Lady Jersey, the prince came half-drunk to a ball given by a great hostess, the Duchess of Gordon, and said to North's daughter, Lady Glenbervie, 'I know none of these fine people of the present day, and none of them know me.' Indeed, people were refusing invitations to dinners at which the heir to the throne would be present.

Pitt's new laws could not silence all bitter comments on high-living prodigals. Peter Pindar's 'Resignation, an Ode to the Journeyman Shoemakers who Refused to Work Except their Wages were Raised' (reprinted by little Thomas Spence) looks at Anne Luttrell, Duchess of Cumberland, merry in widowhood:

Liberty's Last Squeak

Behold a hundred coaches at her door,
Where faro triumphs in his mad career.
We *must* support her—or by hook or crook—
For, lo, her husband was—a royal duke.
We *must* support too her fine gold-laced crew
Behind her gilt coach, dancing molly fellows,   [*effeminate*
With canes and ruffles goodly to the view,
And (suiting their complexions) pink umbrellas.
It must be so, for lordly grandeur rules . . .

Anne Luttrell's brother, the one-time mock-member, had risen to a high command in Ireland and was busy refining the techniques of half-hanging, flogging and pitch-capping.

The fight against democratic ideas became ever more thorough. John Reeves's association 'printed a large number of what they called loyal songs, and gave them to the ballad-singers', the reformer Francis Place recalled twenty-five years later. 'If anyone was found singing any but loyal songs, he or she was carried before a magistrate . . . and told they might have loyal songs for nothing, and would not be molested while singing them.' It was at this time, too, that James Gillray was tamed with a pension.

Pitt broadened his press guidance by sending free copies of his subsidized papers to provincial editors, with articles to be reprinted marked in the margin. He also helped his follower, young George Canning, to launch *The Anti-Jacobin*, a weekly that carried ministerial articles, denounced 'lies' in the opposition newspapers, which Canning called 'Jacobin prints', and lampooned radicals. In a parody on the dactyls of Robert Southey (who in fact had by then renounced all his revolutionary ideas), Canning mocked Jacobinical agitators:

Come, little drummer-boy, lay down your knapsack here:
I am the soldier's friend—here are some books for you,
Nice clever books by Tom Paine the philanthropist.
Here's half-a-crown for you—here are some handbills too—
Go to the barracks and give all the soldiers some.
Tell them the sailors are all in a mutiny . . .

This was just a few months after the suppression of mass mutinies in the navy.

Canning sardonically pictures 'La Sainte Guillotine' in action after a conquest by Napoleon:

And our bishops and judges will stare with amazement
When their heads are thrust out at the National Casement!
When the National Razor has shaved them quite clean,
What a handsome oblation to Sainte Guillotine!

The National Casement is what the French called *la petite fenêtre:* the aperture through which a victim thrust his head before the blade came down.

If Napoleon had invaded, would the home front have been secure? The silencing of the reformers was not accompanied by one concession to the lower orders. They were even told that hunger was good for them. 'Perhaps that very scarcity has been permitted by an all-wise and gracious Providence,' wrote Hannah More in 1801, 'to *unite* all ranks of people *together*, to show the *poor* how immediately they are dependent on the *rich*.' In the same year Thomas Spence, who had already served several terms in jail, published a pamphlet in which he called the great landowners 'a warlike enemy quartered upon us'. He spoke of the Duke of Portland, a Whig now serving as Home Secretary, on whose vast estates it was perilous for a poor man to pick even a nut, and he asked:

What must I say to the French if they come? If they jeeringly ask me what I am fighting for? Must I tell them, For my country? For my dear country in which I dare not pluck a nut? Would they not laugh at me? . . . I would throw down my musket, saying, Let such as the Duke of Portland, who claims the country, fight for it, for I am but as a stranger and sojourner.

This seditious libel got him twelve months. From Shrewsbury Jail he wrote to a friend: 'I have long been reduced to the bare jail allowance, which is a small loaf of bread and an ounce of butter per day. Now I believe very few would think this sufficient aliment. . . . Tea and sugar would very much oblige. . . .' When he came out, reduced at the age of fifty-two to selling books from a barrow in Oxford Street, he and his followers would walk the streets at night to chalk on the walls

'Spence's Plan and full bellies' and 'The land is the people's farm.'

In 1803, when Napoleon's invasion threat had Britain in a patriotic flurry, it was still thought necessary to frighten and cajole poor labourers with broadsides asserting that if the French came, Englishmen would have to work in slave-gangs, would be fed on horse-beans and ditchwater, would see their wives and daughters raped. And this was the reply to Spence:

> There are some labouring people so deluded as to think they have nothing to lose if the French shall conquer this island. Money, they say, they have none; their goods are not worth an enemy's taking; work must be had, whoever is master . . .
>
> What is a day-labourer's condition at present?
>
> . . . It is his own fault if he has not a tight dwelling over his head, warm clothing, and plenty of wholesome food. If he is a good manager in the main, he can afford a pot of beer on a holy-day upon occasion. . . .

A quart pot cost the labourer nearly a third of his day's wage. A fifth of the nation's taxes was being raised on beer alone. Here was the reality behind the propaganda prints that displayed a contented John Bull with his ever-foaming pot.

12

Fond Aged Lover

'I SHALL REJOICE sincerely if any halcyon days are coming to the poor Whigs,' wrote Sydney Smith, the irreverent parson, to Lady Holland, the great Whig hostess, 'but the sovereign has a deplorable knack of recovering.' It was January 1811 and George III had lapsed into delirium for the third time since 1789. He was seventy-two and nearly blind. The Whigs conferred with the Prince of Wales on a Cabinet list and reviewed contenders for 'the loaves and fishes', as political rewards were called. George III did not display his deplorable knack; and yet the Whigs' hopes were dashed. Another royal mind was their undoing: the mind of the prince.

By February 1st a regency had been agreed, and the Tory ministers were sure they were out; on February 2 a few astute Tories at White's Club began putting money on their party staying in; on February 3 they were proved right, and outside Carlton House 'the whole of Pall Mall was crowded with knots of Opposition . . . all in very bad humour'.

> I need not remind you how cursedly bad
> Our affairs were all looking when father went mad.
> A strait-waistcoat on him and restrictions on me—
> A more *limited* monarchy could not well be . . .
> I thought the best way, as a dutiful son,
> Was to do as Old Royalty's self would have done.
> So I sent word to say I would keep the whole batch in—
> The same chest of tools without cleaning or patching.

184

Fond Aged Lover

This parody of a self-justifying letter of the prince came from another frequenter of Holland House, little Thomas Moore.

> Think—only think—if our father should find
> Upon graciously coming again to his mind
> That improvement had spoiled any favourite adviser . . .
> What a shock to his old royal heart it would be!

This had indeed been one of the arguments used on the agitated prince, a notorious vacillator and coward, in an eleventh-hour letter from the queen herself. The queen was asked to write the letter, it was said, by the most Tory of her sons, Ernest Duke of Cumberland, who was bullying the prince to forget the Whigs.

Another influence on the prince was Mrs Fitzherbert. In 1799, with the consent of the Pope, she had resumed living with her bigamous husband, after he had threatened to declare his marriage to her, 'relinquish everything for you, rank, situation, birth, & if that is not sufficient, my life shall go also'. For the next eight years, said Mrs Fitzherbert in her old age, they were 'merry as crickets'. Then she was pushed aside on £6,000 a year, and settled down not far from the prince's pavilion at Brighton. In 1811 she came suddenly to London and saw the prince—the day before he dished the Whigs. Some Tories had been talking of requiring the prince to declare that he was not married to a papist; so that spectre of 1788 may well have helped to keep the Tories in.

Perhaps a Whig prince is in any case unnatural; but a further influence was unquestionably the woman who had supplanted Mrs Fitzherbert: the Marchioness of Hertford, a portly grandmother born in 1760. She and her marquess were high Tories, and one of their nephews was Lord Castlereagh, who would never have been Foreign Secretary and Leader of the Commons for the next ten years if the Whigs had got in. The Hertfords' annual income was at least £100,000; but they were notorious for their avarice, and within a few months the cuckold-husband became the regent's £3,000-a-year Lord Chamberlain, and his son, the disreputable Earl of Yarmouth, Vice-Chamberlain.

And it pleased me to find at the house where, you know,
There's such good mutton cutlets and strong curaçao,
That the marchioness called me a duteous old boy,
And my Y-rm--th's red whiskers grew redder for joy!

Thomas Moore says that cutlets and curaçao are the prince's
'favourite luncheon'.

The prince had become a constant visitor to Hertford House
in Manchester Square (now the Wallace Collection) in 1807. It
was not a platonic attachment. Torn between Mrs Fitzherbert
and the new love, he wept in front of his guests. He made himself ill, and used the illness to woo Lady Hertford (a technique
he had practised with Mrs Fitzherbert twenty years before).
'I really believe his father's malady extends to him, only takes
another turn,' wrote Lady Bessborough in 1807. 'He writes
day and night almost, and frets himself into a fever, and all to
persuade *la sua bella donnone to live with him—publicly!!*'
When the Hertfords were in Warwickshire at their chief
country house, Ragley, he invented crises to bring his 'ever
dearest' back to 'poor me, wretched me'. Yet he still lunged
amorously at other women, including the ageing Lady Bessborough: 'Such a scene I never went through . . . after another
long tirade, threw himself on his knees, and clasping me round,
kissed my neck before I was aware . . . I screamed . . . he
continued sometimes struggling with me, sometimes sobbing
. . . Vows of eternal love . . . he would break with Mrs. F. and
Lady H., I should *make my own terms!!* I should be his sole
confidant, sole adviser—Mr Canning should be prime minister. . . . That immense, grotesque figure flouncing about,
half on the couch, half on the ground. . . .' He gave up after
two hours, then spent two hours telling stories, his other great
pleasure next to eating and drinking.

When this man got the power to make or break governments, he was drinking as unwisely as in his youth, and was
also taking large doses of laudanum—a habit to which he often
returned. The agitations and delights of power (his first
thought was to change the leading regiments' uniforms) so
overset him that his brother Ernest went round saying that the
prince's illness 'was higher than the foot'. From the first he

was assailed with abuse and ridicule, partly inspired by the
betrayed Whigs. 'We all encouraged every species of satire
against him and his mistress,' Lord Holland, the nephew of
Fox, recalled afterwards. As late as 1825, the victim still spoke
bitterly of Thomas Moore's verses, 'in which he introduced in
the most ungentlemanlike and I will even say *unmanly* way
the names of Lady Hertford and other ladies'. Ridicule was
what the prince always feared. He was probably wounded
most by the picture painted by Moore (who had formerly fre-
quented Carlton House) of a prince who was less than a
gentleman. Moore called him a bird of prey, 'half-way/'Twixt
the goose and the vulture, like Lord C-stl----gh'. His way of life
was 'a sick epicure's dream, incoherent and gross'. In *The
Morning Chronicle* Moore printed the mock diary of a Tory
politician:

> Through M-nch-st-r Square took a canter just now—
> Met the *old yellow chariot*, and made a low bow.
> This I did of course thinking 'twas loyal and civil,
> But got such a look—oh, 'twas black as the devil!
> How unlucky! *Incog.* he was trav'lling about,
> And I, like a noodle, must go find him out!
> *Mem.:* When next by the old yellow chariot I ride,
> To remember there *is* nothing princely inside.

An array of wits—Byron, Charles Lamb, Samuel Rogers, even
the young Shelley—joined Moore in firing verse squibs at the
regent in *The Morning Chronicle* and in Leigh Hunt's *Examiner*. A less poetic tormentor of the Tories was an ambitious
Whig barrister, Henry Brougham. His satirical techniques are
well illustrated in some advice he sent a few years earlier to
Holland House:

> Different people should at their spare hours be reading
> Shakespeare and Swift with a view to selecting passages
> suitable to the time, as, descriptions of base courtiers, par-
> ticular characters of bad ministers, hits at bishops (if safe),
> etc. . . . Little biographical sketches of the new ministers—
> extremely concise—not very violent—exposing them rather
> to contempt . . . by leaving out whatever they have done

of a serious or important kind . . . dwelling on the laughable or trifling parts of their history.

There were fewer wits on the Tory side—though according to the prince regent, Lady Hertford herself contributed anti-Whig squibs to *The Morning Herald*, where the ageing Bate Dudley was still earning his subsidy. In the field of higher policy, a subtle operator on the ministerial side was John Wilson Croker—an Admiralty secretary, and much more besides. Years later, to a young man thinking of starting a Tory paper, he described how to convey ministers' thoughts to the public:

> They supplied the *fact* and I supplied the *tact*, and between us we used to produce a considerable effect. . . . Every possible precaution against even a suspicion should be taken. . . . Throw in here and there such a slight mixture of error or apparent ignorance as should obviate suspicion of its coming from so high a source. . . . The success of that period . . . was so complete that it turned the press—I mean the preponderating part of the press—right round.

Whatever the 'preponderating part' might do, the regent was a sad figure, mocked for his wigs and whiskers, his gout and fatness, his drinking, gorging, fetes, palaces, tailors and women. Lady Hertford, 'the Sultana', 'the old Lady of Manchester Square', was denounced in the Lords as 'the matured enchantress'. Lord Grey, leader of the Whigs since the death of Fox in 1806, talked of 'an unseen and separate influence that lurked behind the throne . . . leading to consequences the most pestilential and disgusting'. This inspired a caricature of Lady Hertford manipulating ministerial puppets and saying, 'I can make them do anything. . . . Why, I have had the honour of performing before the regent!' Her puppet-theatre announces, 'The piece called Secret Influence will be continued some time longer.'

It was a high time for caricaturists. James Gillray had by this date withdrawn into madness; but a brilliant successor, George Cruikshank, had arrived. Gillray had been the young Cruikshank's hero. Years later, when Gillray's work-table came up to auction at 27 St. James's Street, Cruikshank bought it, and used it for the rest of his life. Another work-table was a much earlier inspiration: that of his own father, Isaac Cruikshank, who in the 1790s and almost up to his death in 1811 was next in importance to Gillray. George remembered sitting as a little boy and watching his father draw and etch. Soon he was learning the art; and by the time of the regency, though he was not yet twenty, he had produced scores of caricatures.

George Cruikshank had great fun with the bloated regent, his big-breasted sultana, and all his court. In 'An Excursion to R[agley] Hall', the cuckold-horned marquess leads the procession, his son Yarmouth is arm-in-arm with the devil, and Lady Hertford is saying to the regent, 'We have had a glorious ride, my love.' They are passing a Female Asylum; ex-mistresses weep at the windows. 'He has forgot his poor F.,' Mrs Fitzherbert mourns. Another cries, 'There he goes! Oh! oh! oh! O! the gay deceiver.' This was one of a long series of Cruikshank caricatures in a bold new monthly, *The Scourge*. Another, 'The Court of Love,' shows contenders for the regent's bounty stating their claims:

DUKE OF YORK: I am proud to say that the greater part of my life has been passed in the commission of adultery . . .

DUKE OF CLARENCE: I have lived in adultery with an actress for twenty-five years and have a pretty number of illegitimate children.

HERTFORD: My gracious master is personally acquainted with my merits, they live in his bosom.

YARMOUTH: I'm Vice all over.

MARQUESS OF HEADFORT, Lord of the Bedchamber (he had paid £10,000 damages for adultery): Adultery is my motto.

McMahon, the Privy Purse, busy at his pimping, pours golden sovereigns into a bawd's apron and says, 'Let her be forty at least, plump and sprightly.'

A little later *The Scourge* pretends to give the regent some advice: 'You must have a private secretary very like yourself. . . . Suddenly to procure such a man is difficult: therefore bring one up for the purpose. Any little pimp is a good subject to begin with. . . .' And *The Scourge* addresses Pandar Jackall:

Thou art formed those She's to find
Suited to thy master's mind:
And in choosing 'tis thy care
To take *forty, fat and fair.*
. . . Jackall, 'tis thy luck
To get boozy with Old Buck.

It was also his luck to be the person to whom supplicants for jobs and titles came, money in hand. His wife shared in the trade. She is said to have died with £14,000 in a drawer. 'They all came to see her for places,' says William Knighton, who later served the regent. In the end McMahon got too boozy. The regent was worried 'lest there should be a disclosure of secrets', says Knighton. On McMahon's last day at Carlton House, he waited two hours, in vain, for the regent to say goodbye. His secret papers were all in the hands of his successor, Benjamin Bloomfield.

The more the regent was mocked and condemned, the more fawningly was he praised in the papers he paid. In March 1812, Leigh Hunt was disgusted by 'a set of commonplace lines in French, Italian, Spanish and English' in *The Morning Post*, 'literally addressing the prince regent in the following terms. . . . "You are the glory of the people. . . . Wherever you appear you conquer all hearts, wipe away tears, excite desire and love, and win beauty towards you. You breathe eloquence—you inspire the Graces—you are an Adonis in loveliness." ' Who would imagine, Hunt commented in *The Examiner*

> that this Glory of the People was the subject of millions of shrugs and reproaches! . . . That this Conqueror of Hearts was the disappointer of hopes! That this Exciter of Desire (bravo, Messrs of the Post!), this Adonis in Loveliness, was a corpulent gentleman of fifty! . . . A violator of his word, a libertine over head and ears in debt and disgrace, a despiser of domestic ties, a man who has just closed half a century without one single claim on the gratitude of his country or the respect of posterity!

For this, Hunt was jailed for two years and fined £1,000. He went on editing his paper from prison. Nor were other critics silenced; least of all the caricaturists, or the writers who throughout the regency produced a flood of verses in the tradition of Peter Pindar, and often under his name. It would have been difficult to prosecute, for example, *The R---l Brood*, in which George III's children are cocks and hens:

> The foremost of the r---- brood
> Who broke his shell and cried for food
> Turned out a cock of manners rare,
> A fav'rite with the feathered fair. . . .
> But though his love was sought by all,
> Game, dunghill, bantam, squab and tall,
> Among the whole, not one in ten
> Could please him like a tough old hen.

These verse pamphlets were generally not Whig-inspired, but aimed at a public disillusioned with both sides. *The R---l Brood* says the rejected Whigs 'for years at his desire/Had grubbed in every sort of mire', and asks,

> Who heeds their artful cropsick call
> Or feels compassion at their fall?

Another 'Pindar' pamphlet placed the whole profligate history of the regent in another kingdom—Gotham, the traditional land of fools—where

> Husbands would prostitute their wives,
> To live like courtiers all their lives. . . .
> And sons were found to sell their mothers. . . .
> Well-bred cuckolds, pimps and peers,
> And lechers old in sin and years
> Kept sinking Gotham in arrears.

How different from the regent's court!

> No gamesters, cuckolds, pimps are there,
> But gentle lords, and ladies fair. . . .
> There's Y--m--th's lord, who from his birth
> Has proved a miracle of worth,
> And H--t--d, fairest nymph on earth. . . .

The regent was incapable of changing his ways. He sent out

McMahon (and afterwards Bloomfield) to suppress what he could:

> Mac recalled to mind full well
> His tedious journeys through Pall Mall,
> And how one foot outran the other
> To bribe to silence, or to smother. . . .
> How oft to Coutts he used to range . . .
> To give the scribblers what they wanted.

In his first years of power the regent might have hoped to feel more secure. The Whigs were, as usual, weak and split. The war turned at last against Napoleon, and in 1814 London welcomed emperors, kings and princes for a victory celebration. The regent's wife, a constant reminder of his undomestic ways and a focus for popular feeling, left for the Continent, intent on being 'a happy, merry soul'. The regent is said to have drunk a toast to her damnation—'and may she never return to England'.

And yet he was in a bad way. Even at the time of the celebration he was assailed in the streets with hisses, groans and insults. 'All agree that Prinny will die or go mad,' Thomas Creevey, the Whig wit who had formerly been a favourite guest of the prince, wrote to his wife. 'He is worn out with fuss, fatigue and *rage*.' At a dinner with his royal guests he was 'beastly drunk'.

The war had helped to gag reformers for more than twenty years, but it stimulated thought, especially when blatant royal dissipation was accompanied by high taxes and inefficiency and injustice. As early as 1801, the prince's ex-parasite, George Hanger, wrote, 'I am quite dismayed at the learning of the common people; for there is not a tap-boy at a public house, or a ticket porter, that does not every evening read the debates in parliament, and who cannot talk to you now about the Bill of Rights, the fundamental principles of the constitution, and Magna Carta.' (Hanger was by no means against all innovations. He was delighted that women had thrown off their corsetry and were wearing diaphanous dresses.) Statistics support Hanger: the number of newspaper tax stamps issued rose from fourteen million in 1790 to twenty-two million in 1816, even though the tax on knowledge had been raised by then to fourpence a copy. The tap-boys, and all newspaper readers in public houses and coffee-houses, studied debate after debate in which ministers defended strange things against the attacks of a few persistent but powerless critics; things they could comprehend, such as the fact stated by Lord Cochrane, a naval officer, that the £20,000-plus sinecures enjoyed by two peers 'would victual the officers and men serving in . . . 117 sail of the line, 105 frigates, 27 sloops, 50 hulks', or that three such sinecures would maintain the Portsmouth and Plymouth dockyards. And what was that compared to the cost of Prinny? Neither the war nor postwar misery curbed his childish squandering of money he did not have (by 1811 new debts totalled £522,000) among architects, builders, decorators, furniture-makers, jewellers (Lady Hertford adored diamonds), tailors, caterers, wine-merchants, and parasites of both sexes. In 1815, after thirty-two years in Carlton House, and amid riots against the bill that the landed gentry were pushing through parliament to keep up the price of grain, he was still improving and refurnishing the place. A few of the many items that the public heard about were: A clock £735, 2 pair candelabra £1,575, 3 cabinets £1,500, 2 pictures of himself set in diamonds £1,435, a brilliant star £3,155. Out at Windsor he amused himself by having John Nash build The Cottage, a thatched, mock-gothic retreat. Then there was his most splendid hobby, that incoherent £500,000 fantasy, the Brighton Pavilion. On the pavilion's stables and riding-house alone, the prince spent £55,000 during the lowest years of the war— almost enough to raise a new regiment. In 1816 the cabinet told him that if he did not stop all further spending on the pavilion, the government might fall. He spent as much as ever. In a *Scourge* caricature, he exclaims, 'D--n such economy, say I! Why, I might as well turn to eating husks at once!' The large sums that went to the royal family and to the many hundreds of placemen and pensioners whose names could be discovered were listed by a radical publisher in *The Extraordinary Red Book*. A frontispiece shows a starving John Bull watching a procession of the fortunate ones, notably a sly, hideous Queen Charlotte (her jewel collection was worth, according to the royalist John Wilson Croker, £200,000) and a gouty regent on crutches, saying, 'The cash I have is for drinking, eating, sleeping and w---ing.'

Could satire amend a prince who scorned his ministers' pleas—who even insolently kept them waiting in an outer room while he conferred with his tailor? One of the regency Peter Pindars said of his own verses that they

> So moved our r----t great, that he
> Keeps sober now, sometimes, till tea;
> Have made our q---n so generous,
> She lately from her private purse
> Gave *one and threepence* to the *poor*. . . .

And as for the Duke of York

> He now so very chaste has grown,
> He even leaves the maids alone.

A less playful note was increasingly heard, especially in the work of a radical London publisher, John Fairburn. His 'Prayer and Supplication' of John Bull says:

> Send packing each cornuted brute
> And eke each noble prostitute. . . .
> Build no more palaces, lest they
> Should fall about your ears some day. . . .
> If all things rise so high and fast,
> Your people, sire, will rise at last.

And his 'John Bull's Liturgy':

> From rulers who, with pal and punk,
> Spend all the night in getting drunk
> And all the day in titivating
> Their p-----ly persons, business hating,
> > *Good Lord deliver us.*

> From hireling scribblers—venal presses—
> Who'd *write* us out of our distresses;
> Who think fine words as good as meat;
> That only great should drink and eat,
> > *Good Lord deliver us.*

Fond Aged Lover

From quartern loaf which, when we crave,
We must pay *eighteen-pence* to have;
From beer that *fivepence* is a pot;
From beef at *tenpence*, good or not,
Good Lord deliver us.

It was during the regency, which some historians now speak of as a glorious period, that the word 'radical', a political adjective since at least 1769, became a political noun. (Lord Holland's secretary writes in 1816 of the Whigs having 'no communication with the Radicals of any description'.) The poor were no longer willing to keep silent. Hannah More was busy at seventy reviving the dialogues of Jack Anvil and Tom Hod, but the poor were inclined to heed her less than William Cobbett, who was selling 50,000 a week of his *Political Register*, the 'twopenny trash', and was telling them that Hannah's tracts were meant to teach them 'to starve without making a noise'. Neither Robespierre nor Napoleon could be invoked now to stifle them. But the frightened government of Lord Liverpool (son of Charles Jenkinson) and Lord Castlereagh, supported by a parliament as safely ministerial as North's forty years earlier, was determined to yield nothing.

Wherever the new generation of reformers spoke up, the Home Secretary, Lord Sidmouth, had his local agent (a postmaster, lawyer, magistrate, clergyman or simple paid informer) to send reports. And so the Home Office files still contain the news that in Hull in 1816 a grocer was distributing 1,500 a week of Cobbett's paper 'and women who never could talk politics are now warm for Cobbett'; and that in Norwich reformers had established clubs at the King's Head, the Lord Howe, the Bushel, and were 'very industriously' circulating handbills saying

We have been engaged in a long, bloody and expensive war . . . we have beaten Bonaparte, we have shut him up in St. Helena, we have shouted for victory, but alas! in the extravagance of our joy, we forgot the reckoning that was to be paid, the enormous debt of One Thousand Millions which this war had brought upon us, the intolerable burthen of

taxes necessary to pay the interest of this debt. . . . War is
the hotbed of profusion, of plundering jobs without end. . . .

And all this to restore (as a Birmingham handbill put it) 'a
dynasty which had been for ages the scourge of France, the
enemy of England, and the contempt of all the thinking or
benevolent part of mankind'. This Birmingham handbill,
summoning a town meeting which more than 20,000 people
attended, speaks of 'silence in the workshops . . . and the
transformation of our once active, cheerful and high-spirited
artisans into languid, careworn and miserable scavengers'. The
Birmingham artisans demanded what they would have to go
on demanding for nearly thirty years: repeal of the corn law,
and free trade. They also, like every petitioning town, asked
parliament to reform itself, to 'restore frequent elections and
general suffrage'. The word 'restore' was aimed against the
longstanding ministerial denunciation of 'innovation'. Most
working-class reformers flatly demanded annual parliaments
and universal manhood suffrage, which they said would restore
the constitution's primitive purity: a demand that alarmed the
Whigs. Men of the corresponding societies of a quarter-century
before helped to organize a new network of 'union societies'.
New heroes arose, notably an orator in a white hat, Henry
Hunt, a big West Countryman, who invented a potent phrase
for the Red Book sinecurists: The Splendid Paupers. Old men
who could remember the disillusion of 'Wilkes and Liberty'
now shouted 'Hunt and Liberty'. Liberty caps were brought
out again, and even a green-white-red tricolor for the coming
British republic.

A republic did not seem impossible, even to the most hard-
shelled sinecurist, when the monarchy was represented by 'an
old, mad, blind, despised and dying king', a morally blind
regent, and princes and princesses in various states of expensive inutility. (Jeremy Bentham's new watchword, utility,
was then not a boring but a dangerous word.) When the regent
rode in his carriage to open parliament in January 1817, there
was a scene very like that of 1795.

> In Whitehall first rebellious groans
> Broke forth from tongues disloyal,

Fond Aged Lover

> And soon a shower of saucy stones
> Assailed the *caput* royal.

Even when in peril, the regent was a figure of fun. Something, which ministers alleged was a bullet, pierced two panes of his carriage. He is made to tell Sidmouth that he feels 'a little inward pain':

> 'Tis no corporeal hurt, that's plain,
> But perhaps a prick of conscience.

The attack gave Sidmouth the occasion to lay before parliament a collection of reports by informers on various extremists' plots. Among the plotters were a tiny band inspired by the late Thomas Spence, who despairingly dreamed of achieving his plan by violent means. Sidmouth and Castlereagh pushed through the suspension of habeas corpus and other anti-radical measures like those of the 1790s—though now it was peacetime. To check the spread of what he called 'poison', Sidmouth told all justices of the peace they could arrest anyone for selling anything they considered seditious or blasphemous; which meant that many radical hawkers were held indefinitely for lack of bail, and often in irons.

A new generation of press heroes was created. One was William Hone, a reformer since 1796 when, aged sixteen, he joined the London Corresponding Society. He was no revolutionary, but in the English tradition of dissent. He had no wish to be a martyr. As soon as Sidmouth moved to suspend habeas corpus, Hone withdrew from sale three pamphlets that had been going well at his bookshop at 67 Old Bailey: *The Late John Wilkes's Catechism of a Ministerial Member*, *The Political Litany* and *The Sinecurist's Creed*. All three were in a hallowed mode of political parody. The catechism was an adaptation of a piece published during the Wilkite uproar of 1769. Parts of it needed not a word changed:

> Thou shalt not take the pension of thy Lord the Minister in vain. . . .
> Remember that thou attend the Minister's levee day. . . .
> On other days the Minister is inaccessible, but delighteth in the levee day . . . and chatteth. . . .

Our Lord who art in the Treasury, whatsoever be thy name, thy power be prolonged. . . . Give us our usual sops, and forgive us our occasional absences on divisions. . . . Turn us not out of our places; but keep us in the House of Commons, the land of pensions and plenty; and deliver us from the people.

Some of the words of the ministerial member, Lick Spittle, are modernized:

I believe in George, the Regent Almighty, Maker of New Streets and Knights of the Bath;

And in the present ministry, his only choice, who were conceived of Toryism, brought forth of William Pitt, suffered loss of place under Charles James Fox [in 1806], were execrated, dead and buried. In a few months . . . they re-ascended to the Treasury Benches; and sit at the right hand of a little man in a large wig; from whence they *laugh* at the petitions of the people.

Hone's litany (a parody form that was used by both sides in Cromwell's time) is full of reform messages:

From the blind imbecility of ministers; from the pride and vainglory of warlike establishments in time of peace,
Good prince, deliver us!

. . . From all the deceits of the pensioned hirelings of the press,
Good prince, deliver us!

. . . From a parliament chosen only by one-tenth of the tax-payers. . . .
Good prince, deliver us!

It offers a pointed prayer for the regent: 'Keep and defend him from battle and murder and sudden death, and from fornication and all other deadly sins.'

When customers importuned Hone to go on selling the parodies, and offered as much as £1, he refused; and yet ten weeks later he was arrested in the street, and not allowed even to tell his wife before he was carried off to a cell. After a seven-

Fashionable Jockeyship: The grossly fat Prince of Wales is carried to the bed of his
~~mi~~stress of 1796, Lady Jersey, by her complaisant husband, his Master of the Horse.
~~Th~~ey play a variation of a children's game. Gillray makes Lady Jersey a witch-like
~~cr~~one; and pictures an old sow dancing to Cupid's tune. (See page 178)

35, 36 The master and his successor: pencil self-portraits of James Gillray and George Cruikshank. Gillray poses in front of some of his own caricatures. The one behind his head is of Tom Paine measuring the British crown, dating the portrait after 1791

37 *Patent Puppets:* It is 1812, the prince regent has not called on the Whigs, and his mistress, the Tory Lady Hertford, explains to John Bull that she controls the government. Lords Grenville and Grey hang up, left, 'so stiff and stubborn that I cannot do anything with them.' (See page 188)

38 *An Excursion to R[agley] Hall:* George Cruikshank presents the cornuted Lord Hertford, mounted on an ass, conducting his wife and the prince regent to his Warwickshire estate. The devil drives, hugged by the Hertford's son, Lord Yarmouth. Sheridan rides another ass, with a barrel of curaçao for a saddle. At the windows of a Female Asylum, the prince's ex-mistresses weep; notably (front left) 'his poor F'. (See page 189)

39 *Economical Humbug of 1816:* The Chancellor of the Exchequer promises John Bull postwar economies; but a stream of golden guineas pours out for the prince regent and his friends. Economy is what the regent is 'determined not to practise as long as I can get anything.'

40 R[oya]l Hobbies!!!: One of many caricatures inspired by the fad of 1819, the velocipede. 'I'll make you drive it home,' says Lady Hertford. 'You shall remember *pushing your hobby in Hertford'*. The regent is weakening. His brother

41 *A Radical Reformer*: A month after Peterloo, George Cruikshank depicts a monstrous walking guillotine, which he does not quite ask us to take seriously. The regent flees, followed by Lord Liverpool (fallen), Eldon and Castlereagh, whose bags of gold spill on the ground. (See pages 204–7, 222)

THE BATH.   CANVAS AFTER ELECTION.

" 1 2 3 4 ‖ 5 6 ‖ 7 8 9 ‖
——————— The wide sea
" Hath drops too few to wash her clean."
SHAKSPEARE.

" 1 3 5 ‖ ‖ 7 ‖ ‖ 9 ‖
" Put out the light and then ——"
SHAKSPEARE.

42, 43 *The Bath*: *Canvas after Election*: Illustrations from a verse lampoon on Queen Caroline, based on evidence at her 1820 trial that Bergami

44 *Our Fat Friend going to Roost*: December 1820; the king is depicted with uninhibited scorn. 'Our fat friend' echoes Beau Brummell's famous insulting remark about George, 'Who's your fat friend?'

A Pas de Deux or Love at first Sight.

How I'd love you all the day   If with me you'd fondly stray
Every Night we'd Kiss and Play   Over the Hills and far away.

London Published by G. Humphrey 2.nd. S.t. James's S.t. May 14. 1821

45 Queen Caroline and her lover Bergami, 'the courier so rough and so hairy'. Her figu
and strange costume are scarcely exaggerated.

"Georgy loves good Ale and Wine
And Georgy loves good Brandy
And Georgy loves his C...n...g...m
As sweet as Sugar Candy"

Georgy's Delight: The king paid caricaturists to suppress references to Lady Conyng-
am, his new mistress. Here she is named with hardly any disguise.

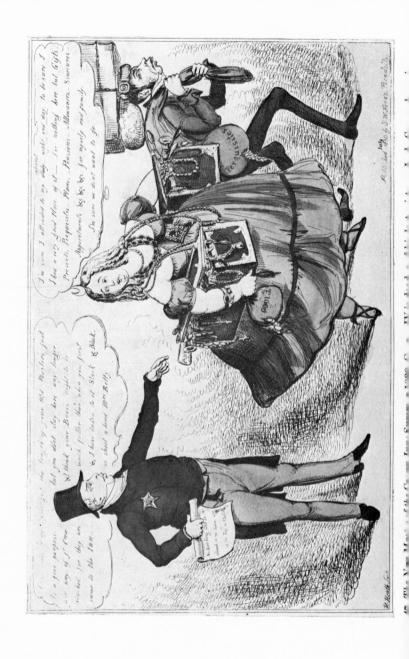

47. The New Mode of the Green Inn Sign. 1800. George Wickstead etc. Heath. Laurie & Whittle.

48 *A Regular Turn Out; or Cleansing the Augean Stable:* November 1830—John Bull, demanding reform, sweeps Wellington's government out of power (by a Commons defeat of 29 votes). The 'Waterloo idol' is pained. (See page 238)

49 *The Bull in a Rage:* The reform crisis of May 1832. The bull refuses to be enslaved
Wellington, Queen Adelaide and the Duke of Cumberland. William IV's crown fa
the hand of justice gives him a fool's cap. A tricolor replaces the tattered Union Ja
A republican message by J. L. Marks. (See pages 240–1)

A GERMAN GOVERNESS;

OR,

A RUMP AND DOZEN.

A German Governess: Adelaide, wearing the breeches, birches William IV, who is held
Wellington. She was blamed for turning the king against reform. The crisis brings out
striking new caricature style. (See page 241)

51 *Something Like Emigration*: Still the 1832 crisis. William IV is not visible on the wagon conveying him on the way to Hanover, but his shadow is thrown on the wall, where there are signs for him to read. Lord Eldon and a bishop hold papers reading 'Decapitation—Charles' and 'Abdication—James.' Wellington is the carter. This was 'a popular

month wait he went on trial at Guildhall for blasphemy—'intent to excite impiety and irreligion'. Once again political hypocrisy was at work. The attorney-general said Hone's catechism, the first item tried, 'has nothing of a political tendency about it'. Hone, conducting his own defence, quoted not from law books but from a quantity of parodies on Scripture which had never been prosecuted—lampoons against Napoleon and against English and French Jacobins—one of which was by the witty George Canning, now a member of the cabinet. 'If I am convicted,' said Hone, 'he ought to follow me to my cell.' He also produced caricatures in which Gillray—'who enjoyed a pension from His Majesty'—used scriptural parody. One pictured the apotheosis of the revolutionary general Lazare Hoche: he rises to a Jacobin heaven, his god is Equality, his commandments savagely twist the true ones.

THE JUDGE: I cannot suffer it to be read. . . . It is a wicked publication.

HONE: It was on the right side—that made all the difference.

The jury took fifteen minutes to acquit Hone. The Lord Chief Justice, the fierce Lord Ellenborough, was so disgusted that he insisted on hearing the next case himself. The attorney-general raised his tone: if Hone's litany were not stopped, the Church of England would be in danger, especially as the pamphlet was sold cheap 'to be within reach of the common people'. Again Hone relied on recent litanies that had not been touched. Some were not even ministerial:

> From four pounds of bread at sixteen-pence price,
> And butter at eighteen, though not very nice,
> And cheese at a shilling, though gnawed by the mice,
> *Good Lord deliver us!*

Ellenborough tried to silence him, but Hone replied with an eye on the jury.

ELLENBOROUGH: I will not let you be wasting time.

HONE: Wasting time, my lord! I am to be tried, not you! When I shall have been consigned to a dungeon, Your Lordship will sit as coolly on that seat as ever.

It did not end like that. The second and third juries acquitted
Hone. Huge cheering crowds sharpened Ellenborough's mortification. The next day he told Sidmouth he was going to retire.

It had been a mixed year for the government. Reform societies went underground, or held meetings on the moors.
Several small risings were smartly crushed—and then it was
revealed that Sidmouth had had not only informers but *agents
provocateurs* at work. The foredoomed risings had served to
entrap desperate men and to stir up feeling against all reformers. Hone himself revealed some other odd happenings in
his weekly *Reformist's Register*. Early in 1817 someone had
sent him an order to print placards for a nationwide display of
force: in every parish people were to assemble in the church-
yard on April 5 'armed with a rake and a small sword or
dagger' (most minute instructions for making which instru-
ments were given in the bill). They were to stay for an hour,
then go home. Hone did not bite: it seemed an excellent plan to
put many thousands of people in the hands of the police and
the yeomanry cavalry. Other London printers were approached.
They found that the person to whom they were to deliver the
placards was a lawyer covertly in touch with Sidmouth.

Hone's victory gave heart (but certainly not immunity) to a
growing force of radical journalists. They were mostly men of
the lower orders. Thomas John Wooler, a printer from Yorkshire, created much of his weekly *Black Dwarf* in his head in
the process of setting it up; and once argued in court that an
indictment for *writing* an allegedly seditious passage could not
stand, as he had not written it. John Wade, publisher of *The
Gorgon*—an advocate of universal suffrage, financed in part by
Bentham—was a former wool-sorter. With John Fairburn he
published a new guide to placemen and pensioners, *The Black
Book, or Corruption Unmasked*; ten thousand copies were sold
in weekly parts. W. T. Sherwin, founder of the Painite *Republican*, was a former Northampton turnkey. His successor,
Richard Carlile, began as a Devon tinplate worker. At the time
of the French Revolution these men were boys, or unborn.
Carlile later recalled his political growth: 'When I first started
as a hawker of pamphlets I knew nothing of political principles; I had never read a page of Paine's writings; but I had a

complete conviction that there was something wrong some-
where, and that the right application of the printing-press was
the remedy.'

What these men did with the printing-press frightened the
middle class; especially when Carlile in particular issued cheap
editions of Voltaire, Diderot and Paine (*Age of Reason* as well
as *Rights of Man*) and advocated a deist republic. Three rebels
of the 1790s, one-time believers in popular rights, were deeply
perturbed. Coleridge, who had long persuaded himself that
educated men should plead '*for* the poor and ignorant, not *to*
them', was moved to write to Lord Liverpool about the radical
danger, urging that everyone must be made to see that men
did not make the state, 'but that the state, and that alone,
makes them men'. Wordsworth was glad habeas corpus was
suspended, and wanted all disaffected journalists to be
silenced. Southey, whom Coleridge had praised in 1795 as 'a
downright upright republican', but who now as Poet Laureate
was writing royal odes, urged Liverpool to close down radical
'rags' and send their editors to Botany Bay.

But a vexing thing happened to Southey—Byron's 'turncoat Southey . . . the epic renegade . . . shuffling Southey,
that incarnate lie'. A radical publisher got his hands on a
verse drama, *Wat Tyler*, that Southey had written in 1794.

> TYLER (to king): Why do we carry on this fatal war
> To force upon the French a king they hate?
> . . . You sit at ease in your gay palaces,
> The costly banquet courts your appetite,
> Sweet music soothes your slumbers; we, the while,
> Scarce by hard toil can earn a little food. . . .
> We pay, we fight, you profit at your ease. . . .
> The hour of retribution is at hand
> And tyrants tremble.

Southey wrote to *The Courier* to declare (what everyone knew)
that these were opinions he had 'long outgrown'. Coleridge
wrote four letters in his defence to the same Tory paper. Reformers revelled and bought the play in tens of thousands.
Southey stimulated sales still further by seeking an injunction

against the publisher—whose counsel cleverly reminded Lord Chancellor Eldon that he had refused a similar injunction to Peter Pindar on the ground that his work was too seditious to merit the protection of the law. Lord Eldon grieved, and ruled the same again.

A year after William Hone was acquitted, he was sitting with his four-year-old daughter on his knee, reading *The House that Jack Built*. 'An idea flashed across my mind. . . . I took it from her. I said, "Mother, take the child, send me up my tea and two candles, and let nobody come near me till I ring." I sat up all night. . . .' Next morning he called in his friend George Cruikshank the caricaturist, who quickly made a dozen wood engravings. Thus was created the best-selling piece of popular satire of 1819–20: *The Political House that Jack Built*. Who could prosecute a parody of a nursery rhyme?

> This is THE MAN—
>   all shaven and shorn,
> All covered with orders—
>   and all forlorn;
> THE DANDY OF SIXTY,
>   who bows with a grace,
> And has *taste* in wigs, collars,
>   cuirasses and lace;
> Who to tricksters and fools
>   leaves the state and its treasure,
> And when Britain's in tears,
>   sails about at his pleasure;
> Who spurned from his presence
>   the friends of his youth,
> And now has not one
>   who will tell him the truth. . . .

Hone's words and Cruikshank's cuts present two sets of symbols. Evil: the regent, the Reasons of Lawless Power (magistrate, soldiers, cannon), the Public Informer, the Vermin that plunder Jack's wealth (courtier, officer, bishop, tax-collector, lawyer). Good: the Thing that will poison the Vermin (the printing press), the Wealth in the House that Jack Built

Fond Aged Lover

(Magna Carta, Bill of Rights, Habeas Corpus), and, of course,
THE PEOPLE—

> all tattered and torn,
> Who curse the day
> wherein they were born.

Anti-radicals hit back with parodies of the parody:

> This is the prince
> of a generous mind. . . .
> Who views with disdain or
> a good-humoured smile
> The libellous trash
> of the base and the vile. . . .

The prince's difficulty was that the facts were against him. He
was not capable even of meeting satire with disdain or a smile.
Neither was he capable of learning from it.

> Be wise in time, wise while you may,
> For Bull will have (I grieve to say,
> Loving old England's constitution)
> Either reform or revo-----n.

This warning, which was to be heeded in high places a dozen
years later, came in a Fairburn pamphlet, *Stripes for Sinecurists*, which went on to present some facts about the regent's
spending:

> . . . Thirty thousand pounds for *glass*
> And *china* for three years, alas!
> . . . Sure Bull may be allowed to say,
> When for *snuff-boxes* he's to pay
> Twenty-two thousand—heaven knows—
> That it is paying through the nose!
> Six thousand pounds for *robes* (don't wince),
> As if 'twas dress that made a p----e.
> Five thousand pounds for *doctor's stuff*. . . .
> Foul and diseased he needs must feel. . . .

Such facts fed the anger of the hundreds of thousands suffering in 1819 from a renewed trade slump. In greater numbers

than ever before they joined penny-a-week political clubs, especially in the growing industrial towns of the Midlands and North. They organized their own reading-rooms and Sunday schools. (Weekday classes were no use: this was the year in which parliament passed, after four years' argument, an unenforceable act to limit children in cotton mills to a twelve-hour day.) Women in Lancashire formed Female Union Societies and dreamed of the vote. Petitions for reform uselessly bombarded the regent. In Birmingham, a town meeting of at least twenty-five thousand men—who had never had an MP, and never would if the government's line held—elected a radical baronet, Sir Charles Wolseley, as their Legislatorial Attorney and Representative. Sidmouth prosecuted Sir Charles and his committee for presuming to flout the constitution. Leeds and Manchester then unaggressively dropped similar election plans. The Lancashire reformers, however, called a mass meeting at Manchester to hear Henry Hunt and to adopt yet another resolution for reform. (The regent's chief concern at this moment was that the government did not dare to ask parliament for more than £150,000 for his plan to convert Buckingham House into a vast palace. He said he must have at least £450,000.)

In column after column more than fifty thousand people marched into Manchester on August 16 behind banners that spoke of both hope and heartache: Vote by Ballot—Success to the Female Reformers—No Corn Laws—No Boroughmongering—Equal Representation or Death—Labour is the Source of Wealth—Hunt and Liberty—Let us Die like Men and not be Sold like Slaves. The meeting opened in St Peter's Fields—and never finished, for it became the event known as Peterloo.

It was bad enough that the Manchester magistrates sent the yeomanry cavalry (shopkeepers and farmers armed with sabres) into the crowd without cause, and so killed eleven people and wounded four hundred. What followed deepened the nationwide sense of outrage. Sidmouth sent a letter to the magistrates announcing 'the great satisfaction derived by His Royal Highness from their prompt, decisive and efficient measures for the preservation of public tranquillity' (just as the prince's father had sent thanks after the St George's Fields killings fifty-one years before). There was no word of sympathy. The prince was 'returning thanks to the *murderers*!!!' said Richard Carlile, who had been on the platform at Peterloo and had hurried to London with a report which he placarded, 'Horrid massacres at Manchester . . . magisterial and yeomanry assassins.'

Lord Eldon, who as attorney-general in 1794 had failed to get convictions for treason, now demanded a treason trial for Hunt and his associates. The magistrates and yeomanry, said *The Black Dwarf*, were the ones who had committed treason, for 'it is treason against the king *to levy war upon his subjects*'. When Hunt came south on bail, there was an extraordinary demonstration which nobody dared to disperse. Dense crowds cheered Hunt as he paraded in his carriage through Islington into the city. Red cockades were worn, the red-white-green tricolor was waved. What Wooler called 'the old red flag with the inscription *Universal Suffrage*' was displayed, and behind Hunt's carriage rode a man with another red flag saying *Liberty or Death*. At a tavern banquet that night, the 'Marseillaise' was played, and one of the toasts was—

> May arms be taken from those who abuse them
> And given to those who have courage to use them.

The Manchester magistrates alleged that the crowd had attacked first, had fired pistols, had thrown enough stones to fill two carts. Castlereagh and other ministers upheld them. *The Times*, converted by Peterloo to the cause of reform, accused Castlereagh of 'matchless, boundless, inconceivable falsehood . . . a degree of inconsideration bordering closely on criminality'. All demands for a public inquiry were blocked. For venturing to favour an inquiry, Earl Fitzwilliam was dismissed as Lord Lieutenant of the West Riding. Sir Francis Burdett, Westminster's radical MP, was fined £2,000 and jailed for three months for writing an open letter in which he said, 'Is this England? This a Christian land? A land of freedom? . . . Will the gentlemen of England support or wink at such proceedings?' Eldon did not get his treason trial; but Hunt and others were jailed for up to two years for 'conspiracy

to alter the law by force and threats'. No sabring yeoman
was punished.

> I met Murder on the way—
> He had a mask like Castlereagh—
> Very smooth he looked, yet grim.
> Seven bloodhounds followed him.
> . . . One by one, and two by two,
> He tossed them human hearts to chew.

So wrote Shelley, a republican poet of a new generation, when
the news of Peterloo reached him in Italy. With an idealist's
self-indulgence, he urged the poor to hold an even larger
national assembly—

> And if then the tyrants dare,
> Let them ride among you there,
> Slash, and stab, and maim, and hew—
> What they like, that let them do.

Thus they could rouse up the people 'in unvanquishable number', Shelley said: 'Ye are many—they are few.' He sent the
poem to Leigh Hunt for *The Examiner*, but Hunt did not court
jail by printing it.

The many did not rise. But the shock of Peterloo won recruits for the reformers, and helped them to speak with a
new boldness. 'There are a few titled and rich boroughmongers who are very vexed that they cannot get into power.
They call themselves Whigs,' says a broadside *Address of the
Reformers of Fawdon to their brothers the Pitmen, Keelmen and
other labourers on the Tyne and Wear*.

> Some of these Whigs in this part of the country have talked
> loudly against the Manchester Massacre, yet they abuse the
> people who met as wicked, dangerous fellows; nor have they
> given one farthing to the sufferers. . . .
>
> The bloated tax-eaters accuse us of conspiracy. Now, the
> rich keep firearms in their houses—they are now training
> their tenants and servants in their halls and parks—their
> obsequious dependants are members of Yeomanry Corps—
> they possess unbounded property and influence . . . and
> they have always a standing army at their call (at least they

think it is at their call)—while were we, who with difficulty
can purchase a dinner, to get arms for our own defence . . .
we would be called daring, rebellious rascals. . . . Is it not
the rich that are conspiring against the unprotected poor?

Sydney Smith wrote at this time to Lord Grey, the great
Northumberland Whig, 'The worst of it all is that a considerable portion of what these rascals say is so very true.'

Wellington feared revolution and raised ten thousand extra
soldiers. Harsher restrictions than ever were imposed on the
radicals' meetings and on their presses; banishment was introduced as a punishment for a second offence of seditious or
blasphemous publishing.

The radicals began a national movement to undermine the
tax revenue by boycotting tea, coffee, beer and tobacco. *The
Republican* advertised Radical Breakfast Powder (roasted peas
and corn) at a shilling a pound instead of three shillings for
taxed coffee.

Vendors of radical weeklies were everywhere being jailed,
sometimes flogged. But savage lampoons could still be found.
Fairburn addressed 'the Grand Lama of the Kremlin'
(Brighton Pavilion):

> Look up, thou lord of double chin,
> Look up, illustrious man of sin
> With glued-on whiskers, oh, look up,
> And kindly take another sup,
> And kindly take another kiss.
> Who *does no wrong* can't do amiss . . .
> Fond aged lover, fat and fair,
> Lord C-------gh's and H--t---d's care. . . .
> Blessed be thy journey through rough life,
> And never mayst thou meet *thy wife*,
> And never may thy conscience prick thee,
> Or *Manchesterian butchers* stick thee.

In a speech from the throne, the regent recommended 'the
cultivation of the principles of religion'. He changed his own
way of life in one way. Weary of the fifty-nine-year-old Lady
Hertford, he fell dotingly in love with the Marchioness

Conyngham, whom wits called 'the new old lady', but who at fifty-one was at least the first *maîtresse en titre* to be younger than the prince. The lampoonists did not discover the change of marchioness for several months, because the prince, to avoid the hisses and missiles of his subjects, was living in great seclusion.

More privately still within Windsor Castle, his father, who now in contrast was spoken of as 'the good old king', began the sixtieth year of his reign, and believing himself already in heaven, lost interest in food and earthly life.

13

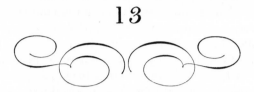

The Lost Mutton

FEW ENGLISH KINGS can have begun their reigns so little loved as George IV was when the news-vendors hurried through the streets on 30 January 1820 blowing their horns and crying 'Death of the king!'

> Blinded with grief, or more probably brandy,
> Were the eyes of this runagate *elderly dandy.*

He had long ago lost the respect of the men who owed their position to him, his ministers and courtiers, because of his ill temper, his greed and his petulant childish selfishness. Now, succeeding in his fifty-eighth year to the father who had bullied, despised and perhaps sometimes envied him, he made his ministers more unhappy than ever. He insisted on getting a divorce from Caroline, his wife of twenty-five years, with whom he had not slept since the morrow of their wedding. Lord Liverpool and his colleagues objected that he would raise a storm that would endanger the throne. George IV furiously accused them of letting him think they would approve a divorce, and then leaving him in the lurch. 'His agitation is extreme and alarming,' says the journal of John Wilson Croker. 'He eats hardly anything—a bit of dry toast and a little claret and water.' He bullied his ministers with threats of dismissal. After two months of argument (and no monarch so wasted his servants' time with rages and three-hour monologues), he agreed to let Caroline be offered £50,000 a year to stay on the Continent and not call herself queen. Her lawyer, Henry Brougham, known to his Whig friends as Old Wickedshifts, worked in such a dilatory and devious way that Caroline had time to persuade herself to do what nobody expected: return to England.

She arrived in London in June, not accompanied by her Italian lover, a general's ex-valet, Bartolomeo Bergami. Vast crowds hailed her as their heroine. No matter if republicans found themselves illogically cheering a royal person: she was the enemy of the hated king. No matter if she was a battered heroine, comically fat, red-faced, hard-drinking, brazen-eyed, in vulgar clothes and a black wig: she was a rallying-point for all despairing reformers. And when the government, on George IV's insistence, brought in a bill to divorce Caroline and deprive her of her crown, millions of people of all ranks persuaded themselves that she had not had a series of lovers for more than twenty years—or if she had, she was in any case the victim of George IV's dissolute cruelty. What right had the king, in the throes of his passion for yet another married woman, to use his parliament to degrade his own wife?

Sir Francis Burdett, the radical MP, said publicly what many people were thinking about the ministers: 'The pit in which they intend to bury the crown of the queen might also serve to bury the crown of the king. . . . If the private conduct of the queen of England is of importance to the country, how much more important is the conduct of the king!' Privately, men in high places began to feel sure that the monarchy was doomed. The king dared not appear in London.

> The time is past when through the town
>   He reeled in open day;
> When riot gave his name renown
>   In many a bruising fray.

He and Lady Conyngham went into retreat in his mock-gothic cottage with her complaisant husband (who became Lord Steward, with his Irish title upgraded to an English one), their son Francis (made a Gentleman of the Bedchamber) and their daughter Elizabeth. Lady Conyngham, whom wits called the Vice Queen or Cunning-game, was delighted that Caroline had brought matters to a head. George behaved like a youth in his first love. 'They spend the evening sitting on a sofa together, holding each other's hands, whispering & kissing,

The Lost Mutton

Lord C. being present,' records a minister's wife, Mrs Charles Arbuthnot.

Wellington was no longer sure he could count on the army. Radical agitators, with a successful army revolt against King Ferdinand of Spain to inspire them, were fraternizing with guardsmen and offering them bribes of money and liquor. Some mutinous guardsmen had to be marched out of town. Many of them were 'drinking the queen's health & had the greatest possible contempt for the king from thinking him a coward & afraid of showing himself,' says Mrs Arbuthnot, an intimate friend of Wellington. 'How much have we cause to bless the memory & mourn the loss of our good old king!'

George III had become the good old king even in radical pamphlets:

> He did not lie snoring with wantons at noon,
> And when he was called, cry, *You've waked me too soon!*
> With one virtuous woman to live he made shift. . . .
> He was not afraid to be met in the street. . . .

These lines are from *A Peep into W-----r Castle after the Lost Mutton*, by John Mitford, whose uncle, the 1st Lord Redesdale, a Tory lawyer, was the ancestor of the latterday writing Mitfords. *A Peep* was one lampoon that George IV tried to suppress. Sir Benjamin Bloomfield, successor to John McMahon as Privy Purse, paid a Soho publisher, J. L. Marks, £35 to give it up. But then a more radical publisher, William Benbow in the Strand, reprinted it with the enticing phrase 'The Suppressed Poem' in its title. It revealed no secrets: it offended chiefly by displaying the king as a grotesque old man, 'sunk, sour and sixty', who rolls up Pall Mall 'like a porpoise on land' and who dallies with old beldames 'who plunder and riot on r---l insanity'. John Bull finds his lost mutton at last in a room marked 'seraglio':

> Stretched at length on a sofa, with fat bloated face,
> He saw the 'lost mutton' of Br------k's lost race.
> He half hid his face, and appeared rather shy,
> And scowled upon John with a lustreless eye,
> Whilst over him bended, to sympathy true,
> The voluptuous form of the famed Mrs Q.

Mitford, writing before Lady Conyngham's role was public, is referring to a subordinate mistress of the regency, the beautiful wife of Colonel George Quintin of the 10th Hussars. Quintin became the king's aide-de-camp, and was knighted.

> If drinking I quit, I shall soon quit this life,
> A thing that would please both Fred and my wife,

says the king to John Bull (Fred being the Duke of York, next in line).

> For the good of the people, I spend on a -----
> What else would be wasted on ten thousand poor.

Having highhandedly seized quantities of jewels on the deaths of his daughter and his mother in 1817 and 1818—

> But the best on't was the time when Old Snuffy she took
>   sickly
> And the people all rejoiced to find her on the go;
> Death sent her soul a-weigh so sudden and so quickly
> I scarce could pack the diamonds up for 'Oh dear oh!'

—and having appropriated everything he possibly could after George III's death (he had to be stopped from selling the royal library), George IV was lavishing gifts on the Conynghams that would indeed have fed ten thousand poor.

The king withdrew to Brighton, and the lampoonists pursued him there:

> 'Tis pleasant at seasons to see how they sit,
> First cracking their nuts, and then cracking their wit;
> Then quaffing their claret—then mingling their lips
> Or tickling the fat about each other's hips. . . .
> The lady is blinkey, she's full half-seas-over,
> And he like a mutton pot-bellied with clover.

This is *The Lost Mutton Found*.

> The RAM turns to this ewe and then turns to that,
> Enveloped in pillows, in feathers and fat. . . .
> The ladies they played in most excellent style,
> And blended their delicate voices the while:

> But the old mutton's *flute*, being *shockingly small*
> And *very much worn*, didn't join in at all.

Dozens of similar lampoons, some running to hundreds of lines, went unsuppressed. J. L. Marks got his £35 because he was one of the publishers who angled for suppression money. A letter of his to Josh Calkin, Bloomfield's go-between, reveals Marks's method. He announces 'a new poem I intend shortly to publish' and says, 'If you will be kind enough to call on me tomorrow morning, I shall be glad, as I shall not advertise . . . till I have your opinion on it.' He calls the poem *Amoroso, King of Little Britain*, and he encloses a title-page proof that lists thirty-four of Amoroso's alleged past mistresses, such as Old Snuffy's Chambermaid, Sherry's Kitten, McMahon's Piece and Cousin Sophy (daughter of George IV's Uncle Gloucester). There is also a sample stanza:

> I've kissed and I've prattled with fifty old jades,
>> And changed them as oft, d'ye see:
> But of all the FAT HAGS I have known in love's trade,
>> The sweet Mrs Coney for me.

This will be recognized as a shameless lift from Isaac Cruikshank's print of twenty-six years before, with Conyngham replacing Jersey. Perhaps Marks failed to convince Calkin that he really had a poem ready; at any rate, there is no receipt for it in the royal archives. But in eleven other deals during 1820, Marks was paid about £500 to suppress caricatures and poems—a useful income, free of printing costs.

During 1819–22 more than £2,600 of the taxpayers' money went in this way. George Cruikshank got £100 for a pledge 'not to caricature His Majesty in any immoral situation', and then ingeniously pictured the king as a repentant sinner in a white sheet. The greatest part of the money went to suppress attacks on Lady Conyngham or her husband; and the reason why 'Mrs Q' continues to appear so often during 1820 may well be that her name was slipped in as a substitute.

The king must have wondered if the outlay was worth it. Never had there been such a year for satirists. Nearly 800 different political caricatures survive from 1820–21. In the

Treasury Solicitor's files there is a collection of ninety-one that were studied for possible prosecution. It is easy to imagine the law officers bending, half-amused and half-angry, over these 'licentious abominations' (as the king called them), in which they themselves sometimes appear, and having to conclude each time that no jury, in the mood of 1820, would convict, and that in any case a prosecution would merely spread the ridicule wider.

The caricature shops knew their wares were being watched. The Treasury messengers who went round buying up seditious material must have become old friends. One radical publisher, Thomas Dolby of 299 The Strand, issued a caricature which joined the Treasury collection, 'His most gracious majesty Hum IVth and his Ministers going to play the Devil with the Satirists'. The attorney-general is armed with 'ex officios' (orders from his office for arbitrary arrests) and his 'select list of Middlesex special jurymen' (a great grievance, this). George IV cries, 'Zounds and fury, down with them! . . . They are ridiculing my very Bomb! I tell you again I am k--g and be d----d to you all, and will do just as I please!!!' The Bomb (pronounced bum), a captured large-bore mortar displayed at the Horse Guards, was the subject of a great deal of rude mockery. The ghost of George III says, 'O my dear son! my dear son! If you persecute them you will make their fortunes— but if you will only conduct yourself like a man and a gentle-man you will destroy their profession'—an argument often used on George III himself. Satirists fly through the air like imps. One of them aims at George IV an arrow labelled 'cradle hymn', thus advertising one of Dolby's own broadsides, which depicts Sidmouth as an old nanny rocking to sleep the Great Babe, while Castlereagh dries its napkins and Liverpool carries away its pot.

> Hush, great babe! Be still and slumber.
>   Troops of Lancers guard thy bed.
> Chinese gimcracks without number
>   Nicely dangle o'er thy head. . . .
>
> Troops of soldiers shall attend you,
>   Muffed and laced, and gilt so fine.

The Lost Mutton

> They shall valiantly defend you
>> From the two-legged rabble swine.

> Hold the press in close submission,
>> Keep the radicals in awe.
> Call reform the worst sedition,
>> Yet observe the *forms* of law!

Even when the law officers were shown caricatures picturing the crown being transferred from George's head to Caroline's, or suggesting that the Duke of York might replace him (George IV to witches: 'Tell me, ye d--ned infernal hags of night, shall Fr------k reign?' Frederick: 'I'll do—I'll do—I'll do!'), they failed to prosecute. George did in fact talk of handing over to Frederick and going to Hanover. But was it not sedition to say that the king was going to hell? Dolby published an elaborate caricature by George Cruikshank's brother Robert, 'The Devil's Ball', in which the devil says:

> Hell ne'er saw so proud a day
> Since the birth of Castle---gh . . .
> Hither, great and mighty HUM!
> Join us with thy monstrous *bomb!*
> You're the 'devil's own', we're sure,
> Who thanked the tr--ps that slew the poor;
> Who led a wicked, useless life,
> And last of all disowned your wife . . .
> I have warmed a berth for you.

Dolby was to be prosecuted; but not for this. Even political pamphlets and weekly papers were not remarkably vulnerable in 1820: there were twenty-eight prosecutions for seditious libel and related offences, against sixty-three in 1819. One reason was that the radicals were no longer on their own. The Caroline affair had aroused a mass of middle-class opinion against the king and his ministers. Juries would be less likely to convict. Besides, the chief purpose of prosecuting a radical publisher was to silence him and frighten the rest, and now newspapers such as *The Times*, which put up its circulation from 7,000 to 15,000 by espousing Caroline's cause, were speaking almost as daringly as the radicals had done. It is true that Leigh Hunt's brother John was jailed for a year for saying in *The Examiner* that the Commons 'for the main part is composed of venal boroughmongers, grasping placemen, greedy adventurers and aspiring title-hunters, or the representatives of such worthies . . . a far greater portion of public criminals than public guardians'; but the jury took two hours to say he was guilty.

The law officers had a further reason for failing to scatter their ex officios: they were desperately busy from June till November preparing and then conducting the 'trial' of Queen Caroline.

There was plenty of material. The Treasury lawyers even looked into her life before marriage: one of them marked a passage in Mary Anne Clarke's suppressed memoirs that told of the Duke of York meeting Caroline while bride-hunting in Germany in 1791. 'The duke . . . was struck with her beauty, but there was something amiss in her *shape*. In fact, he found out that she was then some months advanced in *pregnancy!*' (Caroline often spoke of her early love for a nephew of Frederick the Great.) But what really mattered was her life after marriage. Although the ancient law making adultery with the wife of the royal heir high treason was not now being invoked, it did have some point. When Caroline was pregnant by one of her lovers in 1801, she put about a story that she had spent one or two nights at Carlton House. By the time a son was born in 1801, she had given up the idea of trying to persuade the country that the prince was the father, and made out instead that she had adopted the baby of a poor couple. The actual father was probably a Captain Manby, a natural son of George Townshend, the noble caricaturist of the 1760s. The child was sickly and dull-witted; but had he been a bold and heroic figure, it is possible to imagine his becoming a radical contender for the throne in the 1820s. It was a time when many kings were being made and unmade.

The danger of an illegitimate contender was certainly mentioned when an inquiry was ordered in 1806. The investigators prudently found themselves unable to declare Caroline the mother of the boy, but could not acquit her of unseemly behaviour with a number of men. Among her lovers (though never officially so declared) had been Sir Sidney Smith, a naval hero; a brother of Lord Edward Fitzgerald, the Irish patriot; Thomas Lawrence, who later painted portraits of her husband; and George Canning, who became one of his prime ministers.

Caroline never ceased to find men to commit treason. For several years before 1820, her husband had agents collecting evidence about her in Italy and elsewhere. There was even a Tunisian accoucheur who talked of a baby born in 1816. The day after she returned to England, 'green bags' of papers setting out the case against her were carried into the two houses of parliament. Witnesses were summoned from Italy. And soon the House of Lords became, in effect, a high court, with the attorney-general prosecuting, and Brougham, the most ingenious barrister of his day, defending.

Day after day a huge crowd milled outside to boo, hiss and pelt their villains and to cheer their heroes and the heroine herself. They were well instructed in the virtues of the peers. William Benbow listed scores of them in a pamphlet, *Fair Play, or Who are the Adulterers, Slanderers and Demoralizers?* There is the Duke of Gordon ('This nobleman reminds me of an old sentiment—*May you live to be ninety and tried for a rape*'); the Marquess of Anglesey, involved with the Duke of Wellington's sister-in-law in an unsavoury double divorce; or the duke himself, the man who said to the blackmailing, memoir-writing courtesan Harriette Wilson, 'Publish and be damned' ('As to his chastity, who dare doubt it?'). But although Wellington and others were jostled in the street and had their windows smashed, the general mood was not menacing. There is nothing like a running scandal in high places for creating a cheerful mood. London was 'singularly festive and gay', says Lord Holland. He amused himself in the Lords scribbling epigrams and passing them to brother peers. As the trial dragged on through autumn, peers complained, says Thomas Creevey, that 'it interferes with everything— pheasant shooting, Newmarket, etc., etc.' Every day the papers carried many columns of titillating evidence, but the majority of people refused to lose faith in Caroline. Most ladies of title avoided calling on her for fear of being barred from court forever, but parades of working-men and other Caroline enthusiasts passed through Piccadilly with bands and banners almost every day, bound for the queen's temporary home at Hammersmith. At times, it was remarked, there were crowds far bigger than on the tragic day of Peterloo: but no magistrate dared think of dispersing them. Agitation acquired routine legality. And so did the sharpest satire.

The king made a most vulnerable aggrieved husband. In *The Acts of Adonis* he becomes biblical:

> And he went in unto other men's wives, and he planted horns on the foreheads of his counsellors, and bestowed divers orders and disorders upon them.
>
> Moreover he builded palaces at much cost, and cut out garments of scarlet and garments of blue for the captains of the hosts. . . .
>
> And of the ladies of his court he made concubines, and of concubines he made ladies of his court. And the children of Bull marvelled and were sore afraid. . . .

One Italian witness made his contribution to the merriment of all ranks when, under cross-examination by Brougham, he replied again and again, '*Non mi ricordo.*'

> . . . What chambermaid, what valet,
> Came running to the bell O?
> What footman brought the dinner up?
> *Non mi ricordo quello,*
> Indeed I cannot tell O.
> A damned convenient fellow!

It became a catchphrase, and William Hone quickly produced a pamphlet, *Non Mi Ricordo*, illustrated by George Cruikshank, in which a higher personage is being questioned:

> You are a master tailor, I think? I was cut out for a tailor. . . .
>
> How much money has been expended on you since you were born? Non mi ricordo. . . .
>
> Are you married? More yes than no. . . . I rambled about. Where did you go? To Jersey and elsewhere.

Well, sir, go on. Non mi ricordo.

Do you mean to say that you never went to Manchester Square? More yes than no. . . .

Is the Marquess of C. a married man? (*Order. Order.*)

. . . How many bottles a day do you drink? Non mi ricordo.

How many nights in the week do you go to bed sober? Non mi ricordo.

Are you sober now? More no than yes. . . .

What is your favourite amusement? The C.

After dressing, drinking and dreaming, what time remains for thinking? Non mi ricordo. . . .

Can you produce a certificate of good character from those who *know* you? Yes, from the Minister.

Pho! pho! don't trifle. Can you from any *respectable* person? More no than yes. . . .

Suppose every man in society were to do as you do, what would become of society? And what right have you to do so more than any other man? (*Witness greatly agitated.*)

The strength of this was in its truth to the man. Even Wellington's high Tory friend, Mrs Arbuthnot, when shown it at Lord Westmorland's place, found it 'very ridiculous and clever'.

When George IV went off to Brighton, Hone produced some mock advertisements:

Strayed and missing. An Infirm Elderly Gentleman in a Public Office . . . after dreadfully ill-using his wife about half a crown. . . . He is very deaf and very obstinate, and cannot bear to be looked at or spoken to. It is supposed that he has been seduced and carried off by some artful female. He may be easily known by his manners. He fancies himself the politest man in Europe because he knows how to bow and to offer a pinch of snuff. . . . He is so fond of tailoring that he lately began a suit that will take him his life to complete.

To avoid hostile English eyes altogether, he went sailing in his yacht, the Royal George (with Lady Conyngham's son as vice-commodore); and this move inspired more lampoons. One is a parody of a sea-song of Nelson's day, 'Tom Tough'. The original begins:

> My name d'ye see's Tom Tough, I've see'd a little service
> Where mighty billows roll and loud tempests blow;
> I've sailed with valiant Howe, with Duncan and with Jarvis,
> And in gallant Nelson's fleet I've sung out yo-heave-ho.
> > Yet more would you be knowing:
> > I was coxen to Boscawen. . . .

The king has a different boast:

> I've done duty for a duke, now I do it for a marquess,
> And in matrimony's bed I've sung out yo-heave-ho.
> > And more would you be knowing:
> > I was cockswain to a blowen [*whore*
> Who gave broadside for broadside with friend or with foe.
> > I'm at all in the ring,
> > Of pleasure I'm the spring,
> Except when I'm laid up with my damned gouty toe. . . .
> > In my yacht I'll be a cruiser,
> > I'm a Royal British Boozer,
> And to hell I pitch reform, with a yo-heave-ho.

Another poet thought of the king going overboard:

> > Of *blubber* such a dainty dish
> > > Sharks seldom clap their eyes on:
> > His rotten carcase half the fish
> > > Around Spithead would p'ison.

Gradually it became evident, however, despite every ploy and flourish of Henry Brougham, that even if Caroline had not had so many lovers as her husband, or wasted so much money, or done anything to merit public hatred, she had vied with him in shamelessness. She did not merely take as her lover her Italian courier, Bergami ('six feet high, a magnificent head of black hair, pale complexion, mustachios which reach *from here to London*', as one of Caroline's friends saw him in 1815). She invented an Order of Santa Carolina, made Bergami a baron and Grand Master of the order, and hung a cross of the order round his neck on a lilac-and-silver ribbon—with the same motto as her husband's Garter, *Honi soit qui mal y pense.* She had a touch of style. But more often a touch of vulgar folly. She danced frenziedly at fancy-dress balls with her squat body half-naked—'dressed, or rather undressed, most injudiciously', as her lady-in-waiting recalled. She fondled Bergami lasciviously in front of the servants; and what else she did with him required no guesswork by the time all the evidence had been unfolded.

Caroline's followers did their best to believe she was an innocent victim of perjury, but Bergami set a problem. A Tory pamphleteer asked why Caroline was 'ashamed or afraid' to bring him to England: 'The British people would have been glad to see the faithful servant of their queen.' Another satirist was tickled to find Caroline enthusiasts buying souvenir kerchiefs with 'Bergami's head at the top to be seen/As much as to say, *I'm the man for the queen*'. A few lampoons took a middle-of-the-road course. 'The Kettle Abusing the Pot' gives a George-and-Caroline dialogue:

G. I'll remember the fact—aye, as long as I've breath—
    Your ways in the scullery down at Blackheath;
    Likewise at Southend the pranks you did play,
    On board and on shore, by night and by day. . . .
C. The enjoyments of mine that in private I know
    (Said Pot), Mr Kettle, you could not bestow. . . .
    You monster—ah, have you not, have you not done
    Deeds of darkness that shame the bright rays of the sun?
    . . . My friends may be rogues, and no doubt so are thine,
    But the Kettle's old bottom is blacker than mine.
G. Sometimes I am silly—sometimes I am more,
    And often perplexed 'twixt a rogue and a whore. . . .
    But ah, with his gold the Old Kettle can cover
    His faults and his failings a hundred times over.

Then the evidence about Bergami began to inspire verse and caricatures. *The New Pilgrim's Progress*, illustrated with wood engravings, retails all the delights of Caroline—

Happy all day long to see him,
And to feel him all the night.

Sailing to Palestine, the lovers share a tent on deck:

The dullest mind can understand
What of this scene must be the close,
If *that* be Baron Berghy's hand
And *these* the queen of England's toes!

Bergami officiates at her bath:

The weather's hot—the cabin's free!
And she's as free and hot as either!

. . . Let none but Berghy's hand untie
The garter, or unlace the bodice;
Let none but Berghy's faithful eye
Survey the beauties of the goddess.

While she receives the copious shower
He gets a step in honour's path,
And grows from this auspicious hour
A K-night Companion of the Bath.

A number of caricatures reflected fears of the radicals. And
here George Cruikshank showed his divided mind, and his
willingness to make money from either side—for at that time
he was a fast-living young man, too much devoted, in William
Hone's opinion, to 'late hours, blue ruin and dollies'. In 1819,
Cruikshank had done a powerful print against the 'Manchester butchers'; and a frightening one of radical reformers
pictured as walking guillotines. His sketches for the two are on
the same sheet of paper. In 1820, one of his creations for Hone
was an anti-George 'Matrimonial Ladder'; and he parodied it
himself with a 'Radical Ladder'. Hone decided Cruikshank was
'by no means friendly to reform'.

In the Lords, more and more peers were deciding it was prudent to refrain from giving George IV his divorce. Ministers,
and the king, knew that if the bill went to the Commons, new
issues might be raised that could shake the monarchy.
Brougham had spoken darkly of 'recriminations'. The king had

learned that Caroline's advisers were preparing a pamphlet, based on her private journal, full of details about George's marriage-night drunkenness and about the humiliation she had undergone with Lady Jersey. There was something more serious: the king's first wife was alive, in Brighton. The Fitzherbert marriage was Brougham's 'real trump', he told Croker years later. 'I could have proved it in 1820. . . . I had a communication from her in great alarm. . . .' Recrimination of George's adulteries was nothing, said Brougham, 'but the other meant a forfeiture of the crown, or at least a disputed succession'.

Brougham's trump would have beaten one that George was thinking of playing against Caroline: a written statement by their daughter Charlotte that when at the age of sixteen she was violently in love with a Captain Hesse (a reputed son of the Duke of York), Caroline had locked them up in a room together. But the game ended with the government withdrawing the bill. The queen looked dazed, and wept. In the streets, the decision was hailed as an acquittal, and was celebrated with illuminations and parades. Effigies of Liverpool, Castlereagh, Sidmouth and Eldon were consumed in bonfires. Great men were summoned to their doors and commanded to drink to the queen. Lord Anglesey, or Wellington, retorted, or is said to have retorted, by drinking to 'The queen—and may all your wives be like her.' The story was perhaps inspired by some verses by Theodore Hook:

> May the wives of her champions resemble her all:
> Come join in the wish, and sing tol de rol lol . . .
> Life without love is all tol de rol lol.

Hook, a theatrical song-writer and novelist, was producing quantities of anti-Caroline verse at the end of 1820. It was not a fast-selling line, but it delighted those in power, and especially the king. Hook had a strong incentive for winning ministerial favour: he had been guilty of defalcation in a colonial post, owed the Treasury £12,000, and lived in the shadow of prison. He hit at the radicals in every direction. He mocked the men who were in prison—Henry Hunt at Ilchester, Richard Carlile at Dorchester, Sir Charles Wolseley at

Abingdon, and many others—because they were missing the Caroline furor:

> How's our friend Carlile, ho?
> Dick's fit to hang himself,
> Locked up in time of pelf.

Five weeks after the Bill was dropped, Hook launched a weekly paper, *John Bull*, full of malicious jibes against Caroline and her radical and Whig supporters, with special attention to Whig ladies of dubious virtue. His timing was right. People had digested the evidence, and were ready to be tired of Caroline. Soon Hook was selling 9,000 a week. He also pursued Caroline with a pamphlet in which she and Bergami exchange verse letters. Bartolomeo to Caroline:

> Ah, nothing, my queen, could your courage surpass!
> How surprising the feats you performed on your ass!

(She rode into Jerusalem on a donkey.)

> With how much impatience the curious would burn all
> Were it known you intended to publish your journal.
> Let no *mauvaise honte* from this purpose deter ye.
> If you'd please all the public, you'll send it to Murray.

Caroline, in reply, is already disillusioned:

> This nation so dull and so hard to provoke
> Can seldom be spurred to a desperate stroke. . . .
> And I shrewdly suspect that at length I may feel,
> When the orange is squeezed, what they do with the peel!

So she talks of returning to him:

> Happily clasped in the arms of my dear,
> With him let me share fifty thousand a year!
> . . . Away with all cant about Rights of the People.

She did shake the faith of her followers by accepting her fifty thousand after saying she would not.

George IV said after only four issues of *John Bull* that in the fight to quiet the radicals 'neither he, nor his ministers, nor his parliament, nor his courts of justice all together, had done so much good as *John Bull*. He was also grateful for an anti-radical anthology, *The Loyalist's Magazine*, which was presented to him at a levee. It says of the radicals: 'They would seize all we at present possess by blood and plunder! What mad schemes have not these reformers in view! They have raised corps of women to carry their flags! What next? They would perhaps elect them members of parliament! O! glorious prospect!' And it pictures some future prime minister receiving the following ridiculous news:

> Sir, the reformers in the North have sent
> Twelve Oldham matrons into parliament.
> The dames of Rochdale at your levee press.
> Three Stockport virgins wait with an address.

For Carlile and a few other extremists had been suggesting votes for women.

The Loyalist's Magazine declares that a mood of rebellion is being created by 'parodies—prints—caricatures—ribaldry and ridicule'. Radical publications 'have intimidated the authorities of the land' (though in fact the authorities, especially outside London, had not ceased to intimidate the publishers, and the vendors above all). 'Everything against government is bought up with avidity', but loyalists are slow buyers.

The king wrote to Eldon about the licentious press; and the law officers discussed what could be done about all forms of ribaldry. But what a commentary it would be on the state of the nation if they had to extend their prosecutions to caricatures, which had been immune for so long. However, a useful-seeming voluntary organization, the Constitutional Association, had just been set up to defend all that was sacred. Wellington, one of the sternest anti-reform ministers, led its list of subscribers. Most of the 'subscribing fools', wrote Thomas Dolby a few years later, were 'fat and drowsy dowagers, and other elderly females in small-clothes [breeches] and petticoats; hypochondriacs of all ages; half a dozen crazy lords; an odd bishop or so; and some few straggling, decayed foxhunters'. In February 1821 the association prosecuted London's most radical printseller, William Benbow, over two caricatures of George IV, 'The Brightest Star in the State' and 'The R---l Cock & Chickens'. 'The Brightest Star' depicted

> a grotesque and ludicrous figure of a man meant and intended to represent our said Lord the King in the body of which said figure there was and is represented a certain hole or aperture in which said hole or aperture there was and is represented to be contained (amongst other things) a certain black head with horns thereon meant and intended to represent the head of a devil. . . .

The unmentioned other things in the hole or aperture were the heads of Liverpool, Eldon and Castlereagh, the last saying, 'Hang the people, what a riot they make!' Unmentioned, too, was the fact that the devil says, 'I wish I wasn't the Archbishop of Canterbury.' The indictment does complain that a horned figure is pulling the king's Garter from his leg and saying, 'Down with the Star and Garter, that old sign must be hung on another post.'

One count against 'The Royal Cock' was that on the figure of the king 'there was and is a certain false defamatory and libellous inscription in the words following . . . Fat of the Land'. Worse, there is 'a woman leaning upon and against the left thigh of the said first-mentioned figure . . . in a lascivious and indecent attitude' and the Royal Cock is caressing this woman 'in an indecent and lascivious manner'. while from his mouth emerges what is described, oddly, as a 'false defamatory and libellous inscription': 'To keep thy body in temperance soberness and chastity not to covet or desire other men's goods.' All this was publicized in vain: a Westminster grand jury refused to act on the indictments of the self-appointed association. It served the king no better when it prosecuted Dolby over some verses. For the heart of the charge of malicious libel read:

> If you walk up P--- M--- (*meaning the street called Pall Mall aforesaid*)/You may pass by the gate/Where an old ho- (*meaning hog*) of sixty (*meaning our said Lord the King*)/ Still wallows in state/With his (*meaning our said Lord the King's*) brown wig/And his (*meaning, etc.*) bladder-chops

white./Half drunk with white brandy/O'erheated with lust/
This 'faithful defender' (*meaning our said Lord the King*)/
Of all that is just/In a proud pandemonium/With well-
guarded doors/Is humbugged by st****m*n (*meaning
statesmen*)/And fondled by w***** (*meaning whores*) . . . To
the great contempt and injury of our said Lord the King. . . .

Dolby was also prosecuted over a *Political Dictionary* less
daring than Pigott's of 1795. The shock and worry of his
arrest, he said, killed his wife. After subjecting him to a year of
trouble and expense, the Constitutional Association dropped
the first prosecution; and he was never sentenced on the
second. The association also failed to get anywhere with a
prosecution of Hone's *Non Mi Ricordo*. But it helped to jail a
number of radical journalists, especially agnostic Painite followers of Carlile. For a time Carlile's wife and sister were also
in Dorchester Jail, and volunteers who helped to keep *The
Republican* and its Fleet Street bookshop going were jailed for
up to three years in Newgate, where they slept on mats on the
stone floor, and lived on bread and gruel, with beef on alter-
nate days. Carlile himself was not to be freed until 1825.

The king had other consolations in 1821. There was his de-
layed coronation, which let him indulge to the full his pleasure
in designing uniforms and making an opulent show—at a cost
of £243,000. (Ten years later, William IV's cost £43,000.) His
brother Frederick, expecting to outlive him, said tactlessly,
'By God, I'll have everything exactly the same at mine!'

Caroline said she should be crowned too. Some ministers
thought she might at least be allowed to appear in Westminster Abbey. George raged at them with such frenzy that
they grumbled to outsiders, and Thomas Creevey wrote, 'Geo.
3 was an ill-used man to be shut up for ten years.' On the day,
after George had gone to the Abbey amid cheers, hisses and
groans, Caroline turned up, all in white, escorted by Lord
Hood (one of her naval ex-lovers), was barred by door-
keepers, laughed, was cheered and booed, and drove away.

> *Regas, regat,*
> Good God, what's that!
> The voice is like my deary's!

Leigh Hunt told of the event in a parody of a comic theatre song.

> I decline a
> *C.* Regina,
> *Rex* alone's more handsome:
> O what luck, sir!
> *Exit uxor* . . .

Hunt also makes George say:

> I know where
> A fat and fair
> Sweet other self is doting:
> I'd reply
> With wink of eye,
> But fear the newsman noting.

Here Hunt fails as a newsman. Mrs Arbuthnot watched the king and Lady Conyngham in the abbey: 'He took a diamond brooch from his breast, &, looking at her, kissed it, on which she took off her glove & kissed a ring she had on!!!' Then at the coronation banquet in Westminster Hall, 'The king behaved very indecently; he was continually nodding & winking at Lady C. & sighing & making eyes at her.'

Within a week of her futile gesture at the abbey, Caroline was dying with an abdominal ailment hastened by grief and drink. 'They have killed me at last,' she said. All one night she and her servants burned letters and papers, and also a volume whose loss is a sorrow: a journal in her hand, two feet wide and six inches thick, 'the whole history of her life ever since she came to this country,' says her lady-in-waiting, 'together with the characters of the different persons she had been intimate with'. Outside her door her son stood weeping. 'I am going to die, but it does not signify,' she told Brougham. 'I tell you I shall die, but I don't mind it.'

A few weeks earlier, it was said a zealous courtier had run to George IV with the news of Napoleon's death, and this exchange had taken place:

> Sir, your greatest enemy is dead!
> Is she, by God!

The Lost Mutton

The news of Caroline's actual death reached the king at Holyhead: he was on his way to Ireland on a royal tour (something his father had never ventured to do). It was the night before his fifty-ninth birthday. 'The king was uncommonly well during his passage,' says Croker, 'and gayer than it might be proper to tell. . . . He walked about the cabin the greater part of the night.' Lady Glengall, a Dubliner, goes further: 'He was dead DRUNK when he landed on the 12th of August. They drank all the wine on board the steamboat, and then applied to the whiskey punch till he could hardly stand.'

> Oh, what pleasures do abound
> Now my wife lies under ground!
> Since now I've snapped the nuptial string,
> Come listen while I gaily sing,
>   Let earth cover her,
>   We'll dance over her,
>   To the tune of Pat's mad joy. . . .
>
> Since once again I'm free as air,
> I marry will, and have an heir. . . .
> Fair and forty, fat also,
> Was my toast some years ago,
> But no more that toast I give.
> With blithe sixteen I mean to live.
>   Let earth cover her, etc.

Although he did wish he had an heir to foil his brothers and his niece Victoria, he was still bewitched by Lady Conyngham, 'fair, fat and fifty-two'. In Ireland, says Mrs Arbuthnot, the king 'never drank wine without touching her glass with his, holding her hand under the table all the time he was drinking!!'

He was enchanted, too, with the bacchanalian adulation of the Irish. 'They clawed and pawed him all over,' says Lady Glengall. 'They absolutely kiss his knees and feet. . . . Alas! poor degraded country!' No doubt some of them had a notion that although in 1812 he had betrayed their hopes of Catholic emancipation, as king he would reward them. The servile saturnalia angered Byron. They were kissing the foot of 'the Fourth of the fools and oppressors called George'.

Let the wine flow around the old bacchanal's throne,
Like the blood which has flowed, and which yet has to flow.
But let not *his* name be thine idol alone—
On his right hand behold a Sejanus appears!
Thine own Castlereagh! let him still be thine own!
A wretch, never named but with curses and jeers
Till now. . . .

George gave the Irish nothing. Emancipation (the repeal of laws that made them second-class citizens) came eight years later only as an alternative to rebellion, and after Wellington had undergone months of the king's bullying, betrayals and tearful tantrums.

The king's gifts were for Lady Conyngham. A frequenter of the court, the Russian ambassador's wife, Princess Lieven, who was slim as well as clever, found the infatuation extraordinary: 'Not an idea in her head; nothing but a hand to accept pearls and diamonds with, and an enormous balcony to wear them on.' In January 1822, says Mrs Arbuthnot, Bloomfield said that 'he thinks the king will go mad, such is his infatuation about Lady Conyngham; that it is quite shameful the way in which she is covered with jewels, & that he really believes the king has given her £100,000 worth!!' Bloomfield, who had been indulging George for years, protested at last about state jewels being loaded on Lady Conyngham, and the king dismissed him. He got a peerage and an ambassadorship, for he knew too much. The dismissal brought a caricature from J. L. Marks full of double meanings.

GEORGE IV (fondling Lady Conyngham): Turn him out! . . . Have I not a right to give my *precious stones* to whom I like?
LADY C.: Let me have the care of your *purse*.
GEORGE: You shall, my Cunning-one, and my precious *stones* too.

Marks got £45 for suppressing this—the last such payment, for Bloomfield's successor, Sir William Knighton, stopped the hush-money policy.

Ireland had so flattered George that he went the next year

to Scotland (his father had never been north of Cheltenham).
Sir Walter Scott, his favourite author, helped to create the
romantic custom of putting lowland Scots into the kilt. More
comical still, the bloated German–English figure of George IV
himself was displayed in the kilt, for one night only, at an
Edinburgh ball.

> With his tartan plaid and kilt so wide,
> The ladies blush who stand beside;
> And as he bows, behind each fan
> Exclaim, 'Oh, gallant Highlandman,
> Sing ho, the brawny Highlandman,
> The handy, dandy Highlandman!
> Oh, happy day, when this way ran
> The English–Irish Highlandman!'

Although the Constitutional Association was achieving little
against satire on George IV, it saw a new opportunity when
John Hunt, soon after leaving jail, printed Byron's 'The
Vision of Judgment' in *The Liberal*, a new periodical that
Byron was subsidizing. The poem was Byron's retort to a
hexametric 'Vision' by Southey in praise of the late king—
'rogue Southey', who had accused Byron of seeking to destroy
the social order by 'mingling impiety with lewdness' in his
works. Byron, in his less reverent Vision, said of George III:

> A better farmer ne'er brushed dew from lawn,
> A worse king never left a realm undone.

And (here Satan is speaking):

> 'Tis true, he was a tool from first to last
> (I have the workmen safe). . . .
> He ever warred with freedom and the free:
> Nations as men, home subjects, foreign foes,
> So that they uttered the word 'Liberty!'
> Found George the Third their first opponent. . . .

These lines and various others, 'meaning that his said late
Majesty was a bad king . . . and that his death was un-
lamented and unregretted . . . to the great disquietude and
disgrace of our said Lord the now King', brought Hunt to

trial four years after George III's death. A man who had bought a copy of the poem for the prosecutors, and not for any literary reason, produced, when questioned, this gem:

> Do you know what an hexameter means?
> Why, you are hexamining me.

The trial hardly pleased George IV, or Southey (who is cruelly mocked in the poem), for the whole 848 lines of it were read, were printed in *The Times* next day, and reprinted by the radicals. And Hunt merely paid a £100 fine.

The bitterness of 1819–20 had eased. Trade was improving. Castlereagh had cut his throat. Sidmouth had retired. There were younger Tories who favoured reforms, though not of parliament. George IV, the incorrigible grotesque incarnation of majesty, could not be there much longer. The men who had to deal with him were as willing as the public to look forward to his end. 'A more contemptible, cowardly, selfish, unfeeling dog does not exist,' wrote Charles Greville, clerk to the Privy Council, in his diary. '. . . There have been good and wise kings, but not many of them . . . and this I believe to be one of the worst.'

He tormented his ministers, spent more huge sums on building, sang vehemently, wept sentimentally, fell out of love with Lady Conyngham, made his guards' uniforms gaudier still, drank quantities of wine, sherry, port, brandy, punch and liqueurs, increased his laudanum dose (during 1826–7) to two hundred drops a day, and solicited new women. One of these was Princess Lieven, who reported his wooing methods to Metternich: 'His mistress bores him. She is a fool (he might have found that out sooner). He has been in love with me for thirteen years. He has never dared to tell me. . . . Today, an inner voice told him that I alone could guide him. . . . "But you are satisfied too exclusively with the spiritual side; I can't be content with that. . . ." ' Next month, when she was his guest at The Cottage, he appeared outside her window, appealing to her with 'gestures and passionate looks'. He was nearly sixty-four.

Whoever was in favour had to listen for hours to his stories, in which he was generally the hero. Having been told that his royal leadership defeated Napoleon, he came to believe that he had fought at Waterloo. He remonstrated with Westmacott the sculptor, says Lord Holland, 'for omitting him in the sketch of a *bas-relief* which represented the battle'. To Wellington himself (says Captain Rees Gronow of the Guards) he used to describe how he had charged the French with the Household Brigade and routed Marshal Ney's cavalry—to which Wellington at last replied, 'I have heard you, sir, say so before: but I did not witness this marvellous charge.'

In the kingdom of laudanum, where he reigned on the instructions of the president of the Royal College of Physicians, he found the glory he had forfeited in his own kingdom.

14

'The Day of the Tory is Fled'

THE EARLIEST recorded saying of the child who became George IV dates from 1766. Lady Mary Coke told him she was on her way to visit his great-aunt Amelia. George, aged four years and two weeks, looked her over and said, 'Pray, are you well enough dressed to visit her?' He never lost his concern for the proprieties of form and outward show. As he lay dying, he made a royal comment on a prayer for his recovery formulated by the Archbishop of Canterbury: 'It is in very good taste.'

His last words of all, early in the morning of 26 June 1830, were, 'My boy, this is death'; or (accounts differ) 'Surely this must be death'—a truer statement than many he had made in his self-indulgent life. He was not rewarded with a proper outward show of public sorrow. When the news went round London on that brilliantly sunny morning, the most devout royalist would have been puzzled to find a hint of grief. 'Never saw London so excited or so lively,' Tom Moore wrote in his journal. 'Crowds everywhere, particularly in St James's Street. . . . The whole thing reminded me of a passage in an old comedy: *What makes him so merry?—Don't you see he's in mourning?'*

The jest applied even to the man who that day succeeded to the throne, George's quirky, blunt, excitable brother William. He came into town at once from Bushey Park, and as he drove past the unmourning citizens, he bowed enthusiastically, and was seen to be grinning. He had been treated as a joke for most

234

of his sixty-five years. Now his joy was so great that Charles Greville and others were afraid his erratic mind would slip over into madness. Yet his lack of kingly decorum helped to endear him to his people. At least he did not hide from them. They were willing to forgive him his nine surviving bastards by the actress Dorothy Jordan. It was his ill luck that he did not also produce an heir to the Hanoverian line. In 1818, when the death of George's daughter Charlotte had left the field open, and William and his brothers were hastily choosing German brides, a lampoon had made him say—

> Where, 'mong our brothers, Ge---y, now is
> A man can boast of equal prowess?
> Saving yourself, you must agree
> There's none can do the trick like me.

But no child survived from the three pregnancies of his bride Adelaide; and so the crown went next to Kent's daughter Victoria. An heir of William would certainly have had the benefit of a free-spoken father. At a great dinner after his coronation, with all his ministers and all the foreign ambassadors among his ninety guests, William made an odd, rambling speech which concluded with a toast:

> Les yeux qui tuent,
> les fesses qui remuent
> et le cul qui danse—
> honi soit qui mal y pense.

It was the talk of the town, says Greville. 'Lord Grey was ready to sink into the earth.' Talleyrand, the ancient French ambassador, who had seen and survived many strange things, was asked what he thought. 'With his unmoved, immovable face, he answered only, *C'est bien remarquable.*'

Many changes followed George IV's death. The very first, on that sunlit Saturday, was the departure from Windsor Castle of Lady Conyngham, the last mistress to be openly kept by a reigning British king. In George IV's declining years, when love had died, little but avarice had detained her at Windsor. And though George had heaped wealth on Lady Conyngham, there was a Balzacian scene at his deathbed:

Whiting, one of the pages, said that she had frequently asked the king (but in vain) for the key which he wore suspended to a chain round his neck, and that opened a closet which she supposed contained valuables. On returning to the king's room, which he had left for a short time after his death, he actually found Lady Conyngham trying to take the key from the chain.

So one of the anti-Conyngham prints of this time, 'Packing Up!!!', was fairly sound in showing Lady Conyngham desperately trying to unlock a treasure chest. The story of the key is from Countess Brownlow, who got it from Whiting on being appointed a lady of William IV's court. She records that the Conynghams' carriages left 'loaded with packages of all shapes and sizes', and they descended to taking royal clocks and china. Her word is supported by Greville and others. Caricatures merely exaggerate the baseness of the Conyngham (or Cunning-Hum) rapacity by showing the marchioness pushing a wheelbarrow laden with pots and kettles.

Still, much remained behind, and not least in the old king's wardrobes. 'There are all the coats, etc., he has ever had for fifty years' (Greville reporting); '300 whips, canes without number, every sort of uniform, the costumes of all the orders in Europe, splendid furs, pelisses, etc., hunting-coats and breeches. . . . His profusion in these articles was unbounded. . . . He recollected every article of dress, no matter how old. . . . It is difficult to say whether in great or little things that man was most odious and contemptible.' Mrs Arbuthnot got other details from Wellington:

> . . . Volumes of love letters, chiefly from Lady Conyngham, some foul copies of his own to Lady Conyngham descriptive of the most furious passion, trinkets of all sorts, quantities of women's gloves, dirty snuffy pocket handkerchiefs with old faded nosegays tied up in them. . . . He said he thought the best thing would be to burn them all.

Sir William Knighton saw to the clearing of the sad relics and the embarrassing papers recording a long amorous life; and ordered the burning of 'several drawersful of *free* prints and drawings, the private property of his late Majesty.'

One set of letters could not be lightly disposed of: those of the king's widow. Maria Fitzherbert was still living in Brighton, and indeed had ventured to write to him in his last illness. He did not answer, which 'cut her up', she said. She asked Wellington to send back all her letters. She already had George's letters to her in safekeeping with a friend, Lord Albemarle, and she intended to publish both sides in self-vindication after her death. Wellington, alarmed, demanded a full exchange, letters for letters. A grievous compromise was reached: that they should all be burned. Wellington and Albemarle spent more than a day doing the job in the drawing-room of Mrs Fitzherbert's house in Tilney Street, Mayfair. What Wellington said after several hours will give some notion of their task: 'I think, my lord, we had better hold our hand for a while, or we shall set the old woman's chimney on fire.' Thomas Creevey laments: 'Oh dear, oh dear! That I could have seen them! They began in 1785 and lasted to 1806 . . . when the young man fell in love with Lady Hertford, and used to *cry*, as I have often seen him do, in Mrs Fitzherbert's presence.'

Nine portraits of Mrs Fitzherbert were returned to her. A tenth, a jewelled miniature of her when young, was not. Apparently George did fulfil one of his intentions of 1796. Wellington said that when alone by George's coffin, he saw the miniature round his neck. When this was passed on to Mrs Fitzherbert, 'some large tears fell from her eyes'.

Scarcely a month after William IV's accession, news came that Paris had risen in revolt against Charles X when he tried to dismiss a liberal-minded parliament and gag the press. Within a fortnight Charles X had been replaced by 'citizen king' Louis Philippe. This 1688-style revolution excited British reformers and certainly helped to cause a pro-Whig shift in the elections that were then in progress. When the new parliament met at Westminster that November, Wellington gave the opposition one of those gifts that sometimes come from the Tories. He said the existing parliamentary system had 'the full and entire confidence of the country'; neither he nor anyone else could devise a better one; and he would always resist any reform proposals. A few years earlier it would have been an unsurprising speech. Wellington was never a man to trouble himself about that odd civilian fact, public opinion. 'The duke has undone us!' said his anguished ministers to each other. Riots broke out. Wellington's windows, and many others, were smashed. Fearing a mob attack on Apsley House, he posted armed men at all the windows commanding Piccadilly. As rapidly as Charles X, Wellington was out and Lord Grey, at the age of sixty-six, was in. It was the first time that an election had been followed by a government defeat since the Hanoverians had begun to rule.

And so, seventy years after the accession of George III, his third son found himself presiding—unwillingly, agitatedly, and with the bitter disapproval of his German queen—over a partial reform of the system that George III had so often declared perfect and immutable. Some Tories felt as desperate as George III would have done. A few months later Mrs Arbuthnot, Wellington's friend, wrote in her diary, 'He thinks the revolution is begun and that nothing can save us'. He wrote to her, 'If we are in luck we may have a civil war'. He covered the windows of Apsley House with bulletproof shutters. The country's mood was in fact mainly one of reasoned determination to achieve reform. All through the 1820s, something called The March of Intellect had been at work.

> Mobs, *hélas!* are now at college,
> Where they gain the accursed knowledge
> Of their left hand from their right one,
> And the SCUM thus learn to fight one.
> Servants read the Sunday papers
> 'Stead of scraping masters' scrapers . . .
> The rank and file use pen and ink,
> The radicals begin to think.

What worried Whigs as well as Tories was a whole array of new weekly papers that sold for only a penny by defying the law's demand for the fourpenny Tax on Knowledge. They campaigned for things that Lord Grey could not think of proposing: universal suffrage, the ballot and equal constituencies. Some of them wanted to abolish king, lords and bishops. Their editors and scores of their vendors went to jail; but the papers still came out.

A few innovators in that first age of cheap cotton dodged the tax in a lawful way. The stamp tax law spoke of paper, so they printed on cotton, and very legibly, too. A four-page Political Handkerchief published by H. Berthold addresses 'the Weaver Boys of Lancashire':

> You shall all be as busy as bees, if our Whig taxers do not . . . declare cotton to be paper. . . . Your wives and daughters may become moving monuments of political knowledge. One shall be dressed in a description of king-craft, another in a description of priestcraft, a third in a description of lordcraft. One shall wear the latest news. . . . No policeman (street soldier) can arrest you. . . .

Richard Carlile, still fighting after all his years in jail, issued on William IV's coronation day, 8 September 1831, a three-penny Coronation Handkerchief that exhorted people not to be grateful that the event was costing less than a fifth as much as George IV's, for the cost 'would keep alive a thousand families for a year, that are now perishing from want'.

> This coronation is an entire mummery. . . . It is a festival at which the king, the priests and the lords celebrate their triumph over a conquered and degraded people. . . . DOWN WITH KINGS, WITH PRIESTS, AND WITH LORDS.

A month later came the first crisis of the reform debate. The Lords threw out Grey's bill. The riots that followed were remarkable only in that so few of them occurred. Wellington, of course, was attacked the next time he appeared. One penny paper, Henry Hetherington's *Radical Reformer*, carried this paragraph:

> *'Duke' of Wellington.*—This detestable anti-reform 'thing' called 'lord' was well pelted with mud, and we regret to say with stones, on his way to the House of Noodles on Monday. His carriage was (like his political conduct) covered with filth.

The hated Duke of Cumberland was covered in mud from head to foot. And bishops were so loathed that some of them hid in their palaces—for it was noted that if twenty-one right

reverend fathers in God had not voted against reform, the bill
would have scraped through. The price of muskets went up
from £1 to 25 shillings.

Now both the extreme left and the extreme right were sure
that before long Britain would be a republic. *The Radical Reformer* habitually spoke of 'the *stepping-stone* reform'. Croker,
who looked at the penny papers because he was busy putting
high Tory arguments in *John Bull*, wrote to his old friend, the
Lord Yarmouth of regency days, 'There can be no longer any
doubt that the Reform Bill is . . . a *stepping-stone* in England
to a republic, and in Ireland to separation.' And a little later,
of the twelve-year-old Princess Victoria: 'She may live to be
plain Miss Guelph.' Radical papers were already calling
William IV and Adelaide Mr and Mrs Guelph.

It was a near thing. When Grey had gone to the country,
had increased his majority and had again got his bill through
the Commons, the king refused to create enough peers to get it
through the Lords (though scarcely a Whig peer had been
created since 1782). The king's bastard sons, his sisters, his
cousin 'Silly Billy' Gloucester, and most of all his wife, incited
the puzzled old man to resist the will of the country. For a
week Wellington tried to form a Tory government; as he put
it, he made 'an effort to enable the king to shake off the tram-
mels of his tyrannical minister'—words which might have
been spoken by Bute seventy years before.

Never since has Britain known a week of such passion and
alarm. Reform associations which had grown to great power
during a year's campaigning for 'the bill, the whole bill and
nothing but the bill' held vast meetings to demonstrate to
wavering Tories that if they backed Wellington the country
would rebel. The most potent association of all was the Birmingham Union. In that unrepresented city of 146,000, one
meeting that month was swelled to an estimated 200,000
by marchers from all over Warwickshire, Staffordshire and
Worcestershire. Massed voices sang a new political hymn, 'The
Gathering of the Unions':

> God is our guide! From field, from wave,
> From plough, from anvil and from loom,

'The Day of the Tory is Fled'

We come, our country's rights to save,
    And speak a tyrant faction's doom. . . .

God is our guide! No swords we draw,
    We kindle not war's battle-fires.
By union, justice, reason, law,
    We claim the birthright of our sires. . . .

And a meeting in Birmingham was no longer a local happening. The next day's *Morning Herald* had a five-column report on London breakfast-tables—an astonishing feat of urgent reporting.

If Wellington tried to use the army to break up meetings, said one radical paper, *The Ballot*, every town must hold a meeting at the same moment. There were hints that (as in France) some soldiers would refuse to attack. A 'pay no taxes' movement began to spread over the country. Life was almost suspended. A report from Birmingham said, 'The arrival of a coach from London at an unusual hour empties the workshops in an instant. Very little work is done. The workmen walk about, talking of nothing but the bill.' A run on the banks began, led by reformers. A placard devised by Francis Place, a moderate radical, was posted all over London: 'To stop the DUKE, go for gold.' Inns with Wellington or William IV for their signs turned them upside-down. The king was execrated. *The Cosmopolite*, yet another radical weekly, said:

> The king has shown his cloven foot. The Patriot King is caricatured as the modern Jerry Sneak—as the spoiled child of the royal nursery—as a political cuckold—as the henpecked old man . . . as Silly Billy, an idiot from birth . . . as the nation's expensive toy, costing half a million in the year. . . . His brain cannot long bear all this excitement, and we shall soon hear that he has gone mad.

More than one caricature showed him (in that time of penniless emigrants) making a royal emigration to Hanover. And indeed that became his alternative to recalling Grey, for fighting it out would merely have postponed the emigration.

If William had not lived until 1832, and if the Duke of Kent had not abandoned his mistress in time to father Victoria, the king at this time would have been George III's fifth son Ernest, 'the damnable Duke of Cumberland', the most ultra of Tories. There is no room here for the scandalous life of this extraordinary prince, who at the age of fifty-eight tried to rape the Lord Chancellor's wife; who later pursued an amour with a peer's wife even after he had driven the peer to suicide; and who was alleged to be the father of a son that was born in 1800 to his sister, Princess Sophia (a charge that has been too eagerly doubted by biographers). Ernest would ardently have attempted to suppress reform by force, and could easily have turned the whole family into Guelphs.

As it was, William discovered that the sane thing to do was to recall Grey. Bloodshed had seemed so possible that the joy was intense. 'I witnessed a scene that I never saw equalled,' reported Thomas Attwood, leader of the Birmingham Union. '. . . Resolute and gigantic men shedding tears of joy. . . . I have read of the tears of valiant men. I never saw them until then.'

The emotion was very different in the office of *John Bull*. A few days before, exulting over Wellington's return, it had crowed, 'Lord Grey is gone, fled, run away . . . this lofty hypocrite, this grim and haughty peer,' with much more about Grey's alleged deception and trickery. Now *John Bull* had to say lamely that it had been found impossible to 'extricate the sovereign from the thraldom in which his evil councillors have so cruelly entangled him'.

In what *The Ballot* called 'the well-known House of Incurables', Wellington led a strategic retreat of peers who could see nothing in reform but disaster—peers of whom Grey said, 'Good God, where do they live? What do they do in the country, that they are so ignorant of what is passing among them?' All but twenty-two of them stayed away. The bill passed on 4 June 1832, the ninety-fourth anniversary of George III's birthday; and the one aberrant Whig among his sons, the Duke of Sussex, said loudly in the House, 'Thank God the deed is done at last. I care for nothing now—this is the happiest day of my life.' An old Tory, hearing this, 'lifted up his hands in horror and fervently ejaculated, "O Christ."'

'The Day of the Tory is Fled'

Oh, could the wise, the brave, the just,
Who suffered—died—to break our chains;
Could Muir, could Palmer from the dust,
Could murdered Gerrald hear our strains. . . .

So sang ageing reformers at Sheffield, remembering martyrs of the 1790s, Corresponding Society men transported to Botany Bay. The radical reforms so long demanded had not been won, but they were expected to come soon. 'DEATH EXTRAORDINARY of Tory Power' said one broadside. 'The day of the Tory is fled,' said another. Wellington, Cumberland, bishops and other bogeymen were pictured being thrust into hell. Frantic *John Bull* propagated the idea of coming doom:

On the banks of the Tyne, in Birmingham, in Dudley, in Bradford, the mob is omnipotent. . . . We want another year of Whig misrule . . . to reduce the standard of national feeling to the level of the Marseillois of 1793. . . . A little longer period of ministerial tuition will teach us the ready use of the lamp-post and the guillotine.

Before long, peers and bishops began to notice that they, and the royal family, and even the Conservative Party (as it now was) seemed to be surviving. The outcome of two years of crises was less extreme than the radicals had hoped or the ultras had feared. The war of words became less savage. The leading London political printseller, Thomas McLean, 26 Haymarket, thought it profitable to emphasize that he bore no malice towards anyone. He said in a preface to a bound volume of 1832 caricatures:

Take five hundred conflicting assertions . . . the same quantity of unfulfilled political prophecies, a small portion of charity, and a large measure of disinterestedness; mix; and you will soon have what our transatlantic brethren call 'a pretty considerable' brewing of political indifference. . . . You may laugh with the Whigs at Toryism (I beg pardon— Conservation), with the Tories at the Whigs, with the Radicals at both, and with both at the Radicals. . . .

This line was welcome to the middle classes; but less so, of course, to the lower orders, who could see a closing of the ranks against radical reform. And yet at the start of the Victorian age, the monarchy, that symbol of Conservation, was not yet hedged round with reverence. On Princess Victoria's eighteenth birthday, just before she came to the throne, *Figaro in London*, a wide-selling weekly, parodied the slushy adulation that courtly papers were beginning to lavish on her:

> Her benevolent character was shown from her second to her tenth year, inclusive, by a strong disposition evinced to share with the cat or dog her daily meal of milk-and-water, placing the head of the animal in her own saucer, and then drinking out of it herself with a truly infantine simplicity.

There follows a hit at the secretary and scandalously close friend of the princess's widowed mother: 'Her regard for Sir John Conroy is another praiseworthy trait . . . that highly respectable flunkey and *croupier* to the Duchess of Kent.' *Figaro* pursues the attack on sycophancy when Victoria has become queen:

> If she blows her royal nose, the penny-a-liners must blow their trumpets with a most sweet echo, and swear that they never heard anything so musical as the lower notes of the queen's nasal organ.

Victoria's accession transformed the Duke of Cumberland into king of Hanover, for a woman was never allowed to reign over the electorate. *Figaro* said the Demon Duke had become the Fiend King: 'His dukedom is now at an end, and His Majesty was greeted as he passed with the sincere howls of the populace.' It was a blessing for the court (and for Tories): a terrible relic of the past, the queen's most shameful uncle, was cleared out of sight.

A sovereign who was young and politically sinless, and a female as well, was a difficult target for radicals. The popular weeklies generally made their points jokily. 'We are now under petticoat government,' said the newly-founded *Penny Satirist*. 'Long live the British hen! And may we all be piously resigned to our fate as a henpecked nation!' A week later this paper printed a caricature of the eighteen-year-old queen being wooed by three grotesque German princes. She says:

> Ah, la! Why can't I marry an Englishman? Oh, there's a handsome, noble, charming young subject, and a willing one too, who has actually thrown me into an apoplexy of love . . . and yet, lest I should apply to him for a *prescription* to cure me, they have transported him to foreign climes. . . . I shall be obliged, no doubt, to wed some German adventurer who inherits nothing but a title from his parents, and trusts to that and a pair of fearful mustachios for a royal fortune.

When she had not been a month on the throne, *The Penny Satirist*, more Whig than radical, said, 'Her Majesty . . . has converted a great many radicals already. . . . We know one sour old scoundrel who has not blessed either king or queen for twenty years, who actually exclaimed when he saw her, "God bless the sweet creature, may she live long and happy!" We consider this one of the signs of the times.'

Radicals who looked to the queen in her earliest years were not utterly naive. She was then a devout Whig, 'and the radicals,' she said, 'will also rally round their queen to protect her from the Tories.' The hard truth for the radicals, however, was that scarcely anyone with effective power wanted what they wanted; least of all Lord Melbourne, the extremely conservative Whig who took over from Grey. An age before, Melbourne's mother had been a lover of Victoria's Uncle George; now Melbourne became a treasured uncle-figure to the fatherless queen. This attachment roused some satirical papers to derision. *Nobody in London* in 1838 called fifty-nine-year-old Melbourne the queen's 'chief counsellor and mutton-chop consumer . . . an old, stupid, lame, ugly, toothless foozle—a person that never gives dinners, and never takes in our work—bordering close on his hundredth year, and fitted, in many other respects, to be Her Majesty's grandmother'. The paper goes on to offer a royal letter:

> Dear Melly—How are you, my rum old chap? What shall we have for dinner today?
>
> <div align="right"><i>Tout à vous</i>, VIC.</div>

P.S. Write word directly, as we are very peckish. We think that we could actually masticate a rhinoceros. V.

Distaste for Melbourne was inspired in part by the unworthy role he played in the creation of the Tolpuddle Martyrs. But even such abuse as this, softened with playfulness, was becoming less and less common. Nowhere was this so evident as in the caricature trade, which for so long had thrived on royal and noble misbehaviour.

When Victoria had been scarcely three years on the throne, Thomas McLean was advertising that his caricatures were 'entirely free from whatever could offend the most scrupulous or wound the most susceptible'. The man is betraying his trade, but no doubt knows his customers. What a change since George IV's days! It struck William Makepeace Thackeray, who had been a boy of nine at the time of the Queen Caroline uproar. Writing about George Cruikshank in *The Westminster Review* in 1840, he recalled the old printshops:

Knight's in Sweeting's Alley [Cornhill], Fairburn's in a court off Ludgate Hill, Hone's in Fleet Street—bright, enchanted palaces, which George Cruikshank used to people with grinning, fantastical imps and merry, harmless sprites —where are they? . . . The atrocious Castlereagh, the sainted Caroline (in a tight pelisse, with feathers in her head), the Dandy of Sixty, who used to glance at us from Hone's friendly windows—where are they? Mr Cruikshank may have drawn a thousand better things, since the days when these were; but they are to us a thousand times more pleasing than anything else he has done. How we used to believe in them! to stray miles out of the way on holidays in order to ponder for an hour before that delightful window in Sweeting's Alley! in walks through Fleet Street, to vanish abruptly down Fairburn's passage, and there make one at his 'charming gratis' exhibition! There used to be a crowd round the window in those days of grinning goodnatured mechanics, who spelt the songs and spoke them out for the benefit of the company, and who received the points of humour with a general sympathizing roar. Where are these people now? You never hear any laughing at HB [John

Doyle, McLean's chief caricaturist]; his pictures are a great deal too genteel for that—polite points of wit which . . . cause one to smile in a quiet, gentlemanlike kind of way. There must be no smiling with Cruikshank. A man who does not laugh outright is a dullard. . . . Even the old Dandy of Sixty must have laughed at his own wondrous grotesque image.

Thackeray's last flourish goes too far, and perhaps he makes the crowds outside the printshops a little too goodnatured; but this only amounts to saying that he could well have been sharper in his lament over the decline into quiet gentility. A journalistic innovation associated with the change was perhaps as much a symptom as a cause: caricatures, both social and political, were being offered to the public more and more in magazines and weekly papers instead of through printshops. An editor with his eye on household sales will tend to avoid flights of offensiveness. In the early 1840s, when *Punch* was young, it soon found that to prosper it must give up its radicalism.

Britain was on the way to being elevated, or tidied up, or abashed by what came to be known as Victorianism. Without formal announcement, the monarchy—in the shape of a young woman with none of her uncles' shameful qualities—was put (George III would have said) in shackles. And for men of a rebel mind, it was an ambiguous achievement. Invective was bridled, scoffing became bad form, scurrility went underground. Large questions remained to be fought over—not always in a gentlemanlike way, but certainly with little outright laughing. Now that polemical indecorum is once again thought to be not entirely deplorable, the contenders of this age can profit by a study of the free speaking of pre-Victorian times.

Select Bibliography

A full list of material consulted would be more imposing than helpful. The aim here is twofold: to record my chief sources and to offer signposts to the general reader (who will find further bibliographies in many of the secondary sources listed).

Pamphlets, lampoons, broadsides and caricatures quoted in the text are not listed again here.

MANUSCRIPT SOURCES
Royal Archives, Windsor Castle
British Museum (especially Bute, Fox, Gillray, Hardwicke, Holland, Liverpool, Martin, Place, Robinson, Wilkes, Woodfall papers)
Public Record Office (Home Office, King's Bench and Treasury Solicitor's papers)
Guildhall, London (Wilkes papers)
Warwick County Record Office (Hertford papers)

NEWSPAPERS AND PERIODICALS
(A short-list. A pair of dates indicates the life-span of a short-lived journal. Otherwise, dates cited are of the earliest year inspected, not necessarily year of founding.)
Anti-Jacobin 1797–8, Argus 1789–, Ballot 1831–2, Black Dwarf 1819–24, Bon Ton Magazine 1791–5, Briton 1762–3, Cap of Liberty 1820, Cosmopolite 1831–2
Destructive 1833–4, Examiner 1812–, Figaro in London 1832–9, Freeholder's Magazine 1769–, Gazetteer 1784–, General Evening Post 1771–, Gorgon 1818–19
Hog's Wash 1793–4, John Bull 1820–, London Courant 1780–, London Evening Post 1764–, London Magazine 1760–, London Museum of Politics 1770–1
Medusa 1819–20, Middlesex Journal 1769–, Monitor 1761–, Morning Chronicle 1770–, Morning Herald 1782–, Morning Post 1780–, North Briton 1762–3 (and 1769–70, not Wilkes's)

Select Bibliography

Oxford Magazine 1768–, Parliamentary Spy 1769–70, Penny Satirist 1837–46, Pig's Meat 1793–5, Political Register 1767–, Public Advertiser 1761–

Radical Reformer 1831, Rambler's Magazine 1783–90, Reformist's Register 1817, Republican 1817–26, St James's Chronicle 1761–, Satirist 1808–14, Scourge 1780, Scourge 1811–15, Times 1785–, Town and Country Magazine 1771–, Whisperer 1770–2, White Hat 1819–20

PRIMARY PRINTED SOURCES

Albemarle, 6th Earl of, *Memoirs of the Marquis of Rockingham and his Contemporaries*, 2 vol., 1852

Almon, John, *Anecdotes of . . . Pitt* (the elder), 1793; *Memoirs of a late Eminent Bookseller*, 1790

Archenholtz, Johann von, *Tableau de l'Angleterre*, Brussels, 1788

Aspinall, Arthur, *The Later Correspondence of George III*, 5 vol., Cambridge, 1962–70; *The Correspondence of George Prince of Wales, 1770–1812*, 8 vol., Cassell, 1963–71; *The Letters of King George IV, 1812–1830*, 3 vol., Cambridge, 1938; *Three Early Nineteenth Century Diaries* (1830–2), Williams & Norgate, 1952

Bamford, Francis, and the Duke of Wellington, *The Journal of Mrs Arbuthnot*, 2 vol., Macmillan, 1950

Barnes, G. R., and Owen, J. H., *The Private Papers of John, Earl of Sandwich*, Navy Records Society, 1932

Barrett, Charlotte, *Diary and Letters of Madame D'Arblay* (Fanny Burney), 6 vol., 1904–5

Bessborough, 9th Earl of, *Georgiana*, John Murray, 1955; (with Arthur Aspinall), *Lady Bessborough and Her Family Circle*, John Murray, 1940

Bickley, Francis, *The Diaries of Sylvester Douglas, Lord Glenbervie*, 2 vol., Constable, 1928

Binns, John, *Recollections* (of the 1790s), Philadelphia, 1854

Bladon, F. McKno, *The Diaries of Colonel the Honourable Robert Fulke Greville*, Bodley Head, 1930

Broughton, Mrs Vernon, *Court and Private Life in the Time of Queen Charlotte: being the Journals of Mrs Papendiek, Assistant Keeper of the Wardrobe and Reader to Her Majesty*, 2 vol., 1887

Brownlow, Emma Sophia, Countess, *The Eve of Victorianism*, John Murray, 1940

Bury, Lady Charlotte, *Diary Illustrative of the Times of George the Fourth*, 4 vol., 1838–9

Select Bibliography

Carswell, John, and Dralle, Lewis, *The Political Journal of George Bubb Dodington*, Oxford, 1965

Complete Collection of State Trials (esp. vols. 22–25, 31–33)

Dobree, Bonamy, *The Letters of King George III*, Cassell, 1968

Dolby, Thomas, *Memoirs*, 1827

Fortescue, Sir John, *The Correspondence of King George the Third from 1760 to December 1783*, 6 vol., Macmillan, 1927-8; re-issue, Frank Cass, 1967

Gronow, Captain Rees, *The Reminiscences and Recollections of Captain Gronow*, 2 vol., 1889; abridged edition, ed. John Raymond, Bodley Head, 1964

Hanger, Colonel George, *The Life, Adventures and Opinions of*, 2 vol., 1801

Harcourt, Edward W., *The Harcourt Papers*, 14 vol., Oxford, 1880–1905 (esp. vol. 4 for 1788–9)

Mrs Harcourt's Diary of the Court of George III, Philobiblon Society, 1871

Hardy, Thomas, *Memoir . . . Written by Himself*, 1832

Harris, James, 1st Earl of Malmesbury, *Diaries and Correspondence*, 1844 (reissued 1885)

Holland, 3rd Lord, *Memoirs of the Whig Party*, 2 vol., 1852-4; *Further Memoirs of the Whig Party*, John Murray, 1905

Ilchester, Countess of, and Lord Stavordale, *The Life and Letters of Lady Sarah Lennox* (contains 1st Lord Holland's journal of 1761-3), 1901

Ilchester, 6th Earl of, *Henry Fox, 1st Lord Holland*, 2 vol., John Murray, 1920

Jennings, Louis J., *The Croker Papers*, 3 vol., John Murray, 1885; abridged edition, ed. Bernard Pool, Batsford, 1967

Jucker, Ninetta S., *The Jenkinson Papers 1760–1766*, Macmillan, 1949

Langdale, Charles, *Memoirs of Mrs Fitzherbert*, 1856

Lincoln, Anthony, and McEwen, Robert, *Lord Eldon's Anecdote Book*, Stevens & Sons, 1960

Maxwell, Sir Herbert, and Gore, John, *Creevey*, John Murray, 1948; Gore, *The Creevey Papers*, abridged edition, Batsford, 1963

Place, Francis, *The Autobiography of Francis Place*, ed. Mary Thale, Cambridge, 1972

Quennell, Peter, *The Private Letters of Princess Lieven to Prince Metternich 1820–26*, John Murray, 1948

Reid, W. Hamilton, *Memoirs of the Public Life of John Horne Tooke*, 1812

Select Bibliography

Sedgwick, Romney, *Letters from George III to Lord Bute 1756–1766*, Macmillan, 1939

Sichel, Walter, *The Glenbervie Journals* (for 1793, 1811–15), Constable, 1910; *Sheridan* (with Duchess of Devonshire's 1788–9 diary), 2 vol., Constable, 1909

Smith, William J., *The Grenville Papers*, 4 vol., John Murray, 1852–3

Stephens, Alexander, *Memoirs of John Horne Tooke*, 1813

Strachey, Lytton, and Fulford, Roger, *The Greville Memoirs, 1814–60*, 8 vol., Macmillan, 1938; Fulford, abridged version, Batsford, 1963

Waldegrave, 2nd Earl, *Memoirs from 1754 to 1758*, 1821

Walpole, Horace, *The Letters of*, ed. Mrs Paget Toynbee, 19 vol., Oxford, 1903–25; The Yale Edition, ed. W. S. Lewis, New Haven and Oxford, 1937– (50th vol. scheduled for 1975)

Walpole, Horace, *Memoirs of the Reign of King George II*, 3 vol., 1847; *Memoirs of the Reign of King George the Third*, ed. G. F. Russell Barker, 4 vol., 1894; *The Last Journals . . . 1771–1783*, 2 vol., 1910

Wraxall, Sir Nathaniel, *The Historical and Posthumous Memoirs of*, ed. Henry B. Wheatley, 5 vol., 1884

SECONDARY SOURCES

Aspinall, Arthur, *Politics and the Press, c. 1780–1850*, Home & Van Thal, 1949

Bleackley, Horace, *Life of John Wilkes*, Bodley Head, 1917

Bourne, H. R. Fox, *English Newspapers*, 2 vol., 1887

Brooke, John, *King George III*, Constable, 1972

Butler, J. R. M., *The Passing of the Great Reform Bill*, 1914; reprint, Frank Cass, 1964

Cannon, John, *The Fox–North Coalition*, Cambridge, 1969

Christie, Ian R., *Myth and Reality in Late-Eighteenth-Century British Politics*, Macmillan, 1970

Cobban, Alfred, *The Debate on the French Revolution*, A. & C. Black, 1960

Crane, Verner W., *Benjamin Franklin's Letters to the Press 1758–1775*, Williamsburg, Va., and Chapel Hill, N.C., 1950

Fitzmaurice, Lord, *Life of William Earl of Shelburne*, 2 vol., Macmillan, 1912

Fulford, Roger, *George the Fourth*, Duckworth, 1948; *Royal Dukes*, Pan, 1948

Select Bibliography

George, M. Dorothy, *London Life in the Eighteenth Century*, Penguin, 1966

Hackwood, Fred M., *William Hone, His Life and Times*, 1912

Huish, Robert, *Memoirs of George the Fourth*, 2 vol., 1830, 1831

Laprade, William Thomas, *The Parliamentary Papers of John Robinson 1774–1784*, Royal Historical Society, 1922

Macalpine, Ida, and Hunter, Richard, *George III and the Mad-Business*, Allen Lane, 1969

Maccoby, Simon, *English Radicalism 1762–1785; English Radicalism 1786–1832*, Allen & Unwin, 1955

Morison, Stanley, *The History of The Times*, vol. I, 1935

Namier, Sir Lewis, *England in the Age of the American Revolution*, Macmillan, 1963; *The Structure of Politics at the Accession of George III*, Macmillan, 1960

Pares, Richard, *King George III and the Politicians*, Oxford, 1953

Plumb, J. H., *The First Four Georges*, 1956; Fontana, 1968

Rea, Robert R., *The English Press in Politics 1760–1774*, University of Nebraska, 1963

Rudé, George, *Wilkes and Liberty*, Oxford, 1962

Rudkin, Olive, *Thomas Spence and his Connections*, 1927

Stuart, Dorothy M., *The Daughters of George III*, Macmillan, 1939

Thompson, E. P., *The Making of the English Working Class*, Penguin, 1968

Wickwar, William H., *The Struggle for the Freedom of the Press 1819–1832*, Allen & Unwin, 1928

Ziegler, Philip, *William IV*, Collins, 1971

CARICATURES

Anyone who works in this field is deeply indebted to the late Mrs Mary Dorothy George. Between 1935 and 1954 she produced Vols. 5–11 of the British Museum's Catalogue of Political and Personal Satires, *in which more than 12,500 satirical prints of the period 1771–1832 are described, explained and indexed. (The cataloguing task had been abandoned since 1883, when Vol. 4 appeared.) A few other useful works are:*

Cohn, Albert M., *George Cruikshank. A Catalogue Raisonné*, The Bookman's Journal, London, 1924

Falk, Bernard, *Thomas Rowlandson*, Hutchinson, 1949

Genuine Works of Gillray, McLean, 1830

Select Bibliography

George, M. Dorothy, *English Political Caricature*, 2 vol., Oxford, 1959; *Hogarth to Cruikshank: Social Change in Graphic Satire*, Allen Lane, 1967

Grego, Joseph, *Rowlandson the Caricaturist*, 2 vol., 1880; *The Works of James Gillray, the Caricaturist*, 1873

Hill, Draper, *Mr Gillray the Caricaturist*, Phaidon, 1965; *Fashionable Contrasts: Caricatures by James Gillray*, Phaidon, 1966

Krumhaar, E. B., *Isaac Cruikshank: A Catalogue Raisonné*, Philadelphia, 1966

Wright, Thomas, *Caricature History of the Georges*, 1867 (reissue of *England Under the House of Hanover*, 1848)

Index

(*Figures in bold type indicate illustrations*)

Index

Index

257

Index

Index

Index

Index

Wolseley, Sir Charles, 204, 223

Woodfall, Henry Sampson, 15, 59

Wooler, Thomas John, radical journalist, 200, 205

Worcester, 92

Wordsworth, William, 201

World, 129, 140

Wraxall, Nathaniel, 11, 107, 118

Yarmouth, Earl of (later 3rd Marquess of Hertford), 185–6, 189, 191, 240; **38**

York, Duke of, *see* Frederick

York, Duchess of, 180

Yorktown, 94